DATE DUE   JAN   2003

D1266594

Profit in
the Futures
Markets!

Also available from
BLOOMBERG PRESS

New Thinking in Technical Analysis:
Trading Models from the Masters
Edited by Rick Bensignor

Tom Dorsey's Trading Tips:
A Playbook for Stock Market Success
by Thomas J. Dorsey and the DWA Analysts

Wall Street Secrets for Tax-Efficient Investing:
From Tax Pain to Investment Gain
by Robert N. Gordon with Jan M. Rosen

Investing in REITs:
Real Estate Investment Trusts
Revised and Updated Edition
by Ralph L. Block

Investing in Hedge Funds:
Strategies for the New Marketplace
by Joseph G. Nicholas

Investing in IPOs—Version 2.0:
Revised and Updated Edition
by Tom Taulli

—■—

A complete list of our titles is available at
www.bloomberg.com/books

BLOOMBERG PROFESSIONAL LIBRARY

Profit in the Futures Markets!

■

INSIGHTS AND STRATEGIES FOR FUTURES AND FUTURES OPTIONS TRADING

JAKE BERNSTEIN

BLOOMBERG PRESS
PRINCETON

Books are available for bulk purchases at special discounts. Special editions or book excerpts can also be created to specifications. For information, please write: Special Markets Department, Bloomberg Press.

BLOOMBERG, BLOOMBERG NEWS, BLOOMBERG FINANCIAL MARKETS, OPEN BLOOMBERG, BLOOMBERG PERSONAL, THE BLOOMBERG FORUM, COMPANY CONNECTION, COMPANY CONNEX, BLOOMBERG PRESS, BLOOMBERG PROFESSIONAL LIBRARY, BLOOMBERG PERSONAL BOOKSHELF, and BLOOMBERG SMALL BUSINESS are trademarks and service marks of Bloomberg L.P. All rights reserved.

Portions of the text have been adapted from Jake Bernstein's *New Facts on Futures*.

This publication contains the author's opinions and is designed to provide accurate and authoritative information. It is sold with the understanding that the author, publisher, and Bloomberg L.P. are not engaged in rendering legal, accounting, investment-planning, or other professional advice. The reader should seek the services of a qualified professional for such advice; the author, publisher, and Bloomberg L.P. cannot be held responsible for any loss incurred as a result of specific investments or planning decisions made by the reader.

First edition published 2002
1 3 5 7 9 10 8 6 4 2

Library of Congress Cataloging-in-Publication Data

Bernstein, Jake
     Profit in the futures markets! : insights and strategies for futures and futures options trading / Jake Bernstein -- 1st ed.
          p. cm. -- (Bloomberg professional library)
     Includes index.
       ISBN 1-57660-118-8
       1. Futures market. 2. Futures. 3. Options (Finance) I. Title. II. Series
     HG6024 .A3 B497 2002
     332.64'5--dc21

                                                                            2002003527

Acquired and edited by Kathleen A. Peterson

Book Design by LAURIE LOHNE / DESIGN IT COMMUNICATIONS

Preface

The goals of financial independence and wealth drive millions of investors to seek out vehicles by which such success may be achieved. Whether the method of choice be real estate, business, sales, stocks, or futures, the fact remains that without discipline, education, and persistence the odds of success are slim indeed. Yes, some individuals manage to achieve wealth by pure luck, but such cases are few and far between. In the long run, the fulfillment of financial independence and/or wealth is a function of several factors, not the least of which is knowledge. And knowledge can only be acquired through effort.

Fortunately, those who seek sources of knowledge can readily find them. Whether one seeks to attain knowledge through books, through the Internet, audio tape courses, college classes, video courses, or seminars, there is no doubt that anyone who wants an education in virtually any field can find access to it with minimal effort. However, the process of attaining the knowledge once the information source is found is a far more arduous task.

Profit in the Futures Markets! is intended to provide knowledge to those who seek to achieve financial success using the futures and futures options markets as their vehicle of choice. But buying this book and skimming its contents will not bring you the profits you seek. In fact, a little knowledge may be a dangerous thing—you could very well lose money if your understanding and application of the methods and concepts discussed herein are either faulty or fragmented. The simple fact is that this book must be studied and applied. This is not a "coffee table" book. Nor is this a book whose main function is to look attractive on your desk or bookshelf.

The simple reality is that we must do everything within our power to overcome expectations of immediate success in futures trading (and, for that matter, in life). In fact it is more likely that you will experience instant failure if you cannot apply yourself with persistence, patience, and focus. There's a learning curve, a learning process in everything. And yes, you *can* learn futures trading from books such as this one as long as you practice and apply discipline. This is important because today, more than ever before, it is vital for all traders and investors to understand futures, their workings, the meaning of futures price

trends, and the manner in which trading in the various futures vehicles can benefit a total investment portfolio. Futures and futures options trading strategies
allow for combinations and actions never before available to investors. But you
do need the time and effort and patience and discipline to master the opportunities these vehicles offer.

It is the purpose of this book to educate all investors and potential investors
in futures and futures options trading in a fashion that departs from the traditional approaches taken in teaching this subject. There is little emphasis on history, economic justification, controversial issues, and the hazards of futures trading. The manner in which futures trading is used as a means of hedging risk is
given only brief attention. All of these topics have been adequately and abundantly covered in the past. Virtually every public library is overstocked with books
discussing these aspects of futures trading. However, I do not believe that the
public has ever been offered an opportunity to learn futures and futures options
on a very basic and non-theoretical level.

In effect, the book you are about to read is a layman's guide to futures and
options. It seeks to provide you with the information you will need to get started,
and it will help you determine whether you, in fact, want to get started. It will
help you learn if futures and futures options trading are right for you, and if you
decide that they are, this book will provide you with the direction you will need
to learn more and to profit in your endeavor. Even the experienced trader will
find this book helpful as a refresher course or quick reference guide.

Additionally, and on a more general level, my goal is to teach all investors that
they must, at the very minimum, understand futures trading since futures price
trends tend to forecast or predict economic direction. It is not my intention to
sell anyone on the virtues of futures trading. I do believe, however, that a good
understanding of futures and the meaning of futures price movements can be
very beneficial in understanding, forecasting, and anticipating economic direction and change. I believe that it is the mandate of every investor who claims to
be well-rounded and informed to understand the workings of the futures market
and, above all, to understand how changes in futures prices tend to precede
changes in other sectors of the economy.

With that in mind, use *Profit in the Futures Markets!* according to your particular needs and objectives, whether you are already focused on futures as your
vehicle of choice or are at the stage where you are simply exploring your
options. Whereas there is no cookbook formula to help anyone learn futures
trading, I have some recipes, some methods, some procedures, and many sug-

gestions. This book will give you those. So write in it. Make notes in the margins. Use a highlighter. Read this book until the pages fall out. And if you have a pressing question, feel free to drop me a line: jake@trade-futures.com.

Acknowledgments

I would like to extend my sincere thanks to those who made this book possible either directly by their suggestions, proofreading, and editing, and/or indirectly through their encouragement, support, and feedback. Specifically I wish to offer my thanks to my family and office staff as well as my many clients and website visitors who, through the years, have helped me learn more from them than they have learned from me. Finally, the outstanding editorial and production staff at Bloomberg Press are due a note of thanks. Tracy Tait and Kathleen Peterson have been exceptionally helpful in bringing this project to fruition. They are a joy to work with.

JAKE BERNSTEIN

Contents

Part One

Getting Started: Myths and Realities of the Futures Markets

---

2   THE TWO GENERAL APPROACHES: FUNDAMENTAL VS. TECHNICAL ANALYSIS   37

3   WHAT YOU SHOULD KNOW ABOUT TRENDLINES   51

Part Two

Discipline and Trading

Part Three

The Mechanics of Trading

Part Four

Advanced Trading Strategies and Techniques

Profit in the Futures Markets!

Introduction

There are three ingredients in life: learning, earning, and yearning.

— CHRISTOPHER MANLY

Those who dream of "rags to riches" will find that living in a capitalist society offers many roads to their goal. While some roads are slow and steady with obstacles that are clear and discernible, others are well-known for their numerous pitfalls and frequently invisible traps. Quite often the degree of anticipated reward is a function of the degree of risk and the length of time required to reach the destination.

As the world has become more technologically advanced, hastening the speed of communications and facilitating the growth of a near global economy, opportunities for financial success have increased significantly. We live in an age of "instantism"—a time of immediate communications and far-reaching impact of what in the past have been regional economic events with only limited impact. A banking crisis in Argentina has serious implications in the United States; a recession in Japan affects trade and prices in virtually all countries. Job layoffs in Germany impact the economic well being of all nations in the European Union.

In their search for faster avenues to wealth, investors and speculators have often turned to futures trading as their vehicle of choice. In their desire for speed, however, they have often failed to remember that "speed kills." Driving to your destination at a leisurely pace of 30 miles per hour may take a good deal of time, but the odds of arriving safely are clearly in your favor. On the other hand, breakneck speeds of 150 miles per hour may get you there sooner, but they also require impeccable driving skills and high-speed crash protection gear.

There is always a trade-off between the degree of anticipated reward and the degree of necessary risk. In the end, risk and reward, as well as the vehicle(s) you select to take you to your selected goal(s) at the desired speed(s), are individual matters. Some investors believe that they can achieve their goals quickly and, given their expertise, knowledge, and self-discipline, they are correct in their analysis. Sadly, however, too many investors either overestimate their abilities or underestimate their tolerance under fire. They emerge as losers in the high-stakes, fast-paced game of futures trading.

1

In part, their failures are due to misunderstandings of both the markets as well as their own abilities. Although it is possible to correct factual misunderstandings by education and elucidation, it is an arduous task to correct ignorance of self. Myth and misconception lurk insidiously beneath the thin layer of promise offered by the futures markets. Myths and misconceptions are frequently born of and perpetuated by ignorance, hope, and fear.

History has been unkind to the futures markets. Since the earliest days of grain trading in the futures pits of Chicago more than a century ago, the markets have been shrouded in conflicts and controversies. Well-known speculators such as Jesse Livermore and Arthur Cutten have made and lost fortunes as they manipulated prices and markets to their own ends by means that were often either on the fringe of legality or outright illegal.

Market corners, financial schemes, and clandestine dealings have provided colorful material for books and powerful ammunition for critics of futures trading. To some, the mere mention of the word "futures" conjures up images of overbearing floor brokers, fast-talking traders, flimflam schemes, and ruthless speculators whose one and only goal is to take money from a naive investing public. The sordid reputation sometimes associated with futures trading is no longer warranted due to the numerous regulatory changes that have "cleaned up" the markets since the 1950s. Negative stereotypes are, however, often difficult to eradicate. They fade only with time.

Notwithstanding the persistent negative attitudes about futures trading based on its checkered history, the futures markets have long been considered too risky, too complicated, and/or too sophisticated for the average investor. For too long futures trading was either ignored or shunned in economics texts and, as a consequence, the general public has remained ignorant of how futures trading works, how it serves a vital economic purpose, and how individual investors might benefit financially from trading. Mired in myth and ignorance, the average investor has not been able to make informed choices about the possible benefits of futures trading.

Nevertheless, the individual investor accepts traditional vehicles such as stocks, bonds, and even stock options, as valid and viable investment instruments. For many decades the public has believed that trading in stocks has more historical justification, more stability, less risk, and, therefore, more validity than trading in commodity futures. In the early 1980s, however, with the introduction of stock index futures trading, the "respectability" gap between stocks and futures was bridged.

The hybrid instruments known as stock index futures became the favorite hedging vehicles of mutual fund managers. Then, in 1998, futures trading in individual stocks was initiated at the London International Financial Futures Exchange (LIFFE). Here, at last, was a true hybrid instrument that married stocks and futures. Speculators could now buy a futures contract on 100 shares of a stock. At long last futures trading achieved international acceptance and scope.

In the mind of the new trader, however, myths and misconceptions persist. This book will attempt to dispel the confusion by working from facts rather than by promulgating myths. Education is the key to profits.

Common Misconceptions about Futures Trading

Before launching into an explanation of precisely what futures trading is, let's clear the air of several common misconceptions that contribute to the standard objections often raised about futures trading. Generally, objections to futures trading are based on either partial or distorted facts. Here are a few of the misconceptions and objections followed by factual retorts and/or explanations.

You can lose all your investment capital, or more, if you trade in the futures markets. True. However, the key word is "investment." Trading futures should in no way, shape, or form be considered an investment. As a speculation, however, the rules of the game become substantially different from the rules of investing—high risk is necessary for high reward. Nevertheless, even "high risk" does not mean that the common-sense rules of effective trading and money management (as taught in this book) should be ignored.

By using solid risk management you can substantially reduce the risk of losing all your starting capital. Sense and sensibility are the keys to preserving capital. Following the well-established rules of risk management helps reduce the odds of "losing it all." Finally, it has been demonstrated that a balanced investment portfolio consisting of both stocks and futures performs better, on average, than a portfolio consisting exclusively of stocks. Hence, futures trading should be only part of an overall investment program and, as such, you are unlikely to "go bust."

Trading in futures is a gamble. This is another misconception. Anything in life can be a gamble. A gamble is so defined by its odds of success and its rules of implementation (or lack thereof). Trading in futures is technically and fundamentally no different from trading in stocks. Due to lower margins the odds of making money in futures are probably lower than those of making money in stocks.

Ultimately, however, the possible percentage return in futures trading is considerably greater than the potential return in stocks. Futures trading is, therefore, no more of a gamble than trading in stocks. Carefully and closely following the rules of successful futures trading will help reduce the risk. Traders who fail to follow a plan for, and system of, futures or stock trading are gamblers.

Only "insiders" can profit from futures trading. It's a rigged game. The markets are manipulated to benefit the rich and powerful. These three misconceptions go hand in hand. There is probably less inside information available in futures than in the stock market. The United States Department of Agriculture, the Commodity Futures Trading Commission, and the National Futures Association have imposed very stringent limits on the total number of positions a trader may hold. They monitor the brokerage industry and large trader transactions very closely. The use of inside information is prohibited by law and strictly enforced.

Important government information is guarded and kept strictly secret until the scheduled release date and time. In this way, the markets can function freely and with minimal effects of insider information. In fact, most markets cannot be manipulated for other than very brief periods because they are too complex and diverse for any one individual or group to affect prices over the long run. Although unavoidably some traders will always have an edge based on inside information, success in the futures market is entirely possible without access to such information.

Trading in futures serves no economic purpose. This myth could not be further from the truth. The futures markets serve to stabilize prices. In fact, we often forget that futures markets in the United States were originally created to protect the farmer from volatile price moves. In today's markets, many varied groups need this same price protection: farmers, food companies, banks, and other large institutions, often referred to as "hedgers."

The speculators provide liquidity because they are often willing to take market positions when prices are fluctuating significantly due to news, weather, crop conditions, and so on. They stabilize prices by buffering extreme moves of the traditional players.

Prices would move more viciously and the hedgers could not enter and exit the market as efficiently were it not for the speculators buying and selling regardless of price levels. Supplies would stand a good chance of being disrupted.

One probable cause of the Soviet Union's demise was its lack of a delivery and exchange system for its commodities. A functional futures market would have contributed considerable stability to its economic system while also reducing producer and consumer dissatisfaction.

Futures trading is for short-term speculation only. Myth or misconception, take your pick, but this conclusion is wrong all the same. Futures trading can be either long term, intermediate term, or short term, depending upon the orientation of the trader. In fact, some of the most successful futures traders, referred to as "position traders," hold their positions for an intermediate- to long-term period of time.

The particular time frame that a trader adopts is an individual choice, which does not necessarily have to be short term to be prosperous. Many factors are considered in making the choice, including the trading system used, the purpose of the trade, and the goals of the trader.

Trading in futures options will limit your losses. Yes, this is true if you are a buyer of options. If you sell options short, however, then your risk of loss is unlimited. The good news is that if you buy an option your maximum loss will be the cost of the option plus commission. The bad news is that most options expire worthless, and most options buyers will lose the money they paid for their options.

Why? The simple answer is that most options traders do not employ effective principles of options trading. All too often they hold options too long, allowing them to expire worthless. Buying options can limit your loss on each trade, but in the long run most of your options will be closed at a loss if your system or method is faulty to begin with.

A computer will help you make money in the futures markets. No. Unless you have mastered the basics of trading and unless you employ solid principles of risk management, you will lose money no matter how advanced or expensive your computer may be. The same holds true of trading systems. No system can make you money unless you use the system correctly and thoroughly.

These are just a few of the common myths, misconceptions, and misunderstandings about futures trading, all bred out of either partial information or ignorance. One by one, more myths and erroneous assumptions will be exposed and corrected as your understanding of futures markets and futures trading increases.

Evolution of the Futures Markets

Origins

Futures trading in the United States originated with the development of grain trade in the mid-1800s. Japanese futures trading in silk and rice, as well as the English methods of trading iron warrants, preceded development of the U.S. futures markets.

Futures exchanges and trading in the United States were a natural outgrowth of the need for protection against volatile price moves in physical grain products. Chicago took the leading role as the center of grain futures trading due to its strategic geographical location. The Midwestern United States is the heart of a rich and vast agricultural region, and because Chicago is strategically situated as a shipping center it was a natural site for grain trading. The Mississippi River and its tributaries were available to move grain, and as the railroads expanded, commerce in the grain markets flourished.

The Chicago Board of Trade (CBOT) was organized in 1848 and began trading about 1859. It was formed to meet the needs of producers (farmers) and exporters in order to manage systematically their risk and exposure to unknown elements such as weather, political events, and economic uncertainty. The concept of hedging, upon which futures markets are based, became widely used and continues today to serve as a valuable tool for risk management.

Although the CBOT was originally founded to facilitate trade in the grain markets, the most active contracts traded today are interest rate futures. In addition, the CBOT also founded the Chicago Board Options Exchange (CBOE) where call and put options are traded.

More Recent Developments

Since the late 1880s futures trading throughout the world was restricted to contracts on basic commodities such as grains, meats, metals, tropicals (for example, coffee, cocoa, sugar, and orange juice), cotton, petroleum, and lumber. As economic globalization achieved a strong footing in the early 1970s, the Chicago futures exchanges began trading in currency and interest rate futures. In so doing the traditional banking community entered the futures trading world as a means of protecting its assets from the growing volatility in currencies and the cost of money (i.e., interest rates). Finding such expanded markets very useful, a small but highly vocal minority of traders proposed the initiation of futures trading in stock indices, such as the Value Line Composite Index and the Standard and Poor's 500 Index.

After considerable negotiation with industry leaders and U.S. government regulatory agencies, trading in stock index futures began in the early 1980s. Since then these markets have expanded in volume as well as in the types of contracts traded. Money managers have found the stock index futures markets to be excellent vehicles for hedging their portfolio risk. Futures trading in financial vehicles continues to expand rapidly and is now a worldwide phenomenon. Virtually every stock exchange in the world has adopted a futures contract that correlates with their stock index. This has enabled traders, investors, and speculators to trade futures against a basket of stocks, thereby avoiding the necessity of picking and choosing individual stocks.

The Single Stock Futures Market

In spite of the progress in stock index futures trading, until relatively recently investors, bankers, and money managers still lacked the facility to trade futures in individual stocks. Although such trading was initially opposed by many investors as well as the key government regulatory agencies in the United States, the UK's forward thinking London International Financial Futures Exchange (LIFFE) began trading futures on individual stocks in 1998. The so-called universal stock futures market has grown slowly but steadily since then. After considerable foot dragging, trading in individual stock futures was initiated in the United States in 2002 but not without its skeptics and naysayers. Although the market must still prove itself as a viable trading vehicle, the odds are high that this new market will eventually occupy a vital role in the investment world. The introduction of single stock futures (SSF) in the United States represents a "perfect marriage" inasmuch as it fully bridges the long-standing gap between stocks and futures. The futures markets have, after more than 100 years, gained the "respectability" afforded to traditional investment vehicles such as stocks and bonds. I hasten to add, however, that this does not diminish the risk of trading in SSFs. The mere fact that one is trading a futures contract which requires considerably less margin than traditional stock trading raises the red flag of caution.

How the Market Works

The SSF concept is simple. If you think about the market in the same terms as you would a traditional futures contract, then you'll grasp the situation quickly. Here is a basic example of how the SSF market works compared to either a pure purchase of stock or a pure purchase of futures:

- You buy 100 shares of a stock at $45 per share. Your total cost, not including commission, is $4500.
- You buy 100 shares of stock at $45 per share at 50 percent margin. Your total cost, not including commission, is $2250, which means that you borrowed $2250 from your brokerage firm at their current interest rate.
- You buy one contract of the SSF on the same stock at $45 per share. The contract represents 100 shares of the stock. Your cost, not including commission, is $700 or the prevailing margin rate. You did not borrow any money from your broker to do so. There is no interest charged on the contract margin for futures trading.
- You sell your 100 shares of the $45 stock that you purchased outright at $50. You make $500 in profit, not including commission cost.
- You sell 100 shares of the $45 stock that you purchased at 50 percent margin at $50. You make $500 in profit, not including commission or interest rate charges on the margin money you borrowed from your broker.
- You sell one contract of the SSF on the same stock at $50. You make $500 in profit, not including commission or fees.

As you can see, the futures trader has the advantage in terms of leverage. In the example, by using the SSF to purchase the same stock the trader made a $500 profit on an investment of $700. This represents a much larger percentage return than what was achieved in the case of 100 shares of the stock bought at full margin. The investor who bought the stock at $45 using 50 percent margin in turn achieved a higher return than the investor who bought the 100 shares paying full price.

What's the Downside?

The upside is clear. The advantage in terms of achieving a higher rate of return is clearly to the futures trader. As you well know, futures trading can return a much higher profit for much less initial capital outlay. But what's the possible downside? Without a doubt, there is downside risk when things don't go as planned. Consider the following scenarios:

- You buy 100 shares of a stock at $45 per share. Your total cost, not including commission, is $4500. You exit at $40 per share. You lose $500, not including commissions.
- You buy 100 shares of stock at $45 per share at 50 percent margin. Your total cost, not including commission, is $2250, which means that you borrowed $2250 from your brokerage firm at their current interest rate. You sell the stock at $40 per share. You lose $500 plus commissions and the cost of the interest on the money you borrowed.

- You buy one contract of the SSF on the same stock at $45 per share. The contract represents 100 shares of the stock. Your cost, not including commission, is $700 at the going margin rate. You did not borrow any money from your broker to do so since there is no interest charged on the contract margin for futures trading. You sell the futures contract at $40 per share. You lose $500 plus fees and commissions, losing more than 50 percent of your investment.
- You buy one contract of the SSF on the same stock at $45 per share. The stock declines by $7 per share or $700 for the full contract. You lose 100 percent of your margin plus fees and commissions.

As the above scenarios demonstrate, there are two sides to the SSF coin. This should come as no surprise if one understands how the futures markets work. The simple fact is that if you buy a stock and pay full value for it (that is, 100 percent margin) then you cannot lose more than you invested. On the other hand, buying a stock on 50 percent margin means that you can lose more than you invested. Buying a futures contract at 1 percent to 5 percent margin means that you can lose much more than you invested. Clearly, this is where solid risk management needs to come into play.

Trade Possibilities SSFs Offer

Trading in SSFs opens the door to many possible combinations within the equity and futures markets, most of which professional traders are likely to exploit. Unfortunately, the possibility exists that most participants within the general trading public, by contrast, may be too lax or too inconsistent to educate themselves in the many possibilities. What do I mean by this? Consider the following possible uses of SSFs, each of which has its unique applications, assets, and liabilities:

- You buy a stock and sell an SSF contract as a hedge against the stock.
- You buy an SSF on one stock and go short an SSF on another stock in the same industry group.
- You buy an SSF in one industry group and sell short an SSF in another industry group.
- You buy an SSF on a stock and sell or buy a stock option on that stock.
- You buy an SSF on a stock, sell short an SSF on the stock, and buy a stock option on the stock.

As you can see, such potential combinations are numerous; I have mentioned only a few. It is still too early in the emergence of the SSF market to state with certainty which combinations can be expected to be the most profitable; however, the key, as always, is thorough education. It is very possible that the SSF transaction will prove to be the "best game in town," so don't let time and opportunity pass you by.

The introduction of SSFs represents a new era in the financial markets, one that promises considerable profit potential in the years ahead. Stock traders can now venture into the world of futures trading to amplify their opportunities, and futures traders can now practice their skills on stock trading and thereby open the door to new avenues of profit potential. Yet, as in all market ventures, the risks are ever present and must be considered. As noted above, it is essential to become fully educated in SSF trading before you take on risk. However, the potential benefits of doing so should far outweigh the risk if this hybrid market fulfills its optimistic promise.

What Is Hedging?

Hedging is a procedure used by producers and consumers of commodities and financial institutions as a means of protecting their business interests from severe price fluctuations. The goal of hedgers is to "lock in" or guarantee an approximate future price for the sale or purchase of their product in order to eliminate or minimize the risk of exposure to interim price fluctuations. In practice, the success of the hedger is based upon how accurately he estimates the futures price at which to lock in a sale or purchase.

Hedging is a viable procedure because futures prices fluctuate with the underlying cash markets. In other words, when corn prices on the open market move higher or lower, so do futures prices. Although cash and futures prices do not always move in the same magnitude, they do run sufficiently parallel to permit producers or end users to protect themselves by using the futures markets.

How a Hedge Works

Suppose you are a grain farmer. Your corn crop has been planted, and the summer becomes unexpectedly hot and dry. Rain is scarce in most parts of the corn-growing area. Firms that use large amounts of corn in their businesses become concerned about what will happen to corn prices several months in the future, as the heat and drought damage take their toll on the crop. Prices begin to rise. Fortunately, your area has sufficient rain. You are pleased to see prices moving higher, but you wonder how long the trend will last.

Prices are rising on the futures and cash markets because the end users (grain-processing concerns such as cereal manufacturers, animal feed manufacturers, food processors, and vegetable oil producers) begin buying large quantities of corn from farmers and grain firms that have their harvested crops from previous years in storage. Their buying is massive due to their huge needs. Simple economics tells us that the price of corn will rise as such substantial buying absorbs the supply.

In addition to their buying in the cash markets, the end users of corn also buy futures contracts. They are buying now in order to protect their profits if prices go higher in the future. Their buying is also a way of ensuring that they will have corn in order to meet the needs of their customers, the consuming public. As predicted, prices begin to rise dramatically in the cash market. Other terms for the cash market are the "spot market," "immediate market," or "day-to-day market." All are so termed because they refer to transactions made on the spot, meaning for immediate delivery—not for delivery at some future date.

As an experienced farmer, you know the cost of production for your corn. By following a sensible and complete business plan, you've taken into consideration your fertilizer, fuel, land, labor, and additional costs. You conclude that it costs you $1.85 to produce each bushel of corn. You call the local grain terminal where cash corn is bought and sold to get a price quotation.

The dealer tells you that today in the cash market, corn is selling for $3.25 per bushel. Only two weeks ago it was at $3.00 per bushel, and three months ago it was at $2.75. You know you will be producing over 50,000 bushels of corn this year and, as a consequence, the price difference between what the market was several months ago and today's price is substantial. Each one-penny move in corn prices means $500 in profit or loss to you. Therefore, if corn prices move up $1 per bushel, you stand to make $500 x 100, or $50,000.

Based on your cost of production and the current sale price of corn you stand to make $1.40 profit for each bushel of corn you produce. Is there a way you can guarantee yourself that profit by selling your corn now, before it has come out of the field? What are your choices? You know that by the time your crop has been harvested, prices may be back down again. The government could release grain from its reserves in order to drive prices down; foreign production could be larger than expected, making the U.S. crop reduction less important; or weather could improve significantly, lessening the impact of the problem.

Furthermore, demand could decline, and the grain companies might sell some of the supplies they have recently accumulated as a hedge against higher prices. A plethora of factors could diminish your profit by forcing prices lower.

Regardless of what might happen, you are satisfied with your potential profit. You decide to sell your crop at the current price in order to hedge against a decline in prices from the current high levels. You can accomplish your goal with either of two ways:

1 *You can enter into a "forward contract" with a grain firm.* Such a contract is entered into between you and a grain processor or elevator. (These firms are known as "commercials.") They will quote you a price for your crop to be delivered to them at some point in the future, usually shortly after harvest. Often their price is not as high as the market's current trading level.

2 *As an alternative, you could sell your crop on the futures market.* Prices there will be relatively free of manipulation by large commercial interests, which may have almost complete control over what prices you will be paid for your crops in your hometown area.

Provided your corn meets the proper exchange specifications, you can sell it in advance on the futures exchange. You will not get your money until you deliver the crop to the buyer, but the price you get will be locked in. Regardless of where the price goes thereafter, you will be guaranteed the price at which you sold your crop.

If the cash market is higher by the time the crop is ready, you will not make as much as you might have. If the price is lower, then you are fortunate in having sold prior to the decline. Of course, you have the option of doing nothing, gambling that corn will be much higher at some point in the future. The essence of the futures market vehicle is, therefore, its use as a tool by which the producer and end user can hedge or protect profits. Futures are ideal vehicles for hedging against rising or falling prices.

How Do the Players Benefit?

Who takes the other side of the futures transaction, and why? In other words, who will buy the grain from you, why will they buy it, what will they do with it, and how will they sell it if they change their minds? Essentially, there are three categories of "players" in the futures game. They are as follows:

1 *Producers.* These individuals and/or firms actually produce or process the commodity that is being traded, whether it be silver, gold, petroleum, corn, live cattle, lumber, sugar, or currencies. Producers make the goods available, either by growing them, harvesting them, mining them, or lending them. They need to lock in costs. In other words, they have a product they want to sell at a determined price. They may do this in order to guarantee a profit on an actual com-

modity they have on hand or have produced, or they may want to lock in a price on an item in order to avoid losing more money on it if the price is already declining.

Or, they may not have the goods at all. Rather, they may be protecting themselves from a possible side effect of declining or rising prices. For example, a jewelry store with considerable gold and silver jewelry on hand may fear a decline in the price of precious metals. It stands to lose money on its inventory as prices decline. Therefore, it may choose to sell futures contracts of silver and/or gold in expectation of the decline. Thus, it has profited from the futures sale instead of losing money if the price decline becomes a reality.

2 *End users.* These firms use the commodity that the producers sell. They need to control the cost of their production by advance purchase of raw goods. Therefore, they will either buy on the futures market or enter a forward contract (previously defined).

At times the end user may become a seller as opposed to a buyer. Assume, for example, that the end user has purchased too much or that the final product is not selling well. In such an event, the end user may switch to the sell side and control losses by using the futures market to sell the raw goods they had previously purchased.

The producer may, at times, switch sides as well. Assume that the producer does not have enough production to meet its obligations to others. The producer may then become a buyer as opposed to a seller. Roles are often changed in the futures market as all sides use the market to try to prevent losses and to guarantee profits.

3 *Speculators.* Although the largest group of futures traders, speculators do not necessarily account for the most contracts traded. These individuals are sandwiched between the end user and the producer, providing a market buffer. Perhaps no more than 1–3 percent of all futures contracts are actually completed as deliveries. The balance is closed out before any actual exchange of goods occurs.

Speculators are often willing to take risks in given markets, at given times, and at prices that may not be attractive to the other two groups. Speculators do so in expectation of large percentage profit returns on price fluctuations. **Figure I-1** shows the relationships among the three basic groups of market participants.

FIGURE I-1

Players in the Futures Markets and Their Typical Roles

PRODUCERS	SPECULATORS	END USERS
• Sell to lock in profits. Can buy at times. • Are usually farmers, banks, mining firms, petroleum producers and refiners, airlines, manufacturers. • Often called "hedgers." • Tend to trade large positions.	• Buy or sell to make a profit, but not to use the actual goods or products. • Often called "traders." • Do not take delivery of the goods. • Often trade for short-term price movements.	• Buy in order to use the product in their processing or business concern. • Can be sellers at times. • May not actually use the goods they buy. • Often buy or sell large quantities of given commodities.

Why Trade Futures?

A simple but succinct answer is "in order to profit." Traders trade, or participate in markets, in order to make profits or avoid losing profits. There are numerous ways in which the futures markets may be used for profits. Given the fact that there are literally thousands of other businesses or ventures that can be used as vehicles for profit, why would one want to choose the futures markets? Let's look at a few of the most significant reasons for trading futures.

1 *Futures trading requires relatively small start-up capital.* Typically, one can get started in futures trading for as little as $10,000 to $15,000. In some cases less capital is required. Many professionally managed trading pools require from $2,500 to $5,000 for participation. Although most traders are not successful when starting with limited capital, using small amounts is certainly one way to get your feet wet.

Futures options trading requires even less capital, but the less capital you begin with, the lower will be your odds of success. Trading a small amount of capital most often works against you because you can be wrong only a few times before your capital is gone. The more room you give yourself to be right, the more likely you are to be successful at the futures trading game.

2 *Leverage in futures is immense.* The typical futures contract can be bought or sold for 1–3 percent of its total value. For example, a 100-troy-ounce gold contract at $400 per ounce ($40,000 cash value) can be bought for about $1,500 to

$2,000. The balance of the money will, of course, be due if and when the contract is completed—in other words, if you take delivery. (In practice you will not take delivery of any commodities.)

In the meantime, about $2,000 controls $40,000. In other words, you have immense potential using small amounts of money. But there is another side to the coin! Immense potential often carries immense risk. The futures trader's goal is to make leverage work in her favor.

3 *Futures prices tend to make large moves.* Prices fluctuate dramatically almost every day. There is considerable opportunity to win or lose daily in futures trading. Many markets will permit potential returns of 100 percent or more per day on the required margin money (that is, the money required to buy or to sell a contract). Quick gain and quick loss go hand in hand.

4 *Futures markets are highly liquid.* You can get into or out of a futures position more quickly than you can get into or out of most stock and real estate investments. Some speculative stocks rarely trade, and real estate is often hard to dispose of quickly. With futures transactions, as with active stock transactions, you can enter and exit within minutes or even seconds, which makes the market ideal for the speculator with limited capital.

5 *There are not many secrets to successful trading.* In some areas of investment, you need to know either the right people or the right inside information. Although inside information can always help, it is not necessary to the success of trading futures. Successful trading has few secrets.

Good trading is a skill that can be learned and that can, in fact, be taught specifically, objectively, and successfully to those willing and able to learn. Virtually any individual with speculative capital, self-discipline, and the motivation to succeed has an opportunity to do so in the futures markets—but it's not easy. It requires work, persistence, consistency, and emotional stability.

6 *There are many futures vehicles.* In addition to the traditional buy and sell short positions, there are many vehicles in futures trading, including options, spreads, option spreads, futures versus options positions, and combinations of the above.

As discussed earlier in this chapter, in 1998 the UK's LIFFE initiated futures trading in individual stocks. By 2002, these contracts had begun trading in the United States and other countries, bridging the gap between stocks and futures by offering a hybrid instrument. Traders can now buy and sell futures contracts on stocks by using less margin than would be required for the outright purchase or sale of a stock. This new vehicle may ultimately prove to be the best of all possible worlds.

What about Risk?

As you most likely know, there is considerable risk in futures trading. Clearly, odds of success are not in your favor when it comes to the futures markets. You may have heard, as I have, that 80–95 percent of all futures traders lose money. Why are the odds so low? Why do traders lose? How do you become a member of the elite, winning minority? Here are a few of my thoughts.

Education is vital. You must learn the rules of the game before you attempt to play the game. Rules are often clear and visible. But some rules are subtle and can be learned only with experience, and experience often means trial and error. Here are some basic rules, which, if violated, will most often lead to losses.

First, start with enough capital. Traders who begin with a relatively small amount of capital are most apt to lose. If a trader cannot play the game long enough to get into the highly profitable trades, she will never pass "Go" and collect the prize. The larger your starting amount, the more likely you are to be successful. You must survive the bad times (the losing trades) in order to enjoy the good times (the winning trades).

The second rule is to be persistent. Don't be discouraged. Emotions tend to be destructive to traders. Always remain cognizant of the principles even if you have to write them on index cards or a bulletin board. This book will give you many time-tested principles that, if applied with consistency and discipline, will vastly improve your trading results. Statistically, you can be wrong about the market more than 50 percent of the time and still make money, provided losses are limited. It is the inability to keep losses small that makes most traders losers. Traders tend to make small losses into big losses by refusing to take a loss when their trading system or methods indicates that a loss should be taken.

Third, accept that losses are part of every business. Included in the broad category of losses is the cost of doing business. While not a loss in the strictest sense, these costs—rent, overhead, insurance, and so forth—are deducted from your bottom line. Losses will always happen. It is important not to be scared of them, but to know and understand them. By recognizing a loss and learning from it, you will be better able to achieve the results that differentiate the winners from the losers.

Fourth, recognize the two basic types of losses: losses caused by trader error, and losses caused by your trading system or method. To lose money in the course of following a system or method that has established itself as valid over time is an acceptable loss. To lose money due to a trader error, either from lack of discipline or carelessness, is an unacceptable loss.

In addition to the above basic rules, remember that taking profits quickly and losses slowly can make the statistics work against you. The successful trader is quick to limit losses and tends to ride profits for a relatively long time. I will emphasize this point frequently during the course of this book. Because one of my goals is to teach you the proper philosophy of trading (from which effective actions emanate), I must spend considerable time and space on the topic of trader discipline.

I am convinced that traders can reduce losses by a significant degree if they learn how to limit risk, how to take losses quickly, and how to keep them small. Small losses make every profit that much larger. One of the best ways to improve bottom-line performance is to work directly on the problems you have as a trader, which you can do only by studying your losses and learning from them.

Ultimately, risk is something all investors and traders must evaluate in relation to their financial situation and the potential for profit. Certainly there is more inherent risk in futures trading as it is commonly practiced today. Without risk, however, there cannot be rewards of the magnitude common in futures trading.

Additional Uses of the Futures Markets

As a vehicle for speculating, hedging, or spreading risk, futures trading has significant importance. As a vehicle for stabilizing costs to producers and end users, futures trading is a vital tool.

On a more pervasive level, however, an understanding of futures trading can prove very valuable to the investor not interested in actually trading futures. This book gives considerable attention to the hypothesis that a knowledge of futures price trends and futures market behavior can assist one in understanding economic trends as well as in forecasting the short-term to intermediate-term direction of prices.

Some investors may also find long-range implications in understanding and analyzing futures price trends. Finally, the introduction of futures trading in individual stocks is adding a new dimension to the current status of futures trading throughout the world, opening the door to new trading vehicles and strategies.

Summary

Futures trading is a technique whereby one can buy and/or sell a variety of raw and processed commodity items, as well as contracts on financial instruments, stock indices, and even individual stocks, for anticipated delivery at some point in the future. There are three major categories of participants in the futures markets, each with their own expectations, goals, and market methods.

Futures trading allows producers and end users to lock in costs of production, improving economic stability as well as the stability of their particular business. Speculators, by far the largest category of traders, have no interest in making or taking delivery. Rather, their interest is in playing market swings for dollar profits.

There are many common objections to futures trading. Some have merit; most do not. Most of the misconceptions of futures trading are based on a lack of education. Learning the specific methods, systems, and procedures that are used in futures trading will reduce its inherent risk.

Futures trading involves risk, but this risk can be greatly reduced by consistent application of various principles. Futures trading can be an excellent vehicle for immense profit, or it can lead you on a disastrous road to financial ruin. Those who win often attribute their success to an attitude that reflects self-discipline, courage, consistency, persistence, specific trading techniques, and a willingness to learn from mistakes.

Although the odds of success as a futures trader are clearly stacked against you, the promise of success is real and attainable provided you learn, understand, and follow the rules fastidiously. Yes, you can achieve the American dream, the "rags to riches" success story, but in order to do so you will need knowledge, persistence, self-discipline, patience, motivation, and some money. Notice that I listed money as last on my list. Think about that!

I

Getting Started:
Myths and Realities
of the Futures Markets

CHAPTER 1

Building Blocks and Basics

The only place where success comes before work is in a dictionary.

— VIDAL SASSOON

Students are often tempted to gloss over the introductory portion of a book in order to get on with the "true essence" of the subject. In so doing they often miss the subtle but important points, as well as some of the obvious building blocks that underpin solid understanding. Before you elect to skip lightly or not so lightly over any of this book, let me assure you that this book is all "true essence."

Although trading in futures is by no means rocket science, trading involves money. And where money is concerned caution is advised. Insufficient knowledge or incorrect information can and will cost you money. So if you gloss over any of this book, know that your glossing may prove expensive in the short run as well as in the long run.

Complexity and Simplicity

The stock and futures markets are often seen by the uninitiated as complex. They are, however, relatively simple to understand as long as you do not allow yourself to become intimidated by market lingo, haughty market analysts, or fast-talking brokers who "seem" to know so much. Whether you have had real-time experience trading futures and/or stocks, this chapter will help clarify the journey that awaits you in your efforts to become a profitable trader.

My first exposure to the markets was in an eighth-grade social studies class. The instructor thought it would further our education in economics and the "American Way" if we were to hypothetically invest a thousand dollars in several stocks we selected from the evening newspaper listings. "Why should we do this?" asked one of the students. "To make our capital grow," replied the teacher. He elaborated on our assignment by offering the following concise explanation of how the American capitalistic system works (which I have paraphrased).

Our system of economics functions on the basis of supply and demand. Supply and demand make prices go up and down. In order to meet demand, individuals form associations or businesses to supply the goods, services, or commodities that the public wishes to consume. However, in order to do this, they require capital.

There are many ways in which they can raise the required capital. One of the most common is the issuance of stock. Shares of stock are issued to buyers who will, in effect, lend their money to the company, which will, in turn, produce the products. The shareholders' reward for lending money to the corporation will be participation in the profits.

Of course, there is no guarantee profits will be made, and so the purchase of stock is a gesture of good faith and expectation based on the buyer's perception of the company's ability to make good on its business ventures. If the company does exceptionally well, the demand for its stock will grow and the shareholder can make money in two ways. First, money can be made on a share of profits distributed by the company. Second, money can be made when the stock price goes up in response to demand from more individuals who want to purchase shares of the company.

This definition was simple enough and certainly satisfied every one of us in class. We felt as if the task of making money in the stock market was rather simple. Referring to this oft-shared misconception about the stock market, Will Rogers once commented, tongue in cheek, "Making money in the stock market is simple. Just find stocks that are going to go up and buy them."

My classmates and I readily accepted the simple-minded solution my teacher offered in those days, and it served me well for many years to come. However, with the experience I gained over time, I found that what was once elementary and basic has become complex and involved. And yet, paradoxically, if I stand away from the topic it becomes simple again. It's as if I am looking at an Impressionistic painting. When standing from the painting at a distance I can see the big picture clearly and without confusion. The closer I get, the more blurred the painting becomes until my perspective is gone and I see only the parts of the whole. Each part means very little by itself, but all the parts in unison create a grand scene.

Similarly, there are many other basic issues that appear simple on the surface but become highly complex when examined more closely. The balance of this chapter deals with these issues in considerable detail, although not necessarily in order of importance. Each current or prospective trader must become familiar with these issues and evaluate them. Take your time. Think each issue through thoroughly and, above all, be honest with yourself. Don't take any of these points lightly, even though you may be familiar with all of them.

The facts of futures trading will be helpful to you only if you have a solid philosophical and psychological background against which to apply them. Your experience and knowledge will help you decipher the complexities, turning them into viable realities (in other words, making money).

Grist for the Mill

The world of well-dressed brokers, white-collar executives, the man in the pin-striped suit or the sophisticated woman who "listens while her broker talks" is not the real world of trading. The true facts of trading are neither pristine nor romantic. The futures game is all about professionals versus the public. There is a story behind every trade, and a trade behind every story. More often than not, the story is not a very pleasant one. More often than not, it is one that ends with professionals winning and the uninformed public losing. It's that simple, and it's that complicated.

Trading profitably is not as simple as picking up a telephone or clicking a keyboard to place an order. The true story behind the crisp numbers crossing the brokerage house ticker or flashing on your computer screen is one of competition, psychology, strategy, skill, victory, and defeat. The majority of traders are, and will continue to be, losers. Accept this fact now, or you will be nothing but grist for the market mill—a mill that is run by professional traders, experienced speculators, large hedgers, and a small but successful group of individual traders who have learned profitable trading techniques through experience and persistence.

Information: Is Less More?

Contrary to popular belief, success in the futures markets is not necessarily facilitated by gathering vast amounts of information. If you believe success is achieved by simply acquiring more information, then it is time to reevaluate your thinking process. In order to avoid the unfortunate fate of most speculators, you will need to think and act in a fashion contrary to most traders.

You will need to learn to think for yourself. You will need to respect and have confidence in your own point of view. You will use the same market tools as do many traders, but you will reach different conclusions, and you will take different actions than the majority of traders. In order to do this you will need to

- Examine your trading objectives and recognize the obstacles that might inhibit attainment of them (if any).
- Design your trading plan to include methods and solutions for overcoming the obstacles.
- Make a specific commitment to trading. Base your commitment on the amount of risk capital you plan to use and the length of time you will give yourself to achieve at least some of your objectives. Make your commitments realistic. In other words, begin with enough money and give yourself sufficient time.
- Determine the trading systems, methods, and/or techniques you plan to use as your means to attaining your objectives. If your methods are unclear then get more education (for example, read books like this one, attend seminars, or develop systems) until you have formulated a concise and specific methodology.
- Put your plans into action with consistency and discipline. This often proves to be the most difficult part of the equation.

Remember that knowledge alone is not the key to effective action. You accumulate a vast amount of research time, but without consistent and disciplined action in the markets, your efforts and investment in acquiring knowledge will not help you produce results.

In order to make money in the futures markets, you must find and complete each step of the equation for success thoroughly, consistently, and persistently. You must overcome the failures, disappointments, frustrations, losses, rejection, negativity, sadness, loss of confidence, overconfidence, anger, euphoria, and all the other emotions that are an inseparable part of life.

Define Your Objectives

In formulating your objectives, remember to be realistic. To seek perfection in the futures market is not only impractical, but also impossible. Few of us, including myself, will ever attain the level of success we seek in futures trading. The first caveat in setting your objectives, therefore, is to keep them realistic. Because futures trading is not entirely scientific, results can never be 100 percent predictable or consistent.

What works in one instance may not work in a similar situation. Remember that the percentage of time your trades are correct is not a valid measure of success. Some traders can be right 80 percent of the time and still lose money, while other traders can be wrong 70 percent of the time and make money. Clearly, success depends on whether you make more money in sum total when you're right than you lose when you're wrong.

Although we may secretly wish and hope to surpass the usual standards by a significant amount, we must not err by overestimating our abilities or by setting our expectations beyond the realm of what can realistically be achieved in futures trading. Compare your performance with that of professionals. Set your standards at a level that is realistic considering the results professionals achieve.

What, then, are these standards and how can they be determined? Fortunately, specifics are readily available. A good source of information is the monthly performance statistics of professionally managed funds (published in *Futures Magazine* and other industry publications). By examining these figures over an extended period of time, you will come to recognize what can realistically be achieved and you will also become familiar with which money managers are able to perform consistently.

It would not be unusual, for example to find that of the professionally managed futures-trading mutual funds now in operation, one of the largest cumulative percentage profits since inception was 30.4 percent over a period of six years. Note that since commodity-managed funds began reporting their results, many have been liquidated (in other words, closed down) at losses of 50 percent or greater. Even professional money managers can lose at this high-stakes game!

In order to set realistic objectives, use the following parameters of performance as your guideline: A 15–30 percent profit per year is a realistic expectation. Don't be dismayed—15–30 percent compounded annually works out to be a very high figure. Can you do better than this? Yes, but don't make your goals too lofty at first or you'll be disappointed. And that could very well affect your psychological well being.

Can You Make the Commitment?

Based on the foregoing discussion, note that professional traders, using some of the best tools and information available, commonly have obtained 15–30 percent annual profits. Their work required a major commitment of time, research, money, and effort. Although it is probably true that in the futures markets a one-to-one relationship between profits and efforts does not exist, it is also true that considerable effort is necessary in order to achieve reasonably good results.

You must assess your efforts and objectives realistically in terms of the time commitment you can make. If, after making such a determination, you find that you cannot devote sufficient time or effort to your objectives, then don't blunder by making a commitment you can't possibly keep. Don't set yourself up for failure.

Most individuals are typically long on ambition but short on effort. They have million-dollar dreams on a penny budget of effort. But even hard work, in and of itself, does not guarantee profitable trading results. Effort must be directed at specific goals. It must be guided through proper steps. It must be focused and well timed. And consistency, as well as sufficient speculative capital, must accompany it. Efforts must also be self-correcting. You need patience and a willingness to learn from mistakes. All of this takes time! Perhaps the greatest favor you can do yourself is to give yourself enough time.

How Will You Achieve Your Objectives?

Profits in futures trading can be achieved in many ways—long-term trading, short-term trading, day trading, spreading (the simultaneous purchase and sale of different contract months in the same markets), options trading, option spreads, individual stock futures, and/or floor trading. Being a broker can also provide a vehicle to success. Be forewarned, however, that there are many specious paths and vehicles that can divert you from your objectives.

You must make some important decisions as to how you will achieve your objectives. You can base some of these decisions on your present knowledge. Others, however, cannot be made until you have a broader understanding of the field. The information in this book will help you make these decisions by providing you with the facts and techniques that can help you clarify and/or develop the methods to help you achieve your goals.

The Vehicle

The vehicles that can lead you in either the right or wrong directions are actually the systems and methods of futures trading.

I cannot tell you which system is best for you. All I can do is to acquaint you with the various methods coupled with guidelines to help you decide which methods are best for you, so that you can develop your system. The performance of trading systems is not static. Systems, like traders, go through good times as well as bad. Furthermore, traders and systems interact in a complex and often confusing way.

Because systems and markets are constantly changing, there are no ultimate answers, but there are some "dos" and "don'ts," some facts and fallacies. This book will acquaint you with the tools, their assets, and their liabilities. So you can make your own decisions based upon the facts.

Many roads lead to success, but they can also lead to failure if the trader fails to adhere to the rules. In the same way that an automobile can be used safely to take you from point A to point B, it can also be used recklessly to take you from point A to a brick wall and death. If you have already had some experience in trading, you will recognize the tools that best fit your needs and abilities.

The Fuel

On the road to attaining your objectives, a reliable and well-functioning vehicle is necessary, but even the best automobile cannot take you to your destination without fuel. The energy that drives the wheels of successful speculation is good old-fashioned money. To make it, you have to have it and to multiply it; you have to use it wisely, knowing that the risk is immense and that the odds are stacked against you.

Your chances of making it in the highly competitive world of futures trading are probably five or ten in 100, but they are quickly reduced to near zero if you haven't enough fuel, or starting capital, to give yourself a chance at success. If you have only enough fuel to start the engine of your vehicle, by the time you are ready to take your trip from point A to point B, your fuel tank will be empty and the trip will be over before it begins. Unfortunately, there is no solar power when it comes to trading capital.

Not a Get-Rich-Quick Scheme

Successful speculation is not a get-rich-quick scheme, a no-money-down real estate venture, or a 15-million-to-1 odds lottery ticket. Although some promoters will present futures and options trading as a way to achieve virtually immediate success, the facts refute such claims. Yes, you will get those brochures in your mailbox and via e-mail that claim you can begin with $100 and turn it into $1 million in a year. Whatever you do, don't be foolish enough to fall for those lies.

The facts of futures trading clearly demonstrate that the more money you start with, the greater your odds of success. The less you start with, the greater your chance of failure. It's actually very simple and totally logical. If you begin with $2,500 and lose $500, five times in a row, then you're out of the game. Losing $500 five times in a row is quite common. Hence, beginning with $2,500 or less immediately stacks the odds against you. Does this mean that you can't begin with $2,500? No, it doesn't mean that at all. But it does mean that you'll have to be very accurate in your selection of trades.

"Then how much is enough?" you ask. Here are some guidelines. Based on recent conditions in the futures markets, a beginner should have sufficient capital to meet liberal marginal requirements on at least five futures contracts. If we assume, for example, that the average margin on a futures contract is $1,500 (excluding the very high-margin stock index futures), then we are looking at approximately $7,500 in speculative capital. Yet, if we also assume that traders want a realistic buffer in their accounts, then twice the amount is highly recommended. I therefore believe that $15,000 is a good starting amount. I think it is unrealistic for you to expect success if you begin with less.

Don't be fooled! Some individuals will tell you that you need virtually nothing in the way of starting capital, whereas others will tell you that you need much, much more. I won't argue the fact that the more money you begin with, the better your odds of success will be; however, there is a limit on the lower end of the scale. Although you don't want to risk all your money on a speculative venture such as futures trading, you must be willing to risk a reasonable starting amount.

Take the Test

When someone asks me how much he should risk in futures trading, I answer with a simple question. "How much can you afford to lose?" One answer might be $10,000. "Take this slip of paper on which I have written $10,000," I respond. "Rip it into shreds. Flush it down the toilet. How do you feel?" If you can cope with the loss by not having it affect your lifestyle, then that's how much you can risk.

What if you don't have enough starting capital? Some people will tell you to begin with any amount. "Just get your feet wet," they tell you. Nonsense! That is terrible advice. Why throw the money away? You would be better off buying lottery tickets. At least then you would have one chance in 80 million of winning $120 million. The solution? Save your money until you have a sufficient nest egg. Use the time to sharpen your trading skills or, better yet, invest the small amount of money in secure vehicles so that it can grow a little while you're learning and saving your pennies.

My "flush it down the toilet" test is merely a small experiment that may help you determine how much you can afford to lose in the futures market without too serious an emotional reaction to the consequences. Financially, the answer is different. How much can you afford to risk on futures trading from this standpoint? I suggest that, as a rule of thumb, you risk no more than 10 to 15 percent of your total liquid risk capital.

Should You Borrow Your Starting Capital?

Let me caution you against an ill-advised practice I have witnessed on a number of occasions during my years in the futures markets. It has become more and more common for individuals to borrow money in order to speculate in futures. Specifically, second mortgages, home equity loans, or credit card advances are often used for this purpose. I advise you to *avoid* this foolish practice.

To borrow your starting capital represents poor judgment. The results of such actions can be disastrous. You not only place yourself at financial risk, but also jeopardize your trading by using funds that should not and cannot be placed at risk. Certainly it takes no great insight to see that your trading decisions would be based on fear, which would seriously affect your judgment.

Another pitfall to avoid is the following mental trap: "I'll put more money into my account than I intend to lose, but the rest will draw interest and, of course, I will watch the money closely." This is a rationalization, also based on unrealistic thinking. Even with the best intentions, you are likely to use that "extra" money in the account for trading. Put into your account only what you can afford to lose in its entirety.

Don't be enticed by the lure of interest rate earnings on unused funds, especially so-called "low-risk" trading programs, "fail-safe" programs, "no-risk" option strategies, "minimal-risk" spreading programs, and a host of other seemingly simple "minimal-risk" programs. I've seen many of them come and 99 percent of them go. There are some big winners, but there are many, many more big losers.

Pooling Your Funds

There is one exception to my caveats about borrowing money. If you have one or more friends who would like to join you in a group-trading venture, then my cautionary notes do not apply. You should, however, make some other considerations before you join forces in a trading club or partnership.

Simply stated, the more personalities that are involved in the program, the more room there is for disagreement and petty quarrels that can lead to losses. Yet, if you play to the strengths of the group process, you can achieve some excellent results. Organization, division of labor, and precise procedures are necessary if success is to follow.

Attain Your Objectives by Stages

The most fruitful and consistent way to achieve a goal is through stages or steps. You cannot and will not get from point A to point B instantly. Unfortunately, or perhaps fortunately, the laws of physics, or our current state of knowledge about them, do not permit thoughts to become actions instantaneously, so goals must be attained slowly. All too often traders become aggressive at the wrong time. They are easily influenced by initial successes to begin trading on too large of a scale. Frequently this overeagerness becomes their fatal flaw.

Attain your objectives gradually and steadily. Begin with a reasonable number of futures contracts and progress to larger amounts slowly as you gain experience and your profits increase. Avoid the temptation to "go for the big one" or to "go for broke," risking most of your money on that one big trade. Given the choice, you are better off scoring singles, doubles, an occasional triple, and the rare home run now and then, than you are trying for the home run every time. A solid and effective trading system will take care of this problem for you.

Bank Some Profits

Whether you decide to trade for the short, intermediate, or long term, you should regularly withdraw profits from your account once you have reached a certain level of successful performance. Generally, I recommend removing 10–25 percent of profits from your account. You don't need to do this on a trade-by-trade basis— you can do it weekly or perhaps monthly—but remember to do it!

Withdrawing profits follows the successful methods of most businesses. After a period of learning and initial cost, a business that reaches the point of profitable operation will generate income for its operator(s). The profits are then taken and invested in other vehicles not directly connected with the business itself. Diversification of investments is a solid, time-tested practice. By leaving some of your profits in the account, your base will grow and you can trade bigger positions (in other words, more contracts) and diversify into more markets, thereby spreading your risk.

The history of futures trading is very clear in this respect. Many well-known speculators have achieved tremendous profits in their accounts. However, lured by greed and the promise of even greater profits, they have plowed every penny, if not more, back into the markets, only to lose it all. When all is said and done, they have nothing but frustration and losses to show for their considerable efforts. More speculators would be successful if they approached futures trading as a business.

This is why you must formulate and institute a program for systematically removing a percentage of your profits from your trading account. Do so whether you are speculating for the long-term, short-term or intermediate-term time frame.

Other Important Issues

A number of additional issues and consideration warrant the attention of all futures traders, regardless of their particular trading approach, system, or methodology. Several of them are reviewed briefly now, and discussed in greater detail as the occasions present themselves in later chapters.

Should You Trade Alone or with a Partner?

There are pros and cons to each alternative. If you trade alone, there will be no one to help you with your work (unless you hire employees) and there will be no one who can trade for you in your absence. Furthermore, there will be no one with whom you can discuss various markets, indicators, techniques, and trades.

For individuals who need this type of assistance, a partner or well-trained assistant might be desirable. However, before making a decision consider the potential negatives of having a partner or partners, as noted below. In the final decision, only you know whether you are capable of working with others.

Too many cooks spoil the soup. Futures trading in many ways is a "loner's game." Sometimes a partner or partners will get in your way. You may be influenced to avoid some trades you should have made and to make some trades you should have avoided.

Who's responsible? In developing your trading, it is always good to know that you alone have the responsibility for profits and losses. If you have a partner or partners, it may be difficult to know who is responsible for each decision. Lacking such knowledge will slow the learning process and may, in fact, stall it entirely.

Sharing the profits. Do you really want to share your profits with partners? Granted, they may also share in your losses, but because you may end up with more losses if you have partners, the benefits may prove nil.

Do you want to share your research? Many of us consider our research proprietary. We work long, hard hours to develop trading systems and methods, and we may not want to share these with a partner regardless of what he or she may bring into the relationship.

Slower decision time. Decisions in the futures markets must be made quickly. Many times a trading partner may slow down the decision-making process and, hence, severely limit the speed with which you can execute orders. This, as you can well imagine, can have negative results.

Should You Trade for the Short Term, Long Term, or Intermediate Term?

I could write several books just addressing this subject. There are many variables to consider, not the least important of which are your personality and temperament. Always remember your point of view.

Here are just a few of the factors you should consider in making this decision:

Trading system. Don't attempt to force a system into a time frame that is inconsistent with its method or logic. The system itself will dictate its own length of trade, whether it is short term, long term, or intermediate term.

Time availability. Only you know how much time you have available. To trade for the short term or intraday you must make a major time commitment. If you have another job and you can't make this commitment, don't even try! Be realistic and determine what you can do with the time you have available. Your available time may automatically make your decision for you.

Commissions. Are you paying sufficiently low commissions to permit short-term trading with a positive bottom line?

Personality. Can you take the pressure of short-term or day trading? Are you more in tune with long-term trading, its less demanding pace and required patience?

Health. Believe it or not, health is a consideration. If you are in poor health, then by all means don't push your luck. The stress of trading can often exacerbate existing health problems such as hypertension. If you are prone to react emotionally or if the stress of trading is likely to aggravate any problem condition(s) you have, then do not trade. Assessing your health honestly will help you in making your choice without having to consider any of the other aspects.

Data. Many individuals are under the mistaken impression that they can day trade the market without a steady source of tick-by-tick data. Don't fool yourself! To day trade you need up-to-date, tick-by-tick, accurate, and reliable data. If you can't afford it, if you don't know how to use it, then don't kid yourself. Day trading is not for you.

You. In addition to the above, there are other factors that are specific to your individual situation that you must consider before making a final decision about the type of trading to do. Evaluate where you are in life and what matters most. This is an important decision. Do not take it lightly.

Should You Take a Fundamental or a Technical Approach to Market Analysis?

Another important decision that you should make before you start trading is whether your approach will focus primarily on trading signals from technical indicators or from trading ideas based upon fundamentals. I distinguish here between signals and ideas because they are two distinctly different types of approaches generated by two distinctly different understandings of the futures markets.

Chapter 2 provides a very thorough discussion of the two approaches, outlining their advantages, liabilities, differences, and methods of implementation. For now, suffice it to say that a decision will need to be made, preferably sooner than later, about the approach you wish to use in your trading.

Some individuals may seek to implement a hybrid approach, incorporating what they feel are the best aspects of each technique. I also will discuss the merits of this approach and the hazards.

How Much Risk Do You Want to Take on Each Trade?

Answer this important question before you start trading. Many factors enter into this decision, and there are many different opinions regarding the best answer.

At one extreme are those who belong to the "money management" school. They will tell you that the best approach to take is a per-trade risk based strictly on money management. In other words, you decide ahead of time the maximum risk you want to take, in dollars, based upon your available capital. When a trade goes against you by the predetermined amount, you close it out.

On the other end of the spectrum is the "systems approach." Proponents of this approach claim that each trade is unique. Every trade has specific levels of support and resistance, so it is not possible to determine an *a priori* rule for dollar risk. My approach to determining an appropriate level of risk to take on in futures trading is essentially similar to my approach in other areas. I prefer not to be in the middle of the road. Rather, I would align myself with either of the extremes. Although my rationale for this preference may not be clear to you at this time, I will explain it more fully in Chapter 2. It has been said that you can walk on the left side of the road or the right side of the road, but if you walk in the middle of the road, you will get squashed.

There are merits and drawbacks to each approach, and there is no right or wrong answer to the question. There is, however, an answer that is *your* answer. My job is to help you find it, as one can be successful by following either of the extremes.

Selecting a Broker

This important topic is discussed thoroughly in Chapter 11. You needn't make your decision now. You may, in fact, already have a broker (or brokers). If you do, then you can evaluate your broker in terms of my guidelines and suggestions. In addition, online trading has created a new set of concerns when it comes to the broker selection process, which I also discuss in detail in Chapter 11.

A broker can help you or hurt you. I do not contend that brokers intentionally hurt customers. Certainly, this would not be in their best interest. On various levels, however, the relationship between broker and client is extremely important and insufficient attention has been given to this variable. Virtually no book I've read on successful methods of speculation places adequate emphasis on this relationship as a factor and its potentially positive and negative implications. When you have finished reading this book, your ideas about the broker/client relationship are likely to have changed significantly.

Of course, the advent of online trading that bypasses the need for one-to-one contact with a broker has helped overcome many of the problems that can occur between broker and client. Yet, as is often the case, technology solves some problems but creates others. Online futures trading has been responsible for many blunders in order placement by traders, and, furthermore, it has helped create a new trading addiction. This topic I cover in considerable detail later on.

The foregoing issues are ones you should consider before you undertake serious speculation in the futures markets. This book will raise many other important issues, but the ones outlined in this chapter should incubate within your unconscious mind while you read the chapters that follow.

I want to stress that some of the material discussed in the balance of this book will not be new to you. In fact, I am certain that many of the issues I have discussed in this chapter are ones with which you are already familiar. Don't let your familiarity with these ideas stand in the way of your acquiring new and valuable understanding.

If you consider the fact that most market analysts and speculators have the same information at their disposal, but that some use it with considerably more success than others, you will understand that the difference between losers and winners is not necessarily that winners have better tools, but rather that they use their tools better. How to use these tools for maximum efficacy is what this book will attempt to teach you.

Are Futures Options Your Answer?

If you thought that futures trading was an abstract concept, then get ready for an even more abstract idea. While futures contracts allow sellers or buyers to trade in things that do not yet exist, futures options allow buyers and sellers to buy or sell the right to buy or sell things that don't exist. Futures contracts are one step removed from reality. Futures options are therefore two steps removed from reality.

Instead of buying or selling a futures contract, you buy the right to buy or sell a futures contract. The right, or option, to do so costs you considerably less than the futures contract, but the option has a limited life span and loses value every day that the underlying futures contract goes the opposite way of the option. Options therefore limit the loss you can suffer, but the downside is that they will expire on a given date and have no value if they are not exercised. You'll learn a lot more about options in Chapter 15.

Summary

Success in the futures markets can come only at the expense of other traders' failures, because there is a loser for every winner. Many factors, not the least of which is your own personality, will affect your success in the market. You must set realistic objectives and follow them with persistence and consistency if you intend to succeed.

Before trading, know the amount and sources of the starting capital you'll need. Develop and implement a procedure for withdrawing proceeds from profitable trades. Partnerships, time frame orientation, system type, broker/client relationship, and level of risk are all issues you must deal with in an honest and proactive fashion. If you do not do so before you begin trading, then you are only setting yourself up for failure. Good planning and preparation facilitate success and reduce the likelihood of losses due to errors, misconceptions, and misunderstandings.

CHAPTER 2

The Two General Approaches:
Fundamental vs. Technical Analysis

Opportunities multiply as they are seized.

— SUN TZU

At times it is necessary to challenge existing thoughts, theories, and institutions in order to achieve progress. Many of the beliefs, theories, and trading methods revered and touted as effective by futures traders are based on myth, wishful thinking, and/or misinformation. As in all aspects of life, you must be careful what you believe. Beliefs, although often unsupported by facts, color perception. And perception affects behavior.

Because this book will challenge many concepts and beliefs many traders revere, let's not waste any time before the "feather-ruffling" begins. Let's start by exploring a basic controversy of futures trading. This is what I call the "good, the bad, and the ugly"—fundamental analysis, technical analysis, and the peculiar offspring of their marriage that one might, euphemistically term "eclectic market analysis."

We will take a critical overview of the two major approaches, then examine their hybrid in order to see which, if any, might be the most desirable approach. Please understand that this chapter contains only my opinions. I do not purport to speak for the futures industry or for any particular method or group of analysts. Nor do I represent any favorite methodology or system. My thoughts are based on market experience dating back to the late 1960s.

Does Your Analytical Approach Really Matter?

The ultimate goal of these opinions is not to be right or wrong but to stimulate thought and, in so doing, to promote positive change. All markets function on the basis of opinion combined with fundamental economic factors and investor psychology. Unsupported opinions are plentiful, but opinions based on considerable experience are often catalysts for new insights.

Nothing can replace market experience. No matter what approach you use in trading the futures markets, the end result will be determined by your skill as a practitioner with the method or methods you have selected.

Above all, I am a pragmatist, and I encourage you to adopt the same orientation. I'm interested in whatever works as long as it's legal, moral, and ethical. If someone tells me that they have discovered a method of astrology that predicts market turns with high accuracy, then I'm interested. I hasten to add that many such claims have been presented to me in the past. To date, none have impressed me.

If someone tells me that they have developed a totally computerized black-box approach to trading that produces fantastic results, then I'll look into it and perhaps even use the method once I'm convinced that it has merit. Do I care what's inside the black box? Not at all! Know also that we can often figure out what's going on inside a black box by looking at what comes out of the black box.

Fundamental Analysis

What in heaven's name is a fundamental? I have often asked myself this question. One could argue reasonably that everything is fundamental. Do we mean fundamental as opposed to trivial, do we mean fundamental in the sense of basic, or fundamental as in the sense of a building block? In the world of present-day futures trading, all three definitions are applicable as well as descriptive. Perhaps the best way to understand this approach to market analysis and trade selection is to present an overview of how fundamentals are applied to trading and what kinds of information a "fundamentalist" uses.

Fundamentalists use historical economic information to establish a supply-and-demand price analysis. They then relate estimates of this year's supply-and-demand balance to the historical price to decide if the current price is too high, too low, or just right. The exact fundamentals studied depend on the market being analyzed.

Most often, however, the fundamentals relate to supply-and-demand factors. In the grain markets, for example, the major fundamentals are crop size, weather, demand, and other factors. In the livestock markets fundamentals consist of the number of animals being raised, demand, and other factors. In the interest rate futures markets fundamentals consist of demand for money, government interest rate policy, economic trends, employment statistics, the Gross National Product, and other factors.

Supply and Demand

To arrive at an estimate of current supply and demand statistics in corn, for example, the fundamentalist will often examine reports of the number of acres planted with a particular crop. The fundamentalist also will look at the sales of fertilizer, the sale and cost of diesel fuel for farm equipment, past weather data and predicted weather patterns for both the near and longer term, the impact of competition from substitutes or new products, and changes in eating patterns and per-capita income affecting demand.

This list would have to be extended significantly to include all the primary determinants of price; yet, the accuracy of the current price evaluation would depend on the accuracy of the estimates and the weighting of factors. Do not think, however, that due to the complexity of the information involved, fundamental methods, as we have defined them, are impossible to develop.

Computers can use numerous econometric formulas to massage the data, thereby reducing the often diverse and massive amount of data into specific values and forecasts. A solid analysis of fundamentals can provide highly worthwhile information that can be used effectively for trading purposes when approaching the markets from an intermediate-term to long-term perspective.

The difficulty with the fundamental approach for most speculators is that vast amounts of time and money can be consumed to obtain the past and present data and to work it into reliable formulations. To continue updating the data daily, or even weekly, on all major futures markets would require a full-time staff. Furthermore, the individual trader who wishes to use the fundamental approach competes directly with the largest producers and processors in the world, who have virtually unlimited resources for information gathering and analysis. In such a competition, the usual winner is obvious.

Fundamentals, then, are the economic realities that ultimately affect price. Fundamentalists are those who formulate a trading plan or trading approach on the basis of fundamentals. In other words, they take the basics of supply and demand and determine whether prices are likely to increase or decrease. On the basis of these expectations, they make buy and sell decisions.

Economic Roots

Fundamental analysis has its roots in economics. As there are numerous economic theories, there are many different approaches to fundamental analysis. The common element of all approaches to fundamental analysis is that fundamentalists study the purported causes of price increases and price decreases in the hope that they will be able to ascertain changes prior to their occurrence.

The success of this approach depends on the accurate assessment of the variables analyzed as well as the awareness and correct analysis of variables that may not be known to other fundamental analysts. But timing of market entry is a critical variable. Even when armed with the most solid fundamental analysis, fundamental traders must time their market entry almost perfectly or prices will move against them before their projected trends develop. In the interim they may be forced to abandon their positions if the losses become too large.

The plethora of statistics available to the fundamentalist at any given point in time can be overwhelming. The fundamentalist must be selective in choosing which data to cull and which data to weight more strongly. The true fundamentalist must be prepared to evaluate a massive amount of data.

In recent years the globalization of markets has further complicated the task of fundamental analysis. Economic trends, patterns, and changes in Europe and Asia can and do have a significant impact on price trends in the United States and vice versa. The creation of a common European currency also has had a marked effect on market trends. Clearly, the job of the fundamental analyst is becoming more complicated daily, but advances in the ability of computers to process massive amounts of data quickly and at a low cost have helped offset the increasingly demanding task of fundamental analysis.

There is no one typical fundamentalist. Rather, there are many different types of fundamentalists who evaluate different types of data at different times and for different reasons. There are those who, by virtue of their skill and expertise, can provide accurate forecasts, and there are those who, working with the same tools, make worthless forecasts. Furthermore, some analysts are oriented toward short-term market trends whereas others are focused on secular (in other words, longer lasting) trends.

Some Shortcomings of Fundamental Analysis

The popularity of computer technology has, unfortunately, overshadowed to some degree the excellent work being done by many individual researchers in the area of fundamental analysis. The tendency today to look for high-speed solutions to the problems of economic forecasting (as well as other issues in the social sciences) has been reflected by the trend away from fundamental analysis toward a heavy reliance on technical analysis (to be discussed). On the other hand, the difficulty, complexity, and cost of thorough fundamental analysis have in part been responsible for the contemporary trend toward simpler solutions.

Without considerable training and education, the average trader or investor in futures (and stocks) will have very limited success in understanding, analyzing, and developing massive amounts of fundamental statistics. Furthermore, some of the critically important statistics are not generally available to the public and can be obtained only by conducting private and often costly surveys. Even if all significant fundamental statistics were available to us, the average individual would have difficulty interpreting their meaning as it relates to the important issue of futures trading, which is timing.

There are then, a number of significant drawbacks to the use of fundamental analysis. They are as follows:

Not all fundamentals can be known at any given time. Some of the "unknowns" may be very important and could markedly alter a forecast and/or market timing. For example, the trading public may not be privy to information known only to large firms. Hence, the knowledge that the public has may be dangerously insufficient.

The importance of different fundamentals varies at different times. It is difficult to know which fundamentals are most significant at which time. To correctly interpret the significance of different fundamentals at different times is often more a function of experience and skill than of standardized procedures.

The average speculator may have difficulty gathering and interpreting the wealth of information that is available for every market. This has often meant that thorough fundamental analysis is available only to large corporations and individual investors who have the funds required to gather and to analyze the relevant statistics.

Fundamental analysis often fails to answer the important question that faces most speculators—the question of timing. While our analysis of the fundamentals can tell us that a given crop is in short supply, that world demand has increased, and that current crop conditions are likely to result in lower production, fundamentals cannot necessarily tell us exactly when prices will begin to reflect these conditions.

Many fundamental statistics are available after the fact. By the time various government agencies and/or private reporting services throughout the world gather certain fundamental data, the data is often too old and does not necessarily reflect the immediate situation. Making financial decisions on out-of-date information will often lead to losses.

Fundamentals can be significantly altered by abrupt changes in weather, politics, international events, and economic policies. Although the fundamental statistics lead us to expect certain price trends, current trends could change dramatically in response to unexpected events.

Even though the change may be brief, the resulting temporary reversal in market trends could result in traders' abandoning their positions due to fear of losses. When the momentary impact of the unexpected fundamental developments has subsided, traders are left with losses and no market position in spite of the fact that their fundamental view of the situation was correct.

The amount of effort required in gathering, updating, and interpreting fundamental data may not, in the long run, yield efficient results. Trading is a business. As a business it has fixed and variable costs. Obviously, if the sum total of the fixed and variable costs exceeds the sum total of gross profits, then the business is destined to fail.

The cost and effort of implementing decisions based on fundamental analysis can be a major limitation to profits. Yes, you can buy fundamental research reports from firms that specialize in this field; however, you must remember that most traders who do so will be looking at the same information and most likely acting on such information in the same way.

The odds are that few traders will have a complete picture of the fundamentals, which is the reason why so many traders who use fundamental analysis are so often wrong at major market turning points.

Most fundamental analysis does not provide alternatives based on price action, but rather on changes in underlying conditions. These changes may often be slow to develop. At times there will be no apparent or perceptible alteration in the bullish or bearish trend when, in fact, a major change is developing under the surface.

What I am saying here, in essence, is that markets begin the process of change slowly and often without obvious fundamental changes—and this can be a serious problem to the trader who uses fundamentals as the only means of market analysis and prediction.

Its Value in Spite of the Limitations

Yet, in spite of these often troubling shortcomings, fundamental analysis still has its place in the world of futures trading. Ultimately, the price of every commodity is a function of fundamentals. However, although fundamentals do indeed determine price, the path that prices take to get to from point A to point B may be a meandering one that is more a function of short-term considerations than underlying fundamentals.

Due to this complicating factor (as well as those limitations listed earlier), fundamental analysis has been the whipping boy of market technicians for many years. Whether justified or not, this perception has led to a regrettable understatement of its importance as an analytical tool.

Rest assured that the fundamentals are extremely important. Their proper implementation in developing a trading method can yield significant results over the long term. On the basis of my observations, I conclude that fundamental analysis has its place for the intermediate- and long-term trader. However, for short-term speculators I believe that fundamentals are not likely to yield the results they seek.

The individual who is willing to establish an intermediate or long-term position, who is able to stay with the position, who is also able to give the position plenty of leeway, and who can possibly add to the position on a scale-in basis can do exceptionally well. This is the proper niche for the fundamentalist.

Typically, individuals employed to provide price forecasts, hedging programs, purchasing programs, and planning programs for commercial end users or suppliers using the futures markets are especially good at understanding and implementing fundamentals.

These individuals are not primarily concerned with timing. Frequently they can ride through most temporary price storms within the secular trend. The average speculator, however, cannot use the same approach because capital, time, patience, and tolerance are constrained by very limited resources in comparison to the resources of corporations and/or well-capitalized professional traders.

The Pragmatics of Fundamentals

Fundamental analysis is not the anathema that so many contemporary traders consider it to be. Fundamentals form the basis of the economic equation. Too often they will be proven correct after the fact with virtually 100 percent accuracy. It is easy to see how fundamentals affected prices after the fact, but it is difficult to predict how fundamentals will affect prices before the fact.

Even such unexpected events as changes in weather ultimately will be reflected in the fundamental statistics, forecasting price level, and direction, but response time can be slow. Many a trader has been fooled by a dramatic change in fundamentals, seemingly overnight, that has not affected prices either to the degree or as immediately as the "experts" had expected.

The interpretation of fundamentals is both a science and an art that most speculators and average futures traders will have difficulty implementing. Experience and knowledge are particularly important in the analysis and implementation of fundamentals. They cannot be acquired as quickly as can experience in the area of technical analysis.

If you are interested in learning more about the application of fundamentals, consider the following suggestions:

1 *Study economic theory.* Acquaint yourself with the various micro- and macroeconomic theories, particularly as they apply to production and consumption, in other words, supply and demand.

2 *Acquire a thorough knowledge of the production, consumption, critical factors, and uses of the various commodities you wish to trade.* This can be a daunting task, but it is necessary if you intend to be successful as a fundamental analyst.

3 *Attempt to specialize, but do not exclude all other markets from your perspective.* There are so many factors to consider in the thorough analysis of fundamentals that you cannot keep abreast of all markets and all economic trends throughout the world.

You cannot be in touch with all market factors and all markets at one time, even with the assistance of a computer. Therefore, you may be best off specializing in one or two groups of markets (such as, meats, grains, metals, stock index futures, interest rate futures, or currencies).

4 *Plan to spend several years learning the application of fundamentals.* This is a highly complex field, one that is not mastered easily. Once mastered, however, the benefits can be substantial for the intermediate- and long-term trader.

5 *Always keep in touch with the global economic picture.* As you know, the markets have become global in many respects. Conditions that affect Japanese banks also affect European banks and United States banks. Currency relationships affect grain prices and, at times, interest rates and stock markets.

We live in a world of complex economic actions, reactions, and interactions. To be fully aware of how fundamentals will affect a given market, you must work to understand how the international economic, monetary, and political situations can or will affect the markets you are analyzing.

Technical Trading and Analysis Systems

Excluding the complete novice to futures trading, virtually everyone is familiar with one or several aspects of technical analysis. Technical analysis is loosely defined as a study of market-generated data and its derivatives with the goal of forecasting price and/or determining specific market timing. This means that the technical analyst studies such things as price, volume, open interest, and chart patterns, as well as their interrelations, permutations, and combinations.

The goal of most technical analysis is not necessarily prediction; rather, it is the determination of specific entry and exit levels and/or specific price objectives. Unlike fundamental analysis, prediction is not a significant issue. In fact, there are many excellent market technicians whose motto is "we only follow trends, we don't try to predict them. We let the market tell us what to do, and we follow the directions." For the technical analyst, specific buy and sell points and/or times to buy or sell are sufficient.

Perhaps an example of how a decision might be made using both approaches will help clarify the differences. In mid-2001 cocoa prices began moving higher after many months of a declining trend. Seemingly without warning the price of cocoa futures jumped sharply and continued higher for many weeks. Although the average trader was unaware of the reasons for the move when it first started, the fact that a disease affecting cocoa beans would severely limit the supply of cocoa was well known to the industry professionals and insiders, who were big buyers. Those individuals and firms bought cocoa futures when they learned the news. Technical traders who did not know the news but who saw their chart patterns change from negative to positive also bought the futures markets but not because they knew the news. It was not until the market had made a large move up that the average trader learned of the news. Both types of traders could have made a profit if they had followed their trading signals.

Technical analysis has long been a favorite tool of futures traders. It is difficult to say with certainty when or in what part of the world such methods were first employed. There is evidence, however, that traces of technical analysis go back hundreds of years. For example, in feudal Japan records from 1654 indicate that Japanese rice merchants traded rice contracts using chart patterns similar to what we now call candlestick charts.

Modern-day technical analysis prides itself on having a quasi-scientific basis (I use the term "quasi-scientific" because technical analysis uses elements of scientific methodology combined with subjective aspects.) As a result of this orientation, you can understand how the continued exponential growth of scientific methodology has spilled over into the area of technical analysis (as well as fundamental analysis). As a consequence, there are literally hundreds of trading systems, methods, and techniques based on technical concepts.

Technical Analysis and Short-Term Trading

Technical analysis has a place of prominence in the world of futures trading, but it has its limitations as well. By its nature, technical analysis lends itself more readily to short-term trading than to long-term trading. Although certain technical methods may be applied to long-term charts, futures contracts have a limited time span which makes long-term analysis difficult. The technical analysis of cash prices is indeed possible, but it does not necessarily always yield effective timing in futures.

Long-term technical analysis of price trends must employ long-term data. The only purely continuous long-term data available to futures analysts is cash market data. The variability of prices from one contract to another as a function of such things as carrying charges, storage charges, and interest rates creates a gap that must be filled either by creation of artificial data or by some other statistical manipulation that is not necessarily representative of true underlying conditions.

Some Limitations of Technical Analysis

Critics tend to attack the credibility of technical analysis on several fronts. The most obvious of these contends that the technical analyst attempts to use market-generated data to predict timing and price trends in an insular, almost circular manner. To use a simple analogy, it's akin to asking the elected members of the incumbent political party if they have done a good job.

Additional criticisms of technical analysis are as follows:

1 *"Pure" technical analysis ignores all extraneous inputs such as news, fundamentals, weather, and the like.* Analysts who are pure technicians in fact often consider attention to fundamentals a detrimental distraction. Critics, on the other hand, view technical analysis as a form of tunnel vision, because it accepts input from no other method or technique when employed by its most orthodox adherents. Many in the market feel that a more "holistic" or all-inclusive approach is better, and that pure technical analysis is too narrow in its focus. There is some merit to the argument that ignoring all fundamentals can fail to provide traders with a complete picture.

Technical analysts respond to this criticism by claiming that all fundamentals are reflected in prices and trends, and, because this is the "stuff" that technical analysts study, they are capable of knowing when trend changes are likely to occur or knowing that a new trend has started shortly after it begins.

2 *Technical analysis is so widely used, particularly by computer-generated trading programs, that many systems act in unison, thereby affecting prices in a fashion that is not representative of true price structures.* This type of phenomenon has occurred many times in the markets. The claim is further made that technical analysis has become a self-fulfilling prophecy and that patterns most technical analysts watch fail to follow through after their initial impact, which is caused by technical trading programs. There is also some merit to this criticism.

3 *Technical analysis cannot allow for good forecasting or determination of price objectives, because it does not account for underlying economic conditions.* This is, of course, the crux of the argument between market technicians and fundamentalists. You alone must decide what is right for you given your experiences and observations.

4 *Technical analysis is not a valid scientific approach because most methods study prices based upon price-related data.* In a sense, the technical trader is attempting to predict the outcome of a dependent variable based upon the history of the dependent variable. If the variable is indeed dependent upon circumstances external to it, however, then it is a fallacy to attempt such predictions without knowing the external circumstances.

Those are some of the objections to technical analysis. On the positive side, however, technical analysis attains its strength from the fact that it is a form of disciplined and essentially mechanical application of trading rules. In its ideal form, technical analysis leaves little or no room for interpretation of trading signals. In this way, it permits discipline to regulate trading. Naturally, these are ideal concepts, and their application is most certainly dependent upon the individual.

Advantages of Technical Analysis

The notable advantages of a purely technical trading methodology are:

1 *Objectivity.* The technical approach, in ideal form, is objective and specific. In this sense, it can be considered quasi-scientific, akin to scientific methodology.

2 *Specificity.* The technical approach looks for specific indications from the data that the analysts can then act upon. Hence, there should be little or no room for interpretation in a purely technical method.

3 ***Mechanical decision-making.*** Many technical analysts claim that their approach is totally mechanical. In other words, no "subjective" thought must go into the buying/selling decisions. The system makes all the judgments, and the trader follows them mechanically (when the system is implemented in its ideal form).

4 ***Testable results.*** All results and indicators can be tested and verified historically. This makes the approach more scientific and lends credence to its use and value.

5 ***Cross-user reliability.*** The technical approach should yield similar results regardless of who is using the system, provided the traders' rules are the same. (However, this is not the case with many technical methods, because many traders use different rules that then lead to different trading signals.)

6 ***Ease of application.*** By eliminating judgment calls, interpretation, and even decision making, technical systems are claimed to be easier to implement than are fundamentally based systems.

7 ***Computer application.*** The advent of low-priced personal computer systems has made technical systems even less difficult to test and employ. Most truly mechanical systems can be programmed into computers, which will generate all buy and sell signals accurately. In some cases, computers can even be programmed to send signals online to a broker for electronic execution.

Hybrid Approaches to Market Analysis

There is much to be said in favor of technical analysis. Yet, with the growing capacity of computer systems to work with complex econometric models, I expect to see fundamentally based computer models have an increasing impact on futures trading over the coming decade. The result could very well be a hybrid approach that employs aspects of both trading approaches.

This hybrid should, in theory, yield better performance than any purely technical or fundamental method. However, this is not yet the case. Above all, remember that the weakest link in the performance chain is the trader. Regardless of how promising computer tests of the system may be, whether technical, fundamental, or techno-fundamental, the ultimate action the trader takes will determine the success or failure of any trading system.

What's Best for You?

It is my observation that individuals who adhere strictly to one approach or another can do well in the marketplace. However, individuals who are constantly shifting from one technical approach to another, from one fundamental approach to another, or from an essentially fundamental point of view to a technical point of view will probably not do well. The reason is that they do not allow sufficient time for their trading approach to reach fruition.

The answer to "What's best for you?" is not a simple one. After years of analysis and study, I can tell you that virtually any systematic approach to futures trading can be successful, provided that it contains three essential elements:

1 *Specific entry and exit indicators.* By this I mean that rules for entering and exiting trades must be as specific and mechanical as possible. Interpretation and deliberations about the validity of a given indicator must be kept to an absolute minimum.

There also should be reliability between different users of the method. In other words, two individuals using the same approach on the same market at different locations and without collaboration should ideally reach the same conclusion.

2 *Money management.* In order for a system to be successful, it must have an automatic way to limit losses. There should be a maximum permissible dollar loss or a specific level beyond which losses should not go on, regardless of what the system says.

3 *Flexibility.* The system must be sufficiently flexible to trade both sides of the market, long and short. Furthermore, the system should do well in all types of markets, trending and trendless (although this is a lot to ask).

The technical approach to futures trading can yield excellent results. The same is true of the fundamental approach. As you read on and attempt to find answers best suited to your needs, take into consideration the points I have raised in this chapter and do not make your decisions quickly.

Summary

It may be difficult to decide whether to follow a fundamental or a technical trading approach, but it is a decision you must make on the basis of existing market realities and the reality of your available time and money. Although there has been much negative comment in recent years about the value of fundamentals, the fact remains that fundamentals are the ultimate factors that determine price.

For the average speculator, however, the time, cost, and competition with large firms make fundamental analysis a difficult prospect. Technical trading approaches can work well, provided they are applied in a thorough and disciplined fashion. They are less costly, less time consuming, and more adaptable to today's computer technology. Hence, they are the method of choice for most speculators.

Do not forget the importance of other factors in a successful trading approach. Although the method of market analysis and/or timing that you ultimately select is important, it is also important to remember that risk management and trader psychology are vital determinants of profitable trading. Trading systems that are highly profitable in theory can turn into losing systems in practice if discipline is lacking or if risk management is faulty. Marginally successful trading systems and methods can be transformed into profitable methodologies by traders who are self-disciplined and who practice effective principles of risk management.

Finally, remember that methods of market analysis and trade selection do not provide the "magic bullet" that automatically leads to profits. Trading futures is a business. In addition to an effective methodology, self-discipline, and solid risk management, you need organization, follow-through, consistency, and sufficient starting capital. As you can see, there are numerous aspects, prerequisites that are both tangible and intangible. The bad news is that it takes time and effort to acquire the skills, knowledge, and procedures that facilitate success. The good news is that it can be done!

CHAPTER 3

What You Should Know about Trendlines

Most new discoveries are suddenly seen things that were always there.

— SUSANNE K. LANGER

One of the most popular methods of technical analysis is the charting of trendlines. These charts help determine support and resistance levels, as well as buy points and sell points. "Support" is defined as a price or price level at which a market is likely to stop a decline. "Resistance" is defined as a price or price level at which a market is likely to stop its advance. During the lengthy tenure of this method, it has been studied or used at one time or another by virtually every futures trader.

Some traders feel that trendline analysis is a very effective and simple tool for analyzing the futures (and stock) markets, whereas others feel that the method is subjective and no more accurate than chance, as well as a self-fulfilling prophecy. Still others claim that trendline analysis cannot be thoroughly tested via computer and is therefore not a valid "scientific" (or quasi-scientific) approach to trade selection and/or market analysis.

A common impediment to the successful application of trendline methodology in futures trading is the fact that many traders are unfamiliar with the basic rules of trendline analysis. Before discussing the method, let's examine my working definition of trendline analysis. Clear definitions of the various concepts in trendline analysis will support this methodology as reasonably objective, making procedures consistent and thereby reducing the degree of error.

A *trendline* is a line connecting a minimum of three nonconsecutive turning points on a chart. You can certainly see that a definition of this nature is somewhat general. It leaves considerable room for interpretation (as well as misinterpretation). This is one of the limitations of trendline analysis. Specific examples will help clarify the definition. Let's expand on the definition of trendlines by illustrating the essential types with which you should be familiar.

1 *Support line.* A line connecting at least three nonconsecutive turning points

on a bar chart, slanting in a horizontal or upward direction and running under prices on a bar or line chart. **Figures 3-1** through **3-3** show several typical support lines. As you can see, the term "support" derives from the tendency of prices to recover after coming down to the indicated trendline(s).

2 *Resistance line.* A resistance line consists of at least three nonconsecutive turning points, running above the price on a bar chart and slanting downward or horizontally. Figures 3-1 through 3-3 illustrate several resistance lines. The term "resistance" derives from the tendency of prices to decline again after going up to the indicated trendline(s).

In addition to the two basic types of trendlines, there are two variations on the theme of trendlines.

1 *Support return line.* This is the extension of a support line into the future after the trendline has been penetrated, in order to determine possible future price resistance or support.

2 *Resistance return line.* This is the extension of a resistance line into the future once it has been penetrated by price in order to determine possible future resistance support.

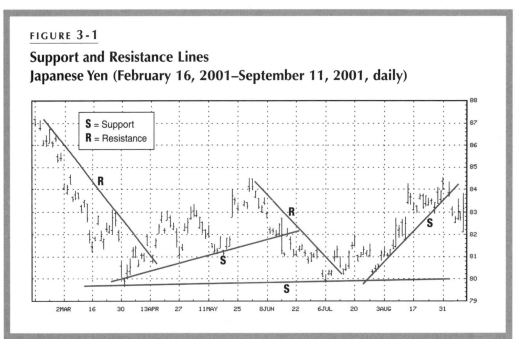

FIGURE **3-1**

Support and Resistance Lines
Japanese Yen (February 16, 2001–September 11, 2001, daily)

Source: Bloomberg

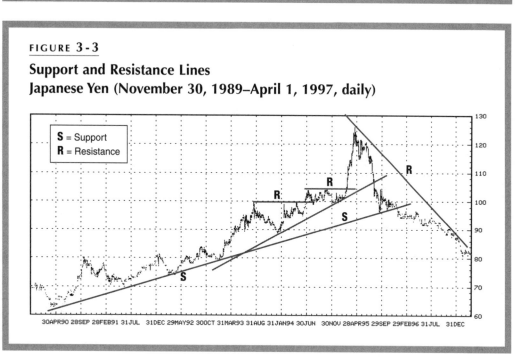

FIGURE 3-2

Support and Resistance Lines
Japanese Yen (December 25, 1998–September 14, 2001, daily)

FIGURE 3-3

Support and Resistance Lines
Japanese Yen (November 30, 1989–April 1, 1997, daily)

FIGURE 3-4

Return Lines
10-Year Treasury Note Yields (April 17, 2001–September 11, 2001, daily)

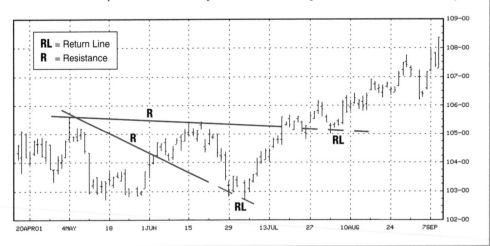

FIGURE 3-5

Return Lines
Swiss Franc (October 20, 2000–March 1, 2001, daily)

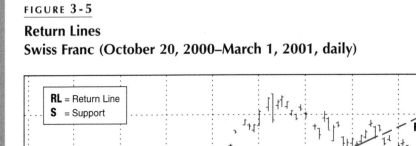

Source: Bloomberg

Source: Bloomberg

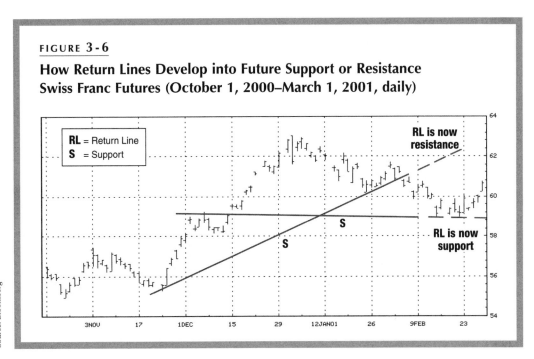

FIGURE 3-6

How Return Lines Develop into Future Support or Resistance Swiss Franc Futures (October 1, 2000–March 1, 2001, daily)

Source: Bloomberg

Examples of support and resistance return lines appear in **Figures 3-4, 3-5,** and **3-6**. Note how prices often revisit their return lines after penetration. The term "return line" describes the tendency of prices to return to a previous support or resistance line once that line has been penetrated. What was once support becomes resistance and vice-versa.

Trading Using Trendlines

You can use trendline analysis and timing indicators to trade in a variety of ways. Traditionally, they have been used as timing tools for buying and selling. This application is based upon the belief that once a trendline has been penetrated in one direction or another, a price move is likely to continue in the direction of the penetration.

Obviously, this is not always the case, but trendlines do appear to have validity as penetration points for buying and selling. I hasten to add that there has been very little solid back-testing information to support the profitability of trendline-based timing methods. **Figures 3-7** through **3-9** illustrate the application of trendline timing.

Trendlines have also been used as indicators of support and resistance (as defined earlier). Once a market has dropped below its support traders assume that the trend has changed to down and they are now willing to sell short as prices move back up and form a new resistance trendline. On the other hand, once a trendline has been penetrated to the upside, forming a new bull trend, traders are willing to buy as prices decline to a support trendline.

Illustrations of all four applications described above (trendline buy signals, trendline sell signals, trendline support for buying, and trendline resistance for selling) are shown in Figures 3-7 through 3-9.

It should be noted that some critics of technical analysis claim that techniques such as trendline methods are self-fulfilling prophecies. In other words, they believe that trendlines work because so many traders act on them at the same time. There is no definitive answer to this long-standing issue, but my view is this: if it works, does it really matter why?

Many traders nowadays prefer more sophisticated computer-generated signals as alternatives to trendline analysis. They have abandoned trendline methods in favor of these more complex, but not necessarily effective, systems. Based on my experience and observations in the markets, the trendline technique of

FIGURE 3-7

Trendlines and Signals
Coffee Futures (December 26, 2000–September 10, 2001, daily)

S = Support
R = Resistance
RL = Return Line

Source: Bloomberg

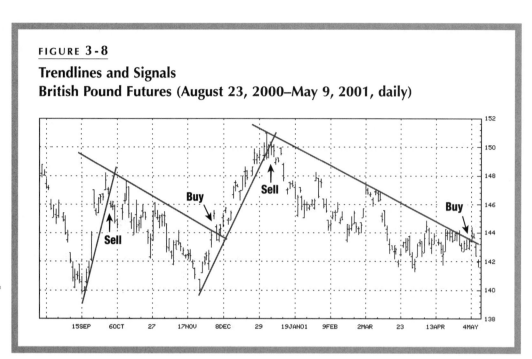

FIGURE 3-8

**Trendlines and Signals
British Pound Futures (August 23, 2000–May 9, 2001, daily)**

Source: Bloomberg

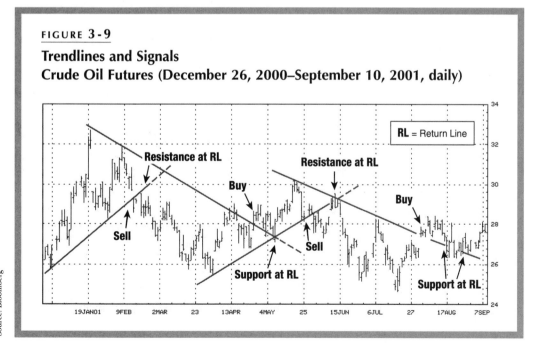

FIGURE 3-9

**Trendlines and Signals
Crude Oil Futures (December 26, 2000–September 10, 2001, daily)**

Source: Bloomberg

buying on reactions to trendline support during an uptrend and selling on rallies to trendline resistance during a downtrend is a simple but potentially effective technique.

It takes very little time to establish trendline points. A computer is not necessary (although it can help). You can use handmade charts. The cost of trendline analysis is virtually nil because you don't need software, hardware, or live price quotations. You can keep your charts manually with paper and pencil, with prices obtained free of charge either online or in the newspaper.

Trendline Trading Rules

The major focus in trendline analysis should be on the accurate interpretation of buy or sell signals and support/resistance points. Trendline followers tend to adapt trendlines to fit their particular needs or market bias. This temptation must be avoided. You should attempt to adhere as strictly as possible to the following suggestions, what we'll call trendline rules for implementing the technique.

1 *Trade with the trend.* This, the single most important rule, is the most frequently stated but most commonly misunderstood and overlooked aspect of successful speculation. Determining the major trend is not an especially difficult task, even for the novice trader. (See Chapter 4 for detailed discussion on trend determination.)

2 *If you have determined that the major trend of prices is up, draw support lines under the market.* In other words, if prices have been moving higher, draw a line connecting the lows.

3 *Extend the trendlines into the future.* This is a simple matter as well. Just continue the trendline beyond where the prices end.

4 *Determine the intersection point of trendline and price for the next market period (day, hour, etc.).* Enter your price order slightly above the support line. I suggest a little leeway in order entry because many other traders will probably be entering their orders at or about the trendline price.

5 *As a rule of thumb regarding stop losses, liquidate your long position(s) as soon as the given market has closed below its trendline.* Such a market move essentially negates its value as support, thereby generating a reversal signal.

Waiting for two consecutive closings below the trendline is advocated as a more accurate method by some traders, provided the first closing below the trendline does not exceed their maximum permissible per-trade losses (if such a limit is being used).

6 *Determine your profit objective.* One technique to do so is to reverse positions once a new trendline signal has formed. Another method is to sell your positions once a resistance line has been touched or approached.

In the absence of a resistance line, other techniques could be used in liquidating a position, such as successively changing stops as the price continues to move in your favor (known as a trailing stop). If you sell short on the penetration of support, you could also lower your stop loss successively as prices decline.

7 *Apply rules 1 through 6 in reverse in response to short sell signals.*

Note that the chart examples in this chapter (and throughout this book) are drawn from real markets and represent real situations. I could have chosen very carefully in order to include examples that illustrate "ideal" or "perfect" market situations, but I have chosen not to do so inasmuch as the real world of futures trading is far from perfect. The perfect situation is the exception rather than the rule. We are far better off knowing what can really happen as opposed to living in a fantasy world of what *should* happen.

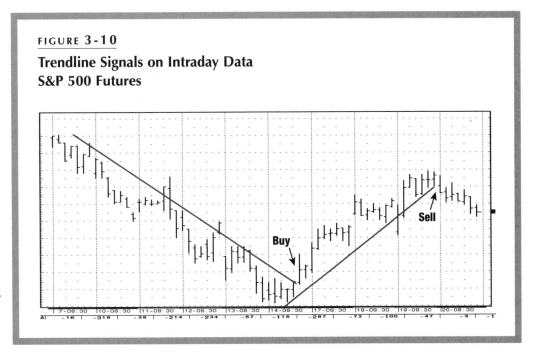

FIGURE **3-10**

**Trendline Signals on Intraday Data
S&P 500 Futures**

Source: © CQG Inc.

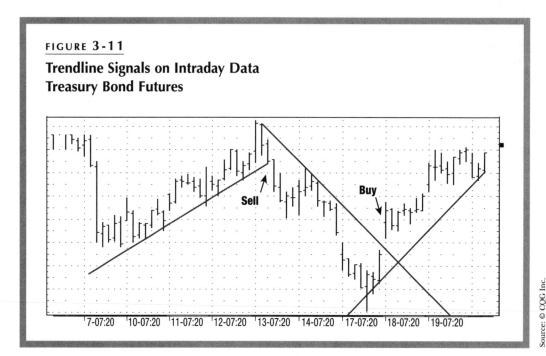

FIGURE 3-11

Trendline Signals on Intraday Data
Treasury Bond Futures

Source: © CQG Inc.

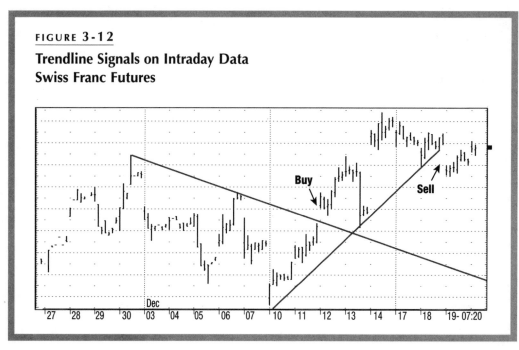

FIGURE 3-12

Trendline Signals on Intraday Data
Swiss Franc Futures

Source: © CQG Inc.

Using Trendlines on Intraday Data

Trendline analysis can also be effective on intraday price data. Ideally, a half-hour or fifteen-minute price chart of active markets is best for this purpose. Support, resistance, and trendline returns can be implemented on an intraday time scale.

Illustrations of these techniques and signals on intraday price charts are shown in **Figures 3-10, 3-11,** and **3-12.** If you find it necessary to trade in ultra short-term time frames, you may want to examine **Figures 3-13** and **3-14.** They show trendline analysis on a one-minute and five-minute price chart.

Summary

Trendline analysis is a good technique for beginners because it is low in cost, simple to understand and use, yet still effective even though not nearly as popular as it has been in the past. Using at least four different types of trendline signals, each adaptable to specific situations, trendline analysis can provide specific exit and entry points based on support and resistance within existing trends,

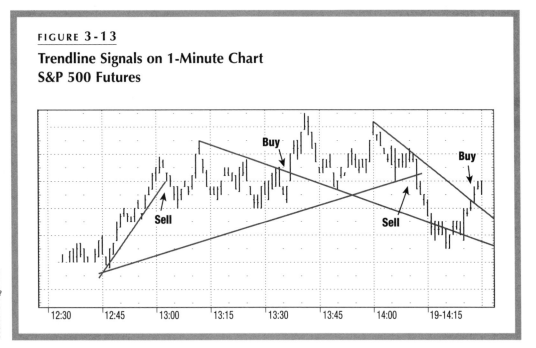

FIGURE **3-13**

Trendline Signals on 1-Minute Chart
S&P 500 Futures

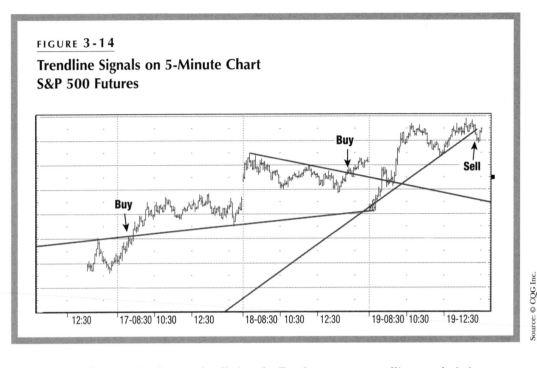

FIGURE 3-14

Trendline Signals on 5-Minute Chart
S&P 500 Futures

Source: © CQG Inc.

as well as precise buy and sell signals. Furthermore, trendline analysis is appropriate to use for intraday trading.

Although trendline trading is not nearly as objective as other technical methods are, this does not necessarily mean that it is less effective. The major problem is one of interpretation. The use of clear rules, consistent application of the rules, and concise definitions can resolve this problem. Remember that an "objective" method is one that follows strict rules. There are levels of objectivity. You can follow the rules religiously, or you can follow the rules less than one hundred percent of the time. Because trendlines can be interpreted in slightly different ways (at times such differences can, in fact, be more than slight), this type of analysis is not as purely objective as other forms of analysis. As an example, consider the red, green, and yellow lights in a traffic signal. Red always means "stop." Green always means "go." But yellow means "caution." What constitutes caution to one driver is different than what may be seen as caution by another driver.

CHAPTER 4

What You Should Know about Cycles

When you steal from one author, it's plagiarism; if you steal from many, it's research.

— WILSON MIZNER

The cyclical method of technical analysis and forecasting has its roots in the work of Edward R. Dewey, who established the Foundation for the Study of Cycles in 1940. Although the Foundation has ceased to exist, its research lives on. Dewey developed his original work and theories by studying time-based patterns in the cash commodity and stock markets. His basic tenet was that virtually all markets and natural phenomena fluctuate in time-based patterns of a given average length.

The number of sunspots, for example, peaks about every 11 years. The population of beef cattle in the United States has followed an approximate 11-year pattern. Interest rates have shown a length pattern of about 54 years, low-to-low, within which approximately five patterns of 10 years also exist. The corn market has shown a cycle of about 5.7 years from one low to the next. In fact, almost every market has shown a number of reliable cycles.

Dewey's pioneering efforts prompted further research by a number of market analysts who expanded and expounded on Dewey's original concepts. With the advent and accessibility of computer technology, the use of price cycles became more popular, but with its inherent complexity, the methodology still has attracted relatively few followers in comparison to other technical methods.

The cyclical nature of prices, although scientifically validated as a measurable phenomenon, is not widely accepted by economists, traders, or governments because it flies in the face of traditional supply-and-demand-based theories. In effect, a cyclical theory suggests that we humans have very little control over the direction of prices. And we would never want to admit that, because it suggests that we are, to a given extent, helpless and powerless. It is not my purpose to debate this controversy within these pages. I can only report the facts as I have come to know them.

I will further preface my remarks about price cycles by warning you that most techniques of contemporary cyclical analysis require a cyclical analysis program and a computer. Though I have been a proponent of cyclic trading for many years, I can say in all honesty that the application of cycles is more challenging than simply demonstrating their existence and performing a simple time count across lows and highs.

Although it is a relatively simple matter to find price cycles (even with limited experience in the futures markets), it is a far more complex matter to apply them correctly. A number of techniques may be employed to find cycles in futures. If you can combine some of the more basic timing indicators used with cyclic price patterns, you can do extremely well as a trader. (This holds especially true for seasonals, a sub-category of cycles that are examined thoroughly in Chapter 6.)

What Is a Cycle?

Let's take a closer look at the definition of a cycle. Stated simply, a price cycle is the tendency for prices to repeat up and down movements in a relatively pre-

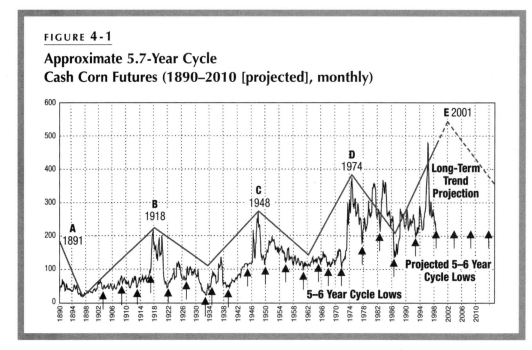

FIGURE 4-1

**Approximate 5.7-Year Cycle
Cash Corn Futures (1890–2010 [projected], monthly)**

Source: MBH Commodity Advisors, Inc.

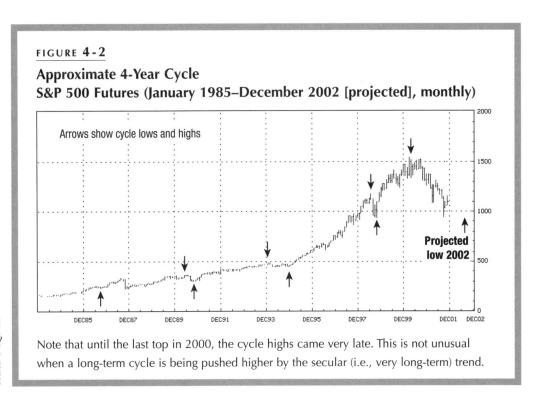

FIGURE **4-2**

Approximate 4-Year Cycle
S&P 500 Futures (January 1985–December 2002 [projected], monthly)

Note that until the last top in 2000, the cycle highs came very late. This is not unusual when a long-term cycle is being pushed higher by the secular (i.e., very long-term) trend.

dictable fashion over essentially similar lengths of time. For example, it is possible to state with reasonable accuracy that corn prices have a price cycle of approximately 5.7 years and that this cycle has been in existence for many years. This price cycle is illustrated in **Figure 4-1**. The long-term cycle in corn has averaged 5.7 years from low to low. Arrows show the cycle lows. As you can see, the lows are not always exactly 5.7 years apart. Some come early and some come late. The larger zigzag lines show the longer-term cycle of about 23 to 35 years. Within the 5.7-year price cycle for corn, there are also 30- to 34-month price cycles.

Price cycles are measured low-to-low, high-to-high, or low-to-high. Various types of measurements are possible. Examples of various price cycles are provided in **Figures 4-1** through **4-4**.

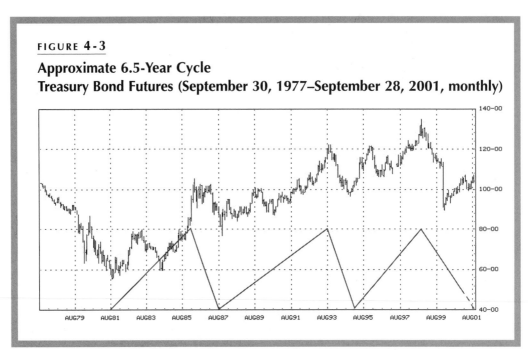

FIGURE **4-3**

Approximate 6.5-Year Cycle
Treasury Bond Futures (September 30, 1977–September 28, 2001, monthly)

Source: Bloomberg

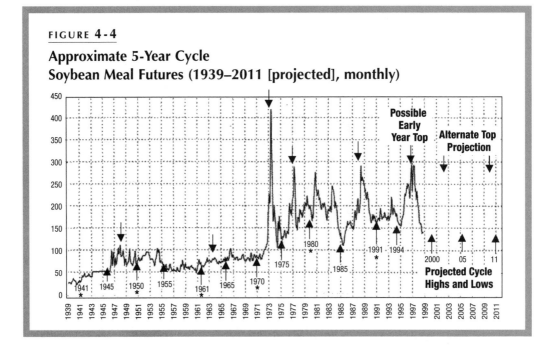

FIGURE **4-4**

Approximate 5-Year Cycle
Soybean Meal Futures (1939–2011 [projected], monthly)

Source: MBH Commodity Advisors, Inc.

Source: © CQG Inc.

FIGURE **4-5**

Approximate 5- to 6-Week Cycle
Sugar Futures (March 19, 2001–December 17, 2001, daily)

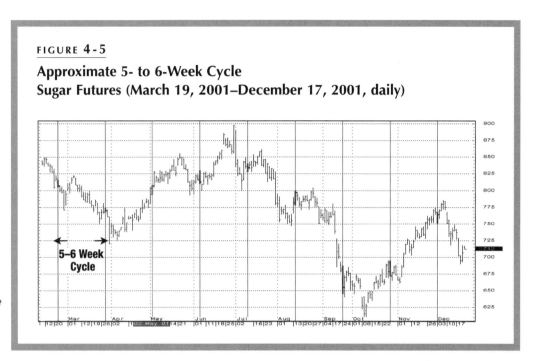

FIGURE **4-6**

Approximate 9-Year Cycle
Wheat Futures (1864–2008 [projected])

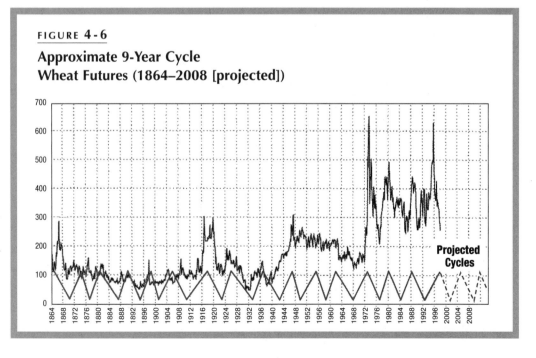

Source: MBH Commodity Advisors, Inc.

Many Markets, Many Cycles

Futures and cash prices demonstrate many different cyclic lengths ranging from the ultra-long term to the ultra-short term. On the short-term end of the spectrum, we can find such patterns as the approximate 4- to 5-day cycle in silver prices. On the long-term end of the continuum, we find the approximate 54-year cycle found in most commodity prices and, in particular, for interest rates. Note that because interest rates are a key indicator of economic strength or weakness, there has long been a marked tendency for interest rate cycles to influence cycles in other commodity markets as well as in stocks. This 54-year cycle is about the longest cycle that commodity traders should study.

In practice the most useful cycles are those that tend to average from 9 to 11 months to as short as 14 days. Most futures trading is likely to be done on the basis of approximately 25- to 32-day cycles.

As a technical yardstick, price cycles are not perfect; they can vary considerably in length. At times there will be an inversion of cyclic highs and lows, with tops occurring when lows should occur. This inversion tends to occur at major turning points in the markets. This can be compensated for by combining cycles with timing.

Trading Using Cycles

The application of the price cycles to futures trading consists of three steps:
1 *Determine or find cycle length.*
2 *Project next cyclical high or low.*
3 *Enter market using timing indicator(s).*

To use cycles effectively you must follow a three-step method. The first step is to know the cycle length for the given market(s) you wish to trade. If you do not know the cycle length for a given market, you can research it in any of several ways. The most simple and cost-effective way to find cycles is by simple visual inspection. All you need to do is to count the number of days between lows and highs, looking for patterns. If you want to use a computer to find cycles, there are a number of programs that can facilitate the process.

Once you know the cycle length, the second step is to forecast the next approximate high or low. Simply counting forward in time and establishing a time frame or time window during which the cycle should ideally top or bottom will allow you to determine the optimum or ideal time frame during which to expect a low or high. Because cycles are not perfect, we allow 15 percent of the length of the cycle as our "window." A cycle low or high can occur as much as 15 percent early or 15 percent late.

Once you have determined the ideal time frame of the next low or high (in other words, the time window), you will wait for the market to enter this time frame, and, regardless of price, you will take action when the timing indicator you are using triggers the trade. (I will explain timing indicators in greater detail later on.)

For example, a cycle in cattle futures is 28 trading days in length. The last low was May 15. You compute 15 percent of 28 days to be 4.2 days. You round the 4.2 days to four days. This means that the earliest a cycle low could come is day 24 from the last low, and the latest a cycle low could come is 32 days from the last cycle low. This *does not mean* that the low must fall within this time frame. It simply means that this is the time frame you will watch for a change in trend. As soon as your selected timing indicator (to be discussed) signals that a reversal in trend is likely, you take action and buy.

Timing Indicators

Timing indicators fall into three basic categories: (1) visual formations on charts, (2) mathematical relationships, and (3) market structure analyses. Such timing

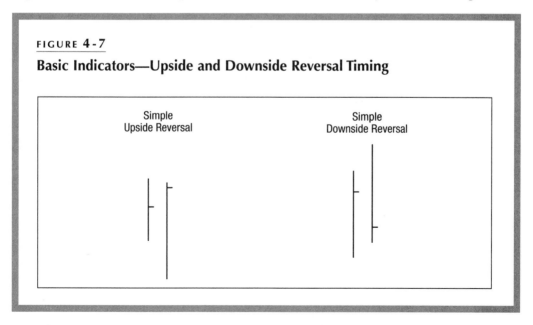

FIGURE 4-7

Basic Indicators—Upside and Downside Reversal Timing

Simple
Upside Reversal

Simple
Downside Reversal

FIGURE **4-8**

Basic Indicators—Low/High and High/Low Close Timing Signals

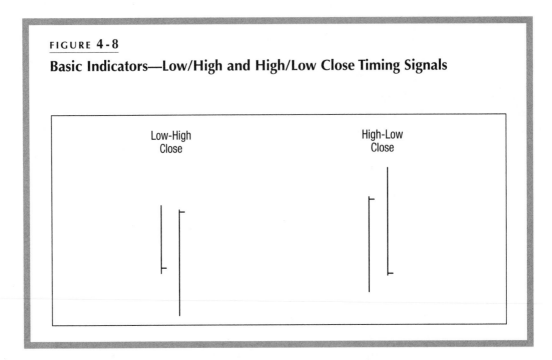

FIGURE **4-9**

Basic Indicators—3 High/3 Low Timing

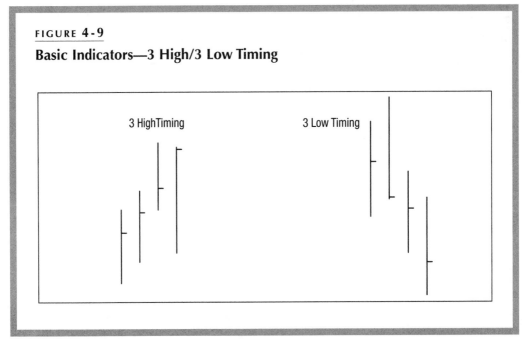

Source: Bloomberg

FIGURE 4-10

Upside and Downside Reversal Timing Signals with a Cycle
CRB Futures Price Index (June 30, 1986–September 28, 2001, monthly)

Source: Bloomberg

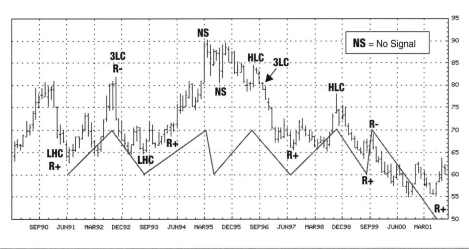

FIGURE 4-11

Combined Timing Indicators with 24-Month Cycle
Swiss Franc Futures (January 1, 1990–October 31, 2001, monthly)

indicators are used within a given time frame or time window as a means of validating or confirming the cycle low or high. A timing indicator confirmation within the ideal cyclical time window for a top or bottom does not, however, guarantee a change in trend. The combination of cycles and timing, while generally useful, is neither perfect nor foolproof as a technical tool and will not guarantee a profitable trade every time.

Many timing indicators may be used within the cyclical time window in order to confirm a low or high. Some are simple and very traditional, while others are not very commonly known. On the traditional side, I suggest three basic timing signals. They are shown schematically in **Figures 4-7**, **4-8**, and **4-9**, and with cycles in **Figures 4-10** through **4-11**.

Variability of Cycle Lengths

As is apparent from the cycle pattern and timing indicators in Figure 4-11 (and others), cycle lengths can be quite variable. At times highs will come very soon after lows, and vice versa. This variability is, in fact, one of the most confusing and potentially limiting aspects of cycles. If you expect to find cycles that are always symmetrical in the futures markets, then this methodology is not the right tool for you. Analysis based on the combination of cycles with timing indicators is designed to reduce confusion resulting from variability in cycle lengths. I recommend against simply buying or selling based on cycle patterns without confirmation by timing indicators.

Even with the use of timing indicators, the cycles can go astray. This problem is clearly indicated in Figure 4-11, which shows an approximate 24-month cycle in Swiss Franc futures with combined timing indicators. As you can see from a close examination of the chart, several cycle lows and highs were incorrect and for trade selection purposes would have resulted in losses even with the use of timing indicators.

Intraday Cycles

Day trading in stocks and futures has become very popular since the mid-1990s. This is, in part, due to two factors: the reduced cost of commissions and significant increases in intraday market volatility. Active markets such as the Standard & Poor's 500 Index, currencies, and interest rate futures have shown themselves to be excellent day-trading vehicles using cycles. For example, consider the cycles shown in **Figures 4-12** and **4-13**.

FIGURE **4-12**

Example of an Intraday Cycle with Timing in S&P Futures

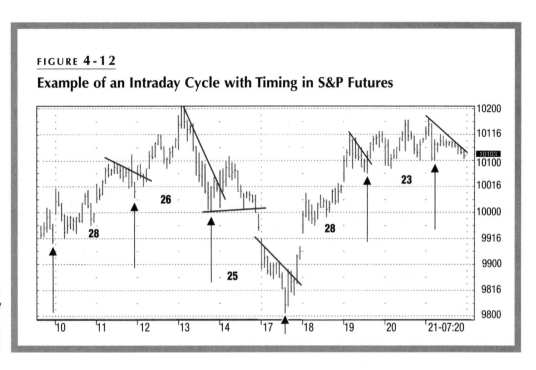

FIGURE **4-13**

Example of an Intraday Cycle with Timing in S&P Futures

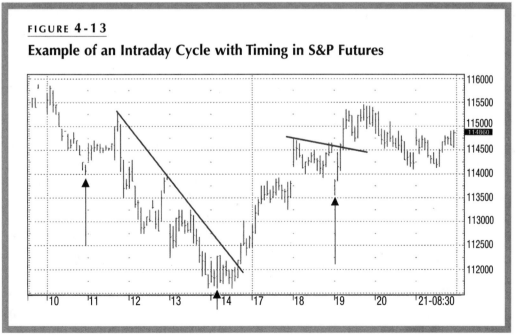

Cycle Trading Rules

Although there are many different approaches to cycles and applications of cyclic theory, some general rules can help you in your study and application of cycles in the futures markets. You will find that cyclical analysis has become very advanced with the proliferation of cyclical software packages and online historical data. Be very careful about which programs you buy, however. As a general rule, avoid programs that are very expensive. Odds are that they are not necessarily any better than the lower-priced programs.

Alternatively, if you want to do your cyclical work manually, follow these eight rules.

1 *Find a market that has reliable cycles.* Currently, reliable cycles include the 20- to 23-week cycle in stock index futures, the approximately 14-day cycle in stock index futures, the 50- to 60-day cycle in soybean futures, the 9- to 11-month cycle in all grain and livestock markets, the approximately 28-day cycle in silver and gold, and the approximately 32-day cycle in interest rate futures.

As market conditions change, cycles become more or less reliable and certain markets begin to exhibit better or worse cyclic tendencies. Focus on the active markets, isolating those that have shown the most reliable cycles for the time frames in which you are trading.

2 *Do not attempt to trade more than two or three markets at once based on cycles.* Trading too many markets at the same time could become confusing and may be a duplication of effort.

3 *Do not duplicate markets.* In other words, do not trade several different markets that are closely related and that follow the same basic cycles (such as silver and gold, cattle and hogs, or soybeans and soybean meal).

4 *Once you have identified markets with reliable cycles for the time frame in which you wish to trade, keep your price charts up-to-date and mark your cycles according to the rules provided earlier in this chapter.*

5 *Project the next cyclic top or bottom within the 15 percent +/- time window.*

6 *Once you have entered the ideal cyclic time frame of a top or bottom, examine timing signals and/or timing indicators to pinpoint as closely as possible the next market turn.* If you are not inclined to use the basic timing indicators suggested above, you can use virtually any of the popular timing tools such as stochastics, multiple moving averages, momentum, or Wilder's Relative Strength Index (RSI). Some of these tools will be discussed later in this book.

7 *Use stop losses specific to each trading signal.*
8 *Develop a trailing stop procedure by which you continually adjust your stop once you are in a profitable position.* This procedure keeps you from losing too much profit back to the market if prices turn against you.

Limitations of Trading with Cyclical Indicators

Although cyclical analysis is an excellent tool for projecting and trading long-term trends and potential changes in trends, timing the cycles can be a difficult proposition due to the variability in their lengths. Methods based on complex mathematical models, such as spectral analysis and Fourier analysis, can help pinpoint the time frame for cyclical turns. However, such methods often are too confusing to new traders. You can use these once you have gained experience in trading. Of course, they, like all technical tools, have their limitations as well and are not foolproof. Various computer programs allow more precise cyclical analysis. Yet here again, use cycle analysis only in conjunction with timing indicators to improve the accuracy of this approach.

Summary

Reliance on cyclical analysis in futures trading is a viable methodology, but due to its inherent variability and the experience it requires, it is not recommended for the novice trader. If you plan to use cycles in your trading, then take your time to study the method and the available computer programs. Although the concept of cycles is appealing and although cycles do seem to have considerable validity, they are not nearly as accurate as one might hope.

When used with an effective approach to timing and a sensible method of risk management, however, this method is capable of generating good profits over the short and long term. The use of futures options can improve cyclic timing by defining maximum risk within the ideal top and bottom time frames.

Traders and investors who are interested in the use of repetitive price patterns with commodity and stock prices also should consider the use of seasonal cycles (discussed in Chapter 6) as an effective tool. Seasonal cycles are considerably more reliable than time-based cycles such as those described in this chapter.

CHAPTER 5

What You Should Know about Moving Averages

The force that through the green fuse drives the flower drives my green age.

— DYLAN THOMAS

In 1955 Richard Donchian advanced the notion that a different type of trend-line could be used to establish buy and sell signals. Rather than the familiar (straight-line) trend method (see Chapter 3), he proposed that a moving average of price could be determined in order to provide a more dynamic tool for market-timing indicators. The moving average method Donchian devised has, to a large extent, remained relatively unchanged through the years except for a few adaptations designed to increase its accuracy. You can use moving averages to determine buy and sell points as well as to indicate support and resistance.

A moving average is a simple mathematical manipulation of raw data that provides regularly updated or "moving" indications of market activity. A 10-day moving average, for example, looks at a window of prices for only the past 10 days, ignoring what has transpired before. In so doing, it provides a measure of market activity that is more closely weighted to recent price history.

The method for calculating a moving average (MA) is very simple. By taking an average of the past 10 days of prices, you have your first MA point. On the eleventh day you drop the oldest day in the data and recalculate the average with the current daily price. Most moving average methods use closing prices, but it is not necessary to use closing prices only. (There will be more about this later.)

Theoretically, when the price of a market closes above the moving average, it is considered bullish. A market that has been in an uptrend and then falls below the moving average line indicates a probable change in trend from bullish to bearish. Conversely, if the market has been moving down (in other words, below the moving average), and if it then crosses above its moving average, this is taken to be a bullish signal.

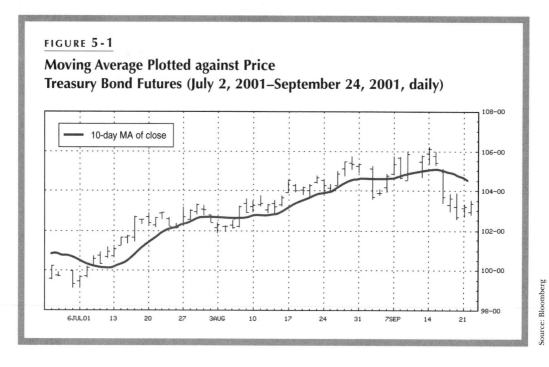

FIGURE 5-1

Moving Average Plotted against Price
Treasury Bond Futures (July 2, 2001–September 24, 2001, daily)

Source: Bloomberg

How Moving Averages Give
Buy and Sell Signals on Price Charts

Figures 5-1, 5-2, and **5-3** show several markets plotted with moving averages of different lengths. The vertical lines show the daily high/low, opening/closing price bars. The solid, gray line shows the moving average plot. Observe the correlation between the length of the moving average and the speed with which it follows price.

Although the examination of a single moving average as a means of timing entry and exit is certainly a potentially useful technique, it has been found that using two moving averages, and perhaps three, provides more accuracy. Such a combined approach could significantly improve results. The use of a multiple MA approach is illustrated in **Figures 5-4, 5-5,** and **5-6**.

The rules of moving average signals are purely objective, however, there are a number of different moving average-based systems. Each system has its unique rules. Generally, however, the following rules apply to most moving average-based systems:

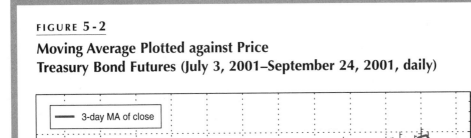

FIGURE 5-2

Moving Average Plotted against Price
Treasury Bond Futures (July 3, 2001–September 24, 2001, daily)

Source: Bloomberg

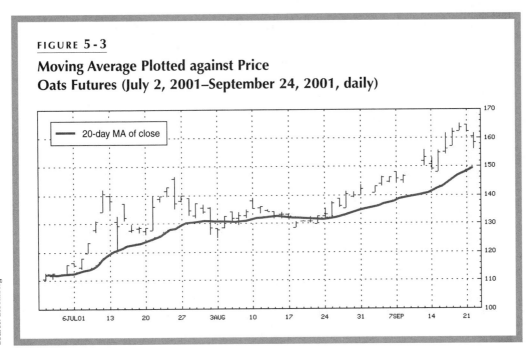

FIGURE 5-3

Moving Average Plotted against Price
Oats Futures (July 2, 2001–September 24, 2001, daily)

Source: Bloomberg

Source: Bloomberg

FIGURE 5-4

Multiple Moving Averages Plotted against Price
Cotton Futures (December 26, 2000–September 10, 2001, daily)

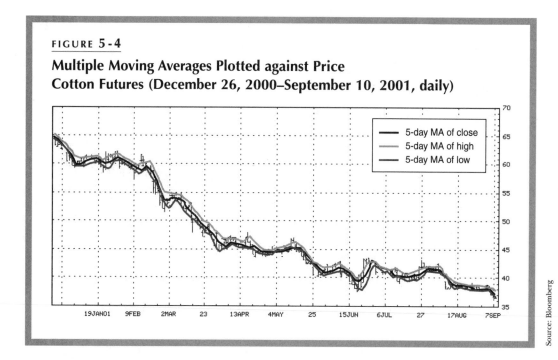

- Prices above their moving average indicates a bull trend
- Prices below their moving average indicates a bear trend
- Prices crossing below their moving average indicates a probable chance in trend from up to down
- Prices crossing above their moving average indicates a probable change in trend from down to up

The advantage of applying various moving averages over multiple time periods to determine buy and sell points has been closely studied over the years. In general, the 4-, 9-, and 18-day moving averages seem to work best together. **Figures 5-7, 5-8,** and **5-9** show this combination and the signals that can be generated from its application. **Figures 5-10** and **5-11** show historical performance records using multiple moving averages in various markets. These illustrations will give you an idea of how moving-average based trading systems perform.

FIGURE 5-5

Multiple Moving Averages Plotted against Price
Soybean Futures (December 27, 2000–September 10, 2001, daily)

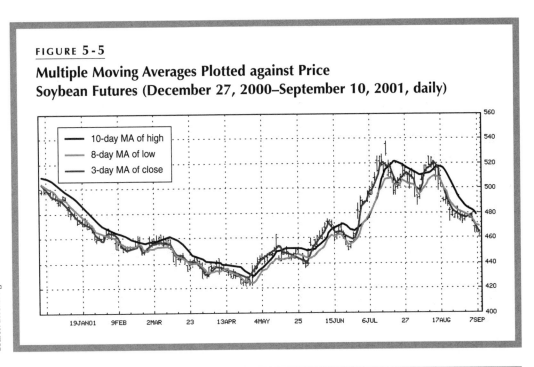

FIGURE 5-6

Multiple Moving Averages Plotted against Price
Swiss Franc Futures (April 18, 2000–January 3, 2001, daily)

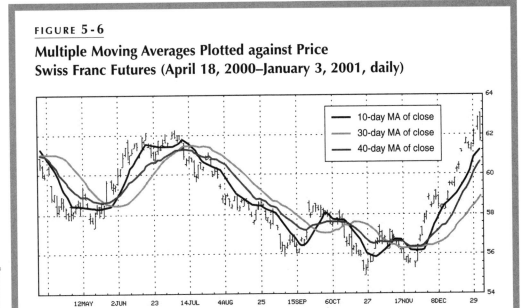

Source: Bloomberg

Source: Bloomberg

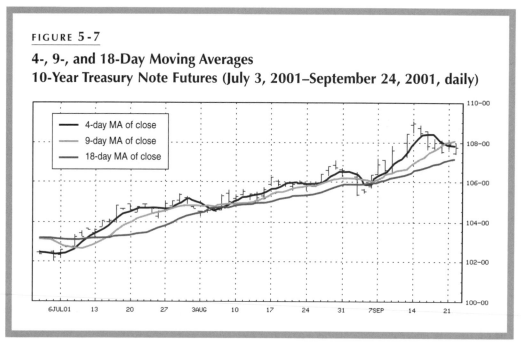

FIGURE 5-7

4-, 9-, and 18-Day Moving Averages
10-Year Treasury Note Futures (July 3, 2001–September 24, 2001, daily)

Source: Bloomberg

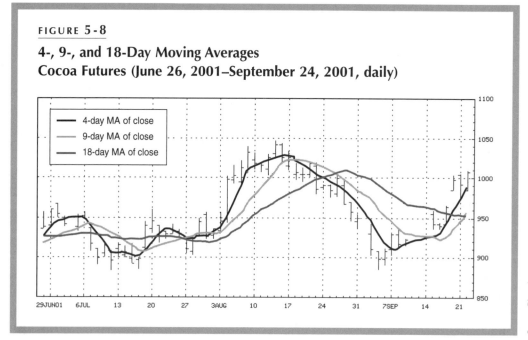

FIGURE 5-8

4-, 9-, and 18-Day Moving Averages
Cocoa Futures (June 26, 2001–September 24, 2001, daily)

Source: Bloomberg

FIGURE 5-9

**4-, 9-, and 18-Day Moving Averages
Natural Gas Futures (July 2, 2001–September 24, 2001, daily)**

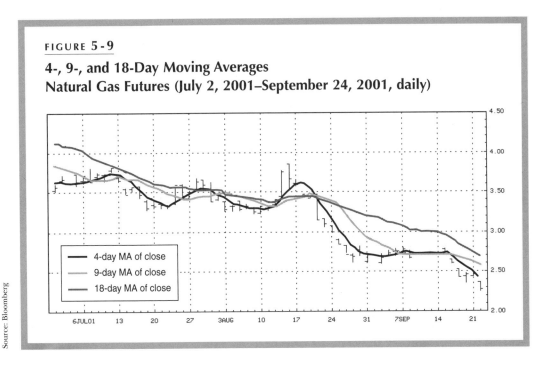

Source: Bloomberg

Pros of Using Moving Averages

Professional money managers frequently use moving-average based systems as a means of selecting trades. The popularity of MA-based systems is derived from the fact that MA signals meet many of the specific and objective criteria that constitute effective systems. These include the following:

1   *Moving average signals are specific and objective.* They are not subject to interpretation. All individuals trained in the system will reach the same conclusions every time (regardless of whether the conclusions reached are ultimately profitable or not).

2   *Moving average signals can keep you positioned in the markets at all times.* For example, they help indicate moves for simultaneously closing out a long position and then going short and covering a short position and then going long. This is a worthwhile approach because it will theoretically allow you to capture most market trends.

3   *Moving averages are trend-following systems.* In other words, when a solid trend is in process, the likelihood of the moving average having a position consistent with the trend is very high.

Cons of Using Moving Averages

Whatever combination of moving averages you use, the fact remains that moving averages are mechanical and easily implemented. There are, however, some significant limitations to MA-based systems. Here are some of the more serious ones:

1 ***Moving averages do not do well in certain types of markets.*** For example, markets that tend to move sideways and markets that have very small trading ranges (in other words, low volatility) tend to give numerous false signals. In such cases the accuracy of MA-based systems is low. In a trending market, however, as noted previously, moving average systems do their best work.

2 ***MA-based systems can give numerous losing trades in a row.*** This means that you could lose a significant amount of capital in your account before the system begins to turn profitable—and this could knock you out of the game before you have had a chance to make money. MA systems are not known for their accuracy. At best, MA-based systems are correct 40 percent of the time. Yet their strength is in their tendency to latch on to large moves.

3 ***MA systems tend to give timing signals quite some time after a change in trend.*** Therefore, if you are using the system for entry and for exit then you may give back a significant amount of profit before a new signal is generated.

4 ***MA systems often give many signals.*** Making frequent trades in response to these signals can cause the trader to spend a large amount in commissions, which, of course, eats into the bottom-line profitability.

5 ***MA-based systems tend to use large stop losses.*** To use MA-based systems profitably you need to accept large risks. This is not always the case in technical trading systems. Hence, unless you are willing to risk a considerable amount of money on each trade, the odds are that you won't be happy with the performance of a traditional MA-based system.

Rules for Trading Using Moving Averages

1 ***Compute the moving average lengths that are required as part of your system.*** The time periods adopted may vary depending on the type of MA system you are using. In general, using three MAs is recommended.

2 ***Buy or reverse your position from short to long when all three moving averages have crossed in an upward direction.*** (If using only one moving average, then buy when the price closes above the MA.)

3 **Sell and sell short or reverse your position from long to short when all three moving averages have crossed in a downward direction.** (If using one moving average, then sell when price closes below the MA.)

4 **Trade at every reversal.** Moving average systems are based on reversals, so when you close out a long position, you enter a short position and when you close out a short position, you enter a long position.

While these steps can be completed manually, they are more easily executed using a computer. There are many low-cost software programs available that will help you address this process quickly and efficiently.

Because moving average systems are relatively simple to follow, they can be valuable to the new trader, but be forewarned that MA systems are notorious for their low level of accuracy. Although they may result in greater than acceptable risk, they require self-discipline and solid risk management, both of which can lead to profitable results. Before you consider using moving averages for trading, study the characteristics of the particular approach you are considering very thoroughly. Of the many variations on the MA theme, some are considerably better than others.

Performance Histories

As an example of how MA-based systems perform, consider the historical back-tests showing the results of two and three MA-based systems in **Figures 5-10** and **5-11**.

FIGURE **5-10**

Performance History Using a Dual Exponential MA
Swiss Franc (February 13, 1975–December 20, 2001, daily)

PERFORMANCE SUMMARY: ALL TRADES			
Total net profit	$88,105.00	Open position P/L	$737.50
Gross profit	$365,635.00	Gross loss	$-277,530.00
Total # of trades	326	Percent profitable	42%
Number winning trades	137	Number losing trades	189
Largest winning trade	$15,167.50	Largest losing trade	$-6,970.00
Average winning trade	$2,668.87	Average losing trade	$-1,468.41
Ratio average win/average loss	1.82	Average trade (win & loss)	$270.26
Maximum consecutive winners	4	Maximum consecutive losers	12

PERFORMANCE SUMMARY: ALL TRADES (CONTINUED)

Average # bars in winners	34	Average # bars in losers	10
Maximum intraday drawdown	$-36,055.00		
Profit factor	1.32	Maximum # contracts held	1
Account size required	$36,055.00	Return on account	244%

PERFORMANCE SUMMARY: LONG TRADES

Total net profit	$57,452.50	Open position P/L	$737.50
Gross profit	$192,470.00	Gross loss	$-135,017.50
Total # of trades	163	Percent profitable	42%
Number winning trades	69	Number losing trades	94
Largest winning trade	$12,455.00	Largest losing trade	$-6,970.00
Average winning trade	$ 2789.42	Average losing trade	$-1,436.36
Ratio average win/average loss	1.94	Average trade (win & loss)	$352.47
Maximum consecutive winners	5	Maximum consecutive losers	7
Average # bars in winners	34	Average # bars in losers	11
Max intraday drawdown	$-19,925.00		
Profit factor	1.43	Maximum # contracts held	1
Account size required	$19,925.00	Return on account	288%

PERFORMANCE SUMMARY: SHORT TRADES

Total net profit	$30,652.50	Open position P/L	$0.00
Gross profit	$173,165.00	Gross loss	$-142,512.50
Total # of trades	163	Percent profitable	42%
Number winning trades	68	Number losing trades	95
Largest winning trade	$15,167.50	Largest losing trade	$-6,445.00
Average winning trade	$2,546.54	Average losing trade	$-1,500.13
Ratio average win/average loss	1.70	Average trade (win & loss)	$188.05
Maximum consecutive winners	4	Maximum consecutive losers	9
Average # bars in winners	35	Average # bars in losers	10
Maximum intraday drawdown	$ -22,530.00		
Profit factor	1.22	Maximum # contracts held	1
Account size required	$22,530.00	Return on account	136%

Source: Omega Research, reprinted by permission

FIGURE 5-11

Performance History with a Triple Exponential MA System
Swiss Franc (February 13, 1975–December 20, 2001, daily)

PERFORMANCE SUMMARY: ALL TRADES			
Total net profit	$85,842.50	Open position P/L	$737.50
Gross profit	$ 368,945.00	Gross loss	$-283,102.50
Total # of trades	352	Percent profitable	42%
Number winning trades	148	Number losing trades	204
Largest winning trade	$16,377.50	Largest losing trade	$-5,997.50
Average winning trade	$2,492.87	Average losing trade	$-1,387.76
Ratio average win/average loss	1.80	Average trade (win & loss)	$243.87
Maximum consecutive winners	4	Maximum consecutive losers	11
Average # bars in winners	29	Average # bars in losers	12
Maximum intraday drawdown	$-34,772.50		
Profit factor	1.30	Maximum # contracts held	1
Account size required	$34,772.50	Return on account	247%

PERFORMANCE SUMMARY: LONG TRADES			
Total net profit	$56,277.50	Open position P/L	$737.50
Gross profit	$191,737.50	Gross loss	$-135,460.00
Total # of trades	176	Percent profitable	43%
Number winning trades	75	Number losing trades	101
Largest winning trade	$12,940.00	Largest losing trade	$-5,735.00
Average winning trade	$ 2556.50	Average losing trade	$-1341.19
Ratio average win/average loss	1.91	Average trade (win & loss)	$319.76
Maximum consecutive winners	5	Maximum consecutive losers	7
Average # bars in winners	29	Average # bars in losers	12
Max intraday drawdown	$-19,370.00		
Profit factor	1.42	Maximum # contracts held	1
Account size required	$19,370.00	Return on account	291%

Source: Omega Research, reprinted by permission

PERFORMANCE SUMMARY: SHORT TRADES			
Total net profit	$29,565.00	Open position P/L	$0.00
Gross profit	$177,207.50	Gross loss	$-147,642.50
Total # of trades	176	Percent profitable	41%
Number winning trades	73	Number losing trades	103
Largest winning trade	$16,377.50	Largest losing trade	$-5,997.50
Average winning trade	$2,427.50	Average losing trade	$-1,433.42
Ratio average win/average loss	1.69	Average trade (win & loss)	$167.98
Maximum consecutive winners	4	Maximum consecutive losers	11
Average # bars in winners	30	Average # bars in losers	11
Maximum intraday drawdown	$-24,730.00		
Profit factor	1.20	Maximum # contracts held	1
Account size required	$24,730.00	Return on account	120%

Source: Omega Research, reprinted by permission

Summary

Consistent application of moving average techniques has validity as a successful methodology for technical traders. The use of two or three moving averages seems to offer more accuracy than the use of a single moving average. Novice traders should not discount the use of such systems inasmuch as these systems are specific, mechanical, trend following, and relatively simple to monitor.

Although there can be large drawdowns and periods of numerous consecutive losses in zigzag ("whipsaw") markets, the potential of moving average systems in trending markets is tremendous. However, before you consider using moving averages for trading, study the approach very thoroughly. Review the examples of moving average performance histories to sharpen your acumen on this subject.

Some traders may be satisfied with the use of simple multiple moving averages as described in this chapter, but there are variations on the theme of moving averages such as oscillators, exponential moving averages, weighted moving averages, moving average convergence–divergence (MACD), and smoothed moving averages that can yield better overall performance results. Some of these methods are described in Chapter 14.

CHAPTER 6

What You Should Know about Seasonality

While the earth remaineth, seed-time and harvest, and cold and heat, and summer and winter, and day and night shall not cease.

— GENESIS 8:22

A major, if somewhat controversial, form of cyclical price behavior in the futures markets is seasonality. Seasonality refers to the tendency of prices to move in certain directions at certain times of the year. Some seasonal price tendencies are extremely reliable, having occurred in excess of 80 percent of the time over a span of many years. Although some traders discount the value of seasonal analysis to trading, I believe strongly that this is one of the best methods, if not in fact *the* best method that traders can use. I further believe that seasonality is an ideal method for new traders for a variety of reasons cited below.

In recent years, the popularity of trading futures and options based on seasonal price tendencies has grown considerably, in part due to the ease of using computers to analyze vast amounts of historical data. On the other hand, considerable controversy has surrounded the use of seasonal trading methods.

Many analysts believe that seasonal factors are already taken into consideration in the current price structure of a market. For this reason, they feel that seasonal analysis is not a viable method of predicting the future direction of prices and, therefore, is also not a worthwhile method of generating buy and sell signals. However, I believe this argument to be based on a thorough misunderstanding of seasonality. If you work with seasonal patterns it quickly becomes apparent that their recurrence is frequent and, at times, the precision with which the patterns repeat can be uncanny.

Time Frames for Seasonals

There are three different types of seasonal tendencies:
1 *Seasonals in cash prices*
2 *Seasonals in futures prices*
3 *Seasonals in futures spreads*

Each type of seasonality can be viewed in different time frames. The time frames are as follows:

- Monthly
- Weekly
- Daily
- Key Dates

The major time frame for seasonals is monthly. The use of monthly prices can give you an idea of how prices behave on a longer-term basis within the year. In other words, you will be able to discern the usual months in which prices typically make their highs and their lows, and the typical yearly trend. Although this longer time frame seasonal is ideal for producers and end users of commodities, speculative futures traders generally can use a shorter term seasonal more effectively. Typically, traders are more inclined to use weekly or even daily seasonals. These short-term seasonal time frames give more precise information of particular value for those who wish to use the patterns for short-term trading.

So-called key-date seasonals are very precise patterns that can indicate for traders the exact date to buy or sell, the exact date to exit a trade, the precise stop loss, and the entire history and probability of the aforementioned strategy. Key-date seasonals are so highly specific and at times so highly accurate that their use has also aroused a considerable amount of controversy among traders as well as interest by some of the regulatory agencies that oversee the markets.

It is beyond the scope of this book to delve into these issues. Suffice it to say that the argument in favor of seasonals being a viable and accurate method of market analysis and trading far outweighs the objections raised to date.

Cash Seasonality

Each commodity market has its own seasonal tendency. These tendencies appear in the cash and futures markets. Given the fact that cash and futures most often move in tandem (although not always with the same magnitude), seasonal trends that appear in the cash market tend to appear also in the futures markets a vast majority of the time.

The study of cash commodity prices over an extended period of time on a month-to-month change basis reveals that during certain months of the year, price tends to go up and/or peak, whereas, during other months price tends to decline and/or bottom. Ample historical and statistical evidence has been documented supporting the existence of seasonal price patterns in the cash commodity markets. I stress this point because, as noted in previous chapters, there is a general lack of statistical evidence supporting many other technical patterns and indicators.

Seasonal Price Tendency Charts

The simplest way to learn about the various seasonal tendencies in cash commodity prices is to refer to books containing these charts. If, on the other hand, such charts are not available and you wish to construct your own, the procedure appears below.

The technique for charting seasonal tendencies in a market is very simple and easily accomplished either manually or using a computer.

1 Obtain monthly prices for the commodity you wish to analyze.
2 List the monthly average cash prices in tabular form.
3 Calculate the differences from one month to the next for the entire period of data.
4 List the differences in columns according to month. For example, notations would appear for January to February differences, February to March differences, March to April differences, and so on.
5 Add the month-to-month differences for each year back to the start of your data.
6 Compute the average of the differences.
7 Plot the first average, then add it to the second average of difference, and plot this figure. Do so until you have plotted all 12 months of differences.
8 Calculate the percentage of time during the history of your data that prices are up or down for a given month. What you will arrive at is a chart that looks like **Figure 6-1**.

Calculating cash price seasonal tendencies will allow you to determine when markets are likely to be at their strongest or weakest and when markets usually top or bottom. As stated previously, the use of monthly cash seasonal charts is primarily advantageous to the producer, hedger, or long-term trader. **Figures 6-1** through **6-5** show some cash seasonals for several markets. As you will note from these illustrations, there are numerous seasonal patterns within each market and within each year. Many reliable and predictable seasonal patterns have emerged in the cash commodity markets. For example, some have persisted for many years. Several examples of seasonal behavior in cash commodity prices will help illustrate my point:

- The price of copper tends to make a low in the November–December period. As builders begin to buy their supplies (i.e., electrical wire, copper gutters, and flashings) the price of copper begins to rise. This price increase tends to last until March when the building season begins.
- Corn and soybean prices often decline from July through October. By July farmers are usually certain about the size and quality of their crop. As harvest approaches, farmers often sell their crop to grain processing firms who will take delivery of the crop when it is harvested. The selling pressure usually causes prices to decline until harvest is over late in the year.
- Home heating oil prices tend to make their low in the summer, when demand is low due to warm weather. Suppliers begin to buy heating oil at the low summer prices as they build up their inventories for the autumn and winter. Their collective buying often causes prices to rise.

In most cases, these patterns are similar to those in the futures markets. Because so many of the seasonal patterns have been so stable for so many years, the charts do not change appreciably from one year to the next.

Figure 6-1 charts the monthly cash seasonal pattern in wheat prices for the indicated period of time. The plot line shows up trends and down trends with-

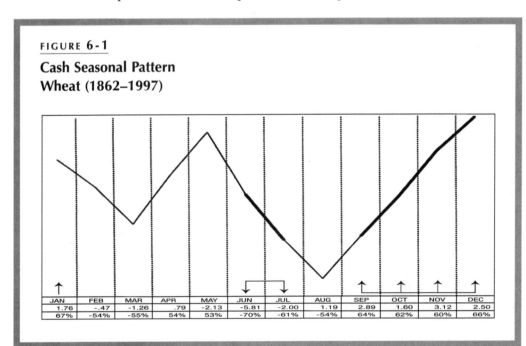

FIGURE 6-1

Cash Seasonal Pattern
Wheat (1862–1997)

	JAN	FEB	MAR	APR	MAY	JUN	JUL	AUG	SEP	OCT	NOV	DEC
	1.76	-.47	-1.26	.79	-2.13	-5.81	-2.00	1.19	2.89	1.60	3.12	2.50
	67%	-54%	-55%	54%	53%	-70%	-61%	-54%	64%	62%	60%	66%

Source: MBH Commodity Advisors, Inc.

FIGURE 6-2

**Cash Seasonal Pattern
Soybean (1930–1997)**

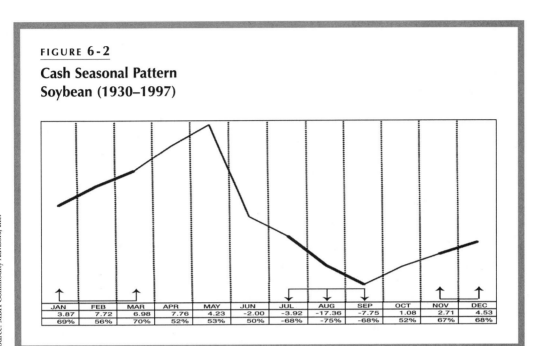

	JAN	FEB	MAR	APR	MAY	JUN	JUL	AUG	SEP	OCT	NOV	DEC
	3.87	7.72	6.98	7.76	4.23	-2.00	-3.92	-17.36	-7.75	1.08	2.71	4.53
	69%	56%	70%	52%	53%	50%	-68%	-75%	-68%	52%	67%	68%

Source: MBH Commodity Advisors, Inc.

FIGURE 6-3

**Cash Seasonal Pattern
Copper (1966–1997)**

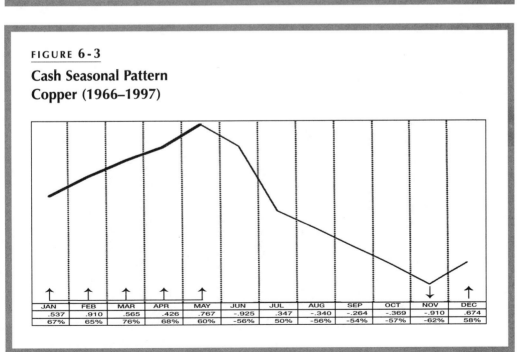

	JAN	FEB	MAR	APR	MAY	JUN	JUL	AUG	SEP	OCT	NOV	DEC
	.537	.910	.565	.426	.767	-.925	.347	-.340	-.264	-.369	-.910	.674
	67%	65%	76%	68%	60%	-56%	50%	-56%	-54%	-57%	-62%	58%

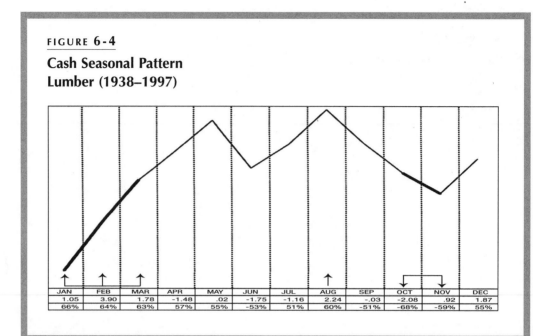

FIGURE 6-4

**Cash Seasonal Pattern
Lumber (1938–1997)**

	JAN	FEB	MAR	APR	MAY	JUN	JUL	AUG	SEP	OCT	NOV	DEC
	1.05	3.90	1.78	-1.48	.02	-1.75	-1.16	2.24	-.03	-2.08	.92	1.87
	66%	64%	63%	57%	55%	-53%	51%	60%	-51%	-68%	-59%	55%

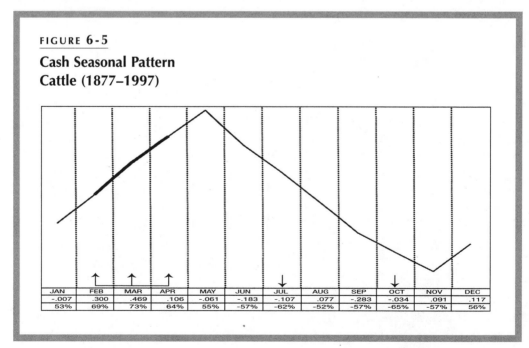

FIGURE 6-5

**Cash Seasonal Pattern
Cattle (1877–1997)**

	JAN	FEB	MAR	APR	MAY	JUN	JUL	AUG	SEP	OCT	NOV	DEC
	-.007	.300	.469	.106	-.061	-.183	-.107	.077	-.283	-.034	.091	.117
	53%	69%	73%	64%	55%	-57%	-62%	-52%	-57%	-65%	-57%	56%

Source: MBH Commodity Advisors, Inc.

in the year. The arrows up and down show time frames during which prices have moved up or down a fairly large percentage of the time. The percentage readings on the bottom row show the portion of time that prices have been up or down for the month. The numbers in the row directly under the month abbreviations show the average percentage price change for the month. As you can see from the chart, there are certain months of the year during which prices have often gone up or down. These are the more predictable moves that we, as traders, seek to uncover (or discover) so as to take long or short positions in advance.

Seasonality in Futures Prices

As noted previously, the use of seasonal futures tendencies on a week-to-week or day-to-day basis as opposed to monthly cash seasonals can be considerably useful to the short-term futures trader. Several methods can be applied in analyzing weekly and daily seasonal futures tendencies. In essence, the approach is quite similar to what was described earlier for monthly seasonal tendencies in the cash market. In this case, however, weekly or daily data are used. Several publications, such as my *Daily Seasonal Futures Charts* and *Weekly Seasonal Futures Charts*, depict weekly and daily futures seasonal tendencies.

Seasonal futures tendencies are specific to the futures contract month. **Figure 6-6** shows a typical weekly seasonal futures chart. As you can see, the seasonal futures tendency of July copper futures shows that prices usually begin moving higher in late December and early January. They tend to peak in late March to early April. While the weekly seasonal patterns for a given futures contract will be reflected in other futures contract months for the same commodity, the weekly percentages are not necessarily the same and the average size of the up or down moves are not necessarily the same. The reasons for this are as follows:

- Different contract months reflect different fundamental conditions.
- Some contract months are more actively traded than others due to the fundamental differences from one delivery month to another. This can result in differences in the percentage of time that up or down moves occur.
- Different contract months tend to make larger up and down moves during the same week as a function of their proximity to the current date. Those futures months that are closest to the current date are more volatile since they more closely reflect current conditions.

The statistics inside the boxes at the bottom of the chart show the percentage

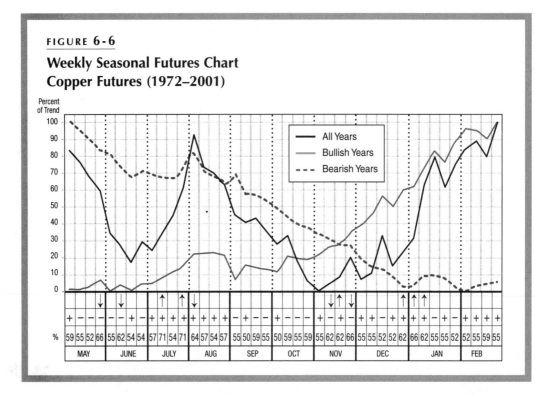

FIGURE 6-6

Weekly Seasonal Futures Chart
Copper Futures (1972–2001)

of time that the price for this market and contract month has closed higher (+) or lower (–) for the given week over the time frame studied. Based on this type of historical data, it is possible to determine when you should ideally be long or short in a given market. Keep in mind that the seasonal charts, whether monthly cash, weekly futures, daily futures (to be discussed), or weekly spreads (to be discussed), do not show what will happen—they show what has happened in the past. In effect, they are a forecast of what is likely to happen in the future based on what has happened with a given degree of regularity in the past.

Seasonals can be wrong on occasion. You need to evaluate the reliability of a seasonal pattern based on the historical accuracy of that pattern as measured by the percentage of time up or down as shown on the seasonal charts. When dealing with seasonals or, for that matter, any technical or fundamental statistic, it is always important to remember that you are dealing with probabilities and not certainties. It behooves the trader to incorporate a variety of factors into the final trading decision. Seasonal price tendencies are studied in order to tilt the odds of success in your favor by virtue of their historical accuracy. Yet even when armed with reliable information, losses can still occur. The goal of market analysis, whether technical, fundamental, or both, is to improve the odds of making a profit.

Note that the analysis of seasonals does not mean that the patterns shown will always be correct. Inherent in all forms of technical and fundamental analysis is a degree of error. However, the results of seasonal analysis can help you determine the usual direction of a market on a week-to-week or day-to-day basis. These tendencies can help you determine both when to buy or sell as well as how to reasonably estimate your potential success.

In addition, you can "filter" seasonals by using a combined approach. Instead of following the weekly seasonal tendencies alone and in a sense "blindly," you instead can study the major market trend and then follow only the daily and/or weekly seasonal readings that coincide with the direction of the major trend.

Daily Seasonal Futures Tendencies

In addition to weekly seasonal futures tendencies, seasonality also exists on a day-to-day basis in the futures markets. **Figure 6-7** shows the daily seasonal futures chart for December cotton futures. Observe that the arrows on the chart point to days that the given market has been up or down a high percentage of the time.

Reliable daily seasonal statistics can be determined for all of the futures markets provided you use an appropriately lengthy database. The weekly seasonal method described earlier is best suited for the majority of futures traders, whereas the daily seasonal tendencies are most appropriate for short-term trading.

Seasonality in Futures Spreads

A commodity spread is the relationship between two different but related markets or between two different contract months in the same commodity. Commodity spreads (also called straddles) are another possible technical tool that exhibits seasonal patterns. Alongside traditional fundamental and/or technical analytical methods, spreads can also be analyzed seasonally using the basic techniques described earlier in this chapter. Some seasonal spread tendencies have been highly predictable, but it is important to keep in mind that spreads are also affected by fundamental conditions such as government programs, weather, supply, demand, interest rates, and carrying charges. For example, the cost of storing grain crops as well as the level of interest rates and government agricultural policies can significantly affect the willingness (or lack thereof) of

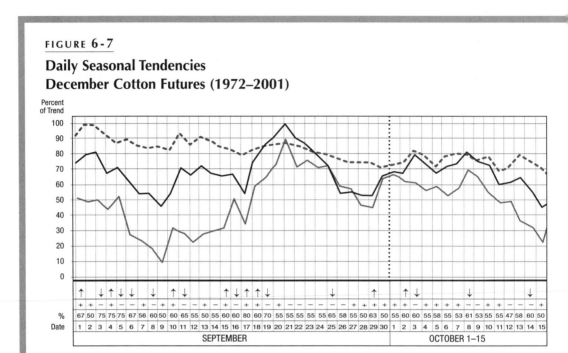

FIGURE 6-7

**Daily Seasonal Tendencies
December Cotton Futures (1972–2001)**

farmers to market their crops. The price of one contract month of a grain crop can be strongly influenced by farmer selling, whereas some contract months of the same commodity (i.e., those farther out into the future) will be only minimally affected by these factors. The differential price movement makes spread trading a viable, and hopefully, profitable, strategy.

You can calculate a seasonal spread tendency in a fashion very similar to the weekly seasonal price tendency. However, you use the three-weekly spread differences as opposed to the week-to-week futures contract differences. A composite seasonal spread chart showing one of the most repetitive seasonal spreads—long April live cattle/short August live cattle—is shown in **Figure 6-8**.

The pattern is very clear. It shows that April live cattle futures tend to gain on August live cattle beginning in early August of the previous year. The tendency becomes very strong beginning in October and November and ends on a very strong note in February through March, just prior to expiration of the April contract.

Ideally, traders would enter the long April live cattle/short August live cattle spread in early August, holding it until mid- to late March. Alternatively, traders

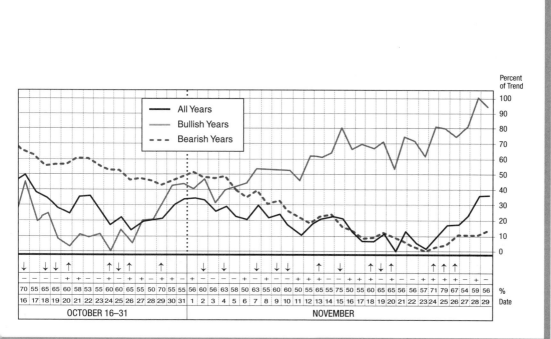

↓		↓	↓	↑			↑	↑	↑			↑			↓		↓		↓		↓	↓		↑		↓		↑	↑	↓	↑			↑	↑	↑		

Source: MBH Commodity Advisors, Inc.

could enter the spread only during the high probability time frames as shown by the up and down arrows. Clusters of arrows in the same direction tend to show the highest probability moves for the spread. See, for example, week numbers 15 through 9, which appear on the bottom row of the chart. Several other seasonal spread relationships are illustrated in **Figures 6-9, 6-10, 6-11,** and **6-12.**

Key-Date Seasonals

The ultimate level of seasonal analysis is the key date seasonal (KDT). Key-date seasonals are the most specific level of seasonality. This aspect of seasonal analysis is specific to the date of entry, the date of exit, and the degree of risk for the given market(s). **Figures 6-13** through **6-16** show key-date seasonals. **Figure 6-17** shows a KDT in a grain spread. As you can see, KDTs are highly specific. They contain virtually all of the necessary information that a trader would require in implementing an objective trading methodology.

Here is the information contained in KDT listings:

● The actual entry date (in the event that a market is closed on the actual entry

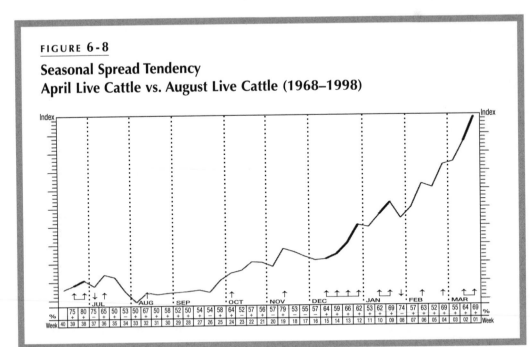

FIGURE 6-8

Seasonal Spread Tendency
April Live Cattle vs. August Live Cattle (1968–1998)

Source: MBH Commodity Advisors, Inc.

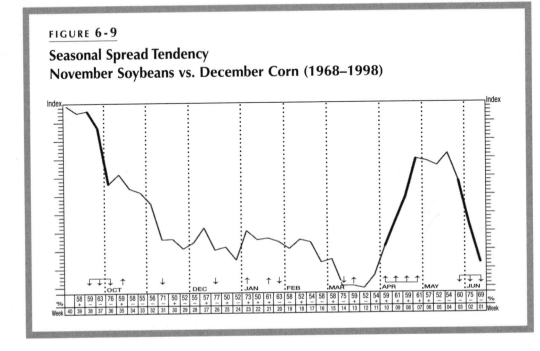

FIGURE 6-9

Seasonal Spread Tendency
November Soybeans vs. December Corn (1968–1998)

Source: MBH Commodity Advisors, Inc.

date, the trade is executed on the close of trading the next business day)

- The specific stop loss as a percentage of the entry price or, for a spread, in points or cents from the entry price
- The actual price change up or down from entry to exit date, or the date the trade would have been stopped out
- The average profit and the average loss for the trade in points and as a percentage of entry price
- The profit-to-loss ratio (total profits/total losses)
- The percentage of time that a trade has been profitable
- The number of years in the historical record
- The cumulative total profit or loss in points, and most important,
- The specific trade rule (e.g., Jan Soybeans SHORT Enter: 9/22 exit: 10/2)

The last item in the list is the specific instruction. It tells you exactly what to do. The importance of having *and following* a specific, objective, and clear rule cannot be overestimated.

Implementing Seasonal Trades

There are several effective techniques for seasonal trading that not only are simple to implement but can also yield very good results. Seasonal futures, the seasonal futures spread methods, and KDTs are excellent methods for novice traders, because they tend to keep you on the right side of the markets and help you trade in the direction of historically valid seasonals. Here are some rules to observe in implementing seasonal trades.

Weekly Seasonal Trading (the simplest approach in using weekly seasonal tendencies)

1 Find weekly seasonal patterns that have had a high percentage of up or down moves (as a rule of thumb, 75 percent or more).
2 Enter a position on the last trading day of the week prior to which the seasonal up or down move is likely to occur.
3 Exit the trade during the last trading day of the week of the seasonal move.
4 As an alternative to exiting the trade per #3, you can determine a profit objective based on support or resistance for the current price chart of the given commodity and month.

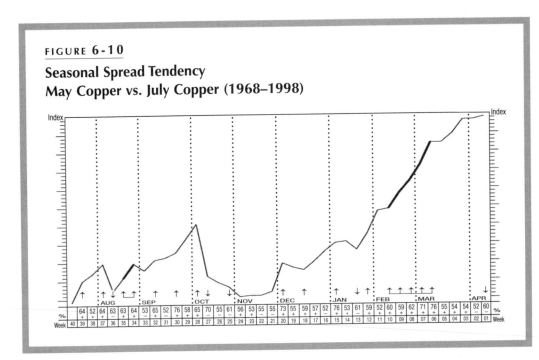

FIGURE **6-10**

Seasonal Spread Tendency
May Copper vs. July Copper (1968–1998)

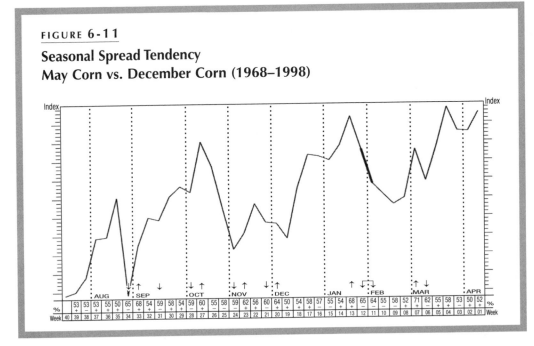

FIGURE **6-11**

Seasonal Spread Tendency
May Corn vs. December Corn (1968–1998)

Source: MBH Commodity Advisors, Inc.

Source: MBH Commodity Advisors, Inc.

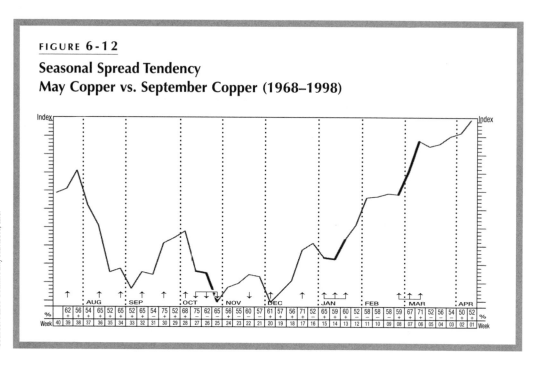

FIGURE **6-12**

Seasonal Spread Tendency
May Copper vs. September Copper (1968–1998)

Filtered Weekly Seasonal Trading

1 Determine the trend of the market.

2 If the trend is up, then follow only those weekly percentage readings that are up at market and implement steps outlined under "Weekly Seasonal Trading." Reliable seasonal moves are those that have been correct 70 percent of the time or more.

3 Conversely, follow only readings that are down for markets in downtrends and then implement the steps for "Weekly Seasonal Trading." Specifically, take only those seasonal trades with high percentages on the downside.

Seasonal Spread Trading

1 Determine which seasonal spread tendencies are reliable.

2 Follow the same procedure outlined for the two techniques above, depending on the orientation and degree of risk you wish to take.

FIGURE 6-13

Key Date Seasonal
January Soybeans (1969–2001)

CONTRACT YR	DATE IN	PRICE IN	DATE OUT	PRICE OUT	PROFIT/LOSS	TOTAL
1969	10/28/68	255.000	11/7/68	258.620	3.620	3.620
1970	10/27/69	249.500	11/7/69	249.370	-0.120	3.500
1971	10/26/70	308.250	11/9/70	305.750	-2.500	1.000
1972	10/26/71	321.250	11/8/71	322.370	1.120	2.120
1973	10/26/72	350.000	11/8/72	356.750	6.750	8.870
1974	10/26/73	556.500	11/7/73	536.500	-20.000	-11.130
1975	10/28/74	777.000	11/7/74	855.500	78.500	67.370
1976	10/27/75	490.250	11/7/75	504.750	14.500	81.870
1977	10/26/76	663.000	11/8/76	674.250	11.250	93.120
1978	10/26/77	544.500	11/7/77	601.000	56.500	149.620
1979	10/26/78	709.000	11/8/78	681.000	-28.000	121.620
1980	10/26/79	655.500	11/7/79	667.000	11.500	133.120
1981	10/27/80	912.000	11/7/80	914.500	2.500	135.620
1982	10/26/81	662.250	11/9/81	667.000	5.000	140.620
1983	10/26/82	546.500	11/8/82	572.500	26.000	166.620
1984	10/26/83	828.500	11/7/83	877.500	49.000	215.620
1985	10/26/84	637.500	11/7/84	639.000	1.500	217.120
1986	10/28/85	512.250	11/7/85	527.000	14.750	231.870
1987	10/27/86	499.250	11/7/86	500.250	1.000	232.870
1988	10/26/87	546.500	11/9/87	553.250	6.750	239.620
1989	10/26/88	784.000	11/7/88	801.250	17.250	256.870
1990	10/26/89	579.750	11/7/89	578.250	-1.500	255.370
1991	10/26/90	611.000	11/7/90	597.500	-13.500	241.870
1992	10/28/91	560.250	11/7/91	557.000	-3.250	238.620
1993	10/26/92	547.250	11/9/92	551.000	3.750	242.370
1994	10/26/93	628.500	11/8/93	639.500	11.000	253.370
1995	10/26/94	560.000	11/7/94	566.000	6.000	259.370
1996	10/26/95	675.500	11/7/95	690.250	14.750	274.120
1997	10/28/96	703.500	11/7/96	685.750	-17.750	256.370
1998	10/27/97	704.500	11/7/97	739.500	35.000	291.370
1999	10/26/98	558.750	11/9/98	573.500	14.750	306.120
2000	10/26/99	479.000	11/8/99	483.000	4.000	310.120
2001	10/26/00	470.500	11/7/00	485.750	15.250	325.370

Trades: 33   Winners: 25   Losers: 8   %Winners: 75.75   Daily PF: 1.37

Avg. Prof: 16.48   Avg. Loss: -10.82   %Avg. Prof: 2.65   %Avg. Loss: -1.74

Source: MBH Commodity Advisors, Inc.

FIGURE **6-14**

Key Date Seasonal
March S&P 500 Futures (1983–2001)

CONTRACT YR	DATE IN	PRICE IN	DATE OUT	PRICE OUT	PROFIT/LOSS	TOTAL
1983	10/26/82	136.800	11/1/82	138.050	1.250	1.250
1984	10/26/83	168.800	11/1/83	167.700	-1.100	0.150
1985	10/26/84	171.100	11/1/84	173.450	2.350	2.500
1986	10/28/85	189.750	11/1/85	193.000	3.250	5.750
1987	10/27/86	240.050	11/3/86	246.600	6.550	12.300
1988	10/26/87	222.000	11/2/87	259.100	37.100	49.400
1989	10/26/88	285.350	11/1/88	283.000	-2.350	47.050
1990	10/26/89	343.650	11/1/89	347.450	3.800	50.850
1991	10/26/90	308.850	11/1/90	311.000	2.150	53.000
1992	10/28/91	392.900	11/1/91	393.900	1.000	54.000
1993	10/26/92	418.300	11/2/92	422.550	4.250	58.250
1994	10/26/93	465.500	11/1/93	470.500	5.000	63.250
1995	10/26/94	466.500	11/1/94	472.250	5.750	69.000
1996	10/26/95	583.350	11/1/95	593.100	9.750	78.750
1997	10/28/96	706.750	11/1/96	712.750	6.000	84.750
1998	10/27/97	884.400	11/3/97	955.400	71.000	155.750
1999	10/26/98	1090.200	11/2/98	1131.500	41.300	197.050
2000	10/26/99	1301.700	11/1/99	1379.500	77.800	274.850
2001	10/26/00	1391.300	11/1/00	1453.000	61.700	336.550

Trades: 19   Winners: 17   Losers: 2   %Winners: 89.47   Daily PF: 3.33

Avg. Prof: 20.00   Avg. Loss: -1.72   %Avg. Prof: 3.15   %Avg. Loss: -0.73

Source: MBH Commodity Advisors, Inc.

FIGURE 6-15

Key Date Seasonal
Treasury Bonds Futures (1978–2001)

CONTRACT YR	DATE IN	PRICE IN	DATE OUT	PRICE OUT	PROFIT/LOSS	TOTAL
1978	10/28/77	101.188	11/23/77	101.688	0.500	0.500
1979	10/30/78	91.094	11/27/78	92.313	1.219	1.719
1980	10/29/79	80.219	11/23/79	81.531	1.313	3.031
1981	10/28/80	68.594	11/24/80	69.438	0.844	3.875
1982	10/28/81	56.656	11/23/81	63.094	6.438	10.312
1983	10/28/82	74.781	11/23/82	76.750	1.969	12.281
1984	10/28/83	70.375	11/23/83	71.063	0.688	12.969
1985	10/29/84	69.281	11/23/84	72.531	3.250	16.219
1986	10/28/85	74.938	11/25/85	79.438	4.500	20.719
1987	10/28/86	95.313	11/24/86	99.375	4.063	24.781
1988	10/28/87	85.250	11/23/87	88.625	3.375	28.156
1989	10/28/88	90.188	11/23/88	87.688	-2.500	25.656
1990	10/30/89	99.063	11/24/89	99.688	0.625	26.281
1991	10/29/90	90.156	11/23/90	94.000	3.844	30.125
1992	10/28/91	97.563	11/25/91	98.156	0.594	30.719
1993	10/28/92	101.438	11/23/92	102.563	1.125	31.844
1994	10/28/93	117.844	11/23/93	114.438	-3.406	28.437
1995	10/28/94	97.688	11/23/94	98.188	0.500	28.937
1996	10/30/95	116.438	11/24/95	117.594	1.156	30.094
1997	10/28/96	110.438	11/25/96	115.094	4.656	34.750
1998	10/28/97	116.375	11/24/97	118.594	2.219	36.969
1999	10/28/98	129.000	11/23/98	127.281	-1.719	35.250
2000	10/28/99	92.688	11/23/99	94.281	1.594	36.844
2001	10/30/00	100.375	11/24/00	101.563	1.188	38.031

Trades: 24   Winners: 21   Losers: 3   %Winners: 87.50   Daily PF: 0.08

Avg. Prof: 2.17   Avg. Loss: -2.54   %Avg. Prof: 2.65   %Avg. Loss: -2.33

FIGURE 6-16

Key Date Seasonal
Gold Futures (1975–2001)

CONTRACT YR	DATE IN	PRICE IN	DATE OUT	PRICE OUT	PROFIT/LOSS	TOTAL
1975	4/14/75	168.300	5/14/75	171.300	-3.000	-3.000
1976	4/14/76	129.100	5/14/76	129.000	0.100	-2.900
1977	4/14/77	154.900	5/16/77	150.000	4.900	2.000
1978	4/14/78	180.600	5/15/78	178.900	1.700	3.700
1979	4/16/79	237.100	4/25/79	249.500	-12.400	-8.700
1980	4/14/80	535.700	5/14/80	534.900	0.800	-7.900
1981	4/14/81	504.400	5/14/81	501.200	3.200	-4.700
1982	4/14/82	384.800	5/14/82	347.300	37.500	32.800
1983	4/14/83	449.600	5/16/83	446.700	2.900	35.700
1984	4/16/84	391.300	5/14/84	382.600	8.700	44.400
1985	4/15/85	337.600	5/14/85	329.800	7.800	52.200
1986	4/14/86	347.500	5/14/86	346.300	1.200	53.400
1987	4/14/87	460.200	5/14/87	471.200	-11.000	42.400
1988	4/14/88	461.100	5/16/88	459.800	1.300	43.700
1989	4/14/89	394.700	5/15/89	380.000	14.700	58.400
1990	4/16/90	383.600	5/14/90	374.600	9.000	67.400
1991	4/15/91	366.100	5/14/91	363.900	2.200	69.600
1992	4/14/92	342.700	5/14/92	339.900	2.800	72.400
1993	4/14/93	342.100	5/6/93	359.800	-17.700	54.700
1994	4/14/94	382.900	5/16/94	386.700	-3.800	50.900
1995	4/17/95	399.900	5/15/95	388.800	11.100	62.000
1996	4/15/96	397.700	5/14/96	395.800	1.900	63.900
1997	4/14/97	351.400	5/14/97	351.000	0.400	64.300
1998	4/14/98	312.200	5/14/98	301.900	10.300	74.600
1999	4/14/99	285.200	5/14/99	278.000	7.200	81.800
2000	4/14/00	287.200	5/15/00	279.300	7.900	89.700
2001	4/16/01	265.400	5/14/01	269.700	-4.300	85.400

Trades: 27   Winners: 21   Losers: 6   %Winners: 77.77   Daily PF: 0.22

Avg. Prof: 6.55   Avg. Loss: -8.70   %Avg Prof: 1.90   %Avg. Loss: -2.86

Source: MBH Commodity Advisors, Inc.

FIGURE 6-17

Key Date Seasonal Spread
July Corn vs. July Oats (1969–1999)

CONTRACT YR	DATE IN	PRICE IN	DATE OUT	PRICE OUT	PROFIT/LOSS	TOTAL
1969	7/17/69	-61.075	8/4/69	-53.900	7.175	7.175
1970	7/17/70	-63.000	8/3/70	-59.550	3.450	10.625
1971	7/19/71	-70.550	8/2/71	-60.925	9.625	20.250
1972	7/17/72	-51.550	8/2/72	-51.350	0.200	20.450
1973	7/17/73	-106.850	8/2/73	-129.000	-22.150	-1.700
1974	7/17/74	-136.000	7/29/74	-168.750	-32.750	-34.450
1975	7/17/75	-110.500	8/4/75	-129.000	-18.500	-52.950
1976	7/19/76	-104.750	8/2/76	-98.750	6.000	-46.950
1977	7/18/77	-96.000	8/2/77	-93.000	3.000	-43.950
1978	7/17/78	-106.000	8/2/78	-95.500	10.500	-33.450
1979	7/17/79	-140.250	8/2/79	-123.750	16.500	-16.950
1980	7/17/80	-137.000	8/4/80	-145.750	-8.750	-25.700
1981	7/17/81	-155.250	8/3/81	-142.750	12.500	-13.200
1982	7/19/82	-90.750	8/2/82	-88.250	2.500	-10.700
1983	7/18/83	-130.250	8/2/83	-155.250	-25.000	-35.700
1984	7/17/84	-108.750	8/2/84	-106.500	2.250	-33.450
1985	7/17/85	-98.250	8/2/85	-95.000	3.250	-30.200
1986	7/17/86	-66.750	8/4/86	-59.250	7.500	-22.700
1987	7/17/87	-18.500	8/3/87	-4.250	14.250	-8.450
1988	7/18/88	-26.500	8/2/88	-15.750	10.750	2.300
1989	7/17/89	-83.000	8/2/89	-78.250	4.750	7.050
1990	7/17/90	-124.500	8/2/90	-116.250	8.250	15.300
1991	7/17/91	-108.250	8/2/91	-128.000	-19.750	-4.450
1992	7/17/92	-94.500	8/3/92	-86.250	8.250	3.800
1993	7/19/93	-103.500	8/2/93	-100.500	3.000	6.800
1994	7/18/94	-102.250	8/2/94	-98.000	4.250	11.050
1995	7/17/95	-123.500	8/2/95	-103.750	19.750	30.800
1996	7/17/96	-147.750	8/2/96	-134.000	13.750	44.550
1997	7/17/97	-99.250	8/4/97	-98.750	0.500	45.050
1998	7/17/98	-112.500	8/3/98	-106.000	6.500	51.550
1999	7/19/99	-93.500	8/2/99	-108.250	-14.750	36.800

Trades: 31   Winners: 24   Losers: 7   %Winners: 77.42

Avg Prof: 7.44   Avg Loss: -20.24

Source: MBH Commodity Advisors, Inc.

Summary

The existence of seasonal price tendencies in cash commodity prices, stocks, futures, and futures spreads is an observable fact with which many traders may become familiar. In spite of the availability of a number of computer research studies on the topic, however, few traders are well versed in this important approach to futures trading.

Given the historical reliability of many seasonal price patterns, novice traders can take considerably less risk by learning how to use seasonals and by using them in their trading approach. There are many different seasonal tendencies and many different ways in which to employ them. Choose what best fits your situation and resources as discussed in Chapter 17.

Inasmuch as seasonal data is relatively simple to obtain and relatively simple to evaluate, the potential value of seasonality in most trading approaches is significant. In fact, it can be argued that seasonality can be used as an effective addition to other trading systems, and, when combined with even the most elementary timing indicators, this approach can yield very good results. Although the analysis of seasonals does not mean that the patterns shown will always be correct, it can help you significantly improve your odds of success in comparison to the many marginal or losing methods used by traders.

CHAPTER 7

What You Should Know about Computers and Computerized Trading Systems

It is better to ask some of the questions than to know all the answers.

— JAMES THURBER

Today many aspiring futures traders feel that they cannot be successful without a computerized price quote system and/or a computerized trading system. The reality is that success is not computer-dependent in today's futures markets, however counter-intuitive this may sound. This chapter offers some insights and direction about the advantages and limits in the use of a computer in futures trading. Before we explore this topic more fully I would like to emphasize the following points:

- A computer will not necessarily make you a more profitable futures trader.
- A computer, if used incorrectly, can help you lose money.
- Bigger, better, and faster computers do not necessarily mean bigger, better, or faster profits.
- It is not necessary to trade online in order to make money in futures.
- You do not need trading software in order to make money in futures.
- You do not need expensive trading systems, historical data, or charting programs in order to be successful in the futures markets.
- You do not need a degree in electronics or programming in order to use a computer for trading futures and/or to use a futures trading system.
- You do not need to visit online chat rooms, advisory services, or chart services in order to be a successful futures trader.
- You do not need to be a day-trader in order to make money in the futures markets with your computer.
- You do not need to take classes or seminars on how to use your computer profitably in the futures markets.

Reinvent the Wheel?

The almost continuous stream of futures trading software that now dominates the marketplace has turned from a slow trickle into a virtual waterfall of programs. Competition is becoming greater every day, and rarely a day passes without a new program or system being presented to the public for sale or lease. The response in the marketplace has been quite positive, and futures software sales have been booming.

In some cases, there may be so many users of a particular system that this could, to a certain extent, affect its operations. However, the large number of alternatives and competitive systems on today's market makes the likelihood of too many traders following any one particular system rather small. This speaks favorably about the possibility of profiting from one of the commercially available systems.

The independent trader will probably want to avoid most commercially available trading systems in favor of developing his own trading approach using concepts and techniques he has developed. This approach is, of course, the ideal application of computer systems, and the results may justify the entire cost of the system many times over.

If you are interested in trading software development, a utility program may considerably cut down on your work. Specifically, you can purchase a prewritten program that will allow you to input various parameters for test purposes. These programs can be found through an Internet search for "trading software." You may then generate hypothetical trading results more quickly and specifically without having to go through all of the programming work from start to finish. Although the decision to develop or use prewritten software is certainly an individual one, the rapid changes and accelerating progress in futures trading software research make it worth your while to consider a prewritten program as opposed to developing your own systems. Consider also the possibility of modifying existing software to suit your needs more closely or, perhaps, to improve its performance vastly.

Computerized Quote Systems

The days of the large mechanical quote board that clicked and ticked away in the broker's office are almost history. The familiar clicking sound of rapidly changing prices on the old mechanical quote boards has been replaced by the stark silence of the glowing screen, and the occasional beep of a computer reminding its master that something of importance has occurred. The hand-drawn chart has been replaced by the multicolored computer screen version. Laser-printed color charts have replaced the colored lines and colored pencils of earlier times.

Yet, in spite of our wonderful technology, there are still many significant differences among the available quote systems. The single best way to determine the type of quotation system best suited for your purposes is to test-drive a few. If you cannot arrange for a no-cost trial period, then attempt to visit a broker or friend who has a system and use it for a while to see how you relate to it. Different systems have different strengths and weaknesses. Certainly you would hate to purchase a system and be stuck with it if it is not ideally suited to the precise applications you require.

Pros and Cons of Trading Systems

Trading systems facilitate discipline. Computerized systems offer additional advantages. The speed and efficiency with which a computer identifies patterns and generates trading signals is one obvious advantage. It is impossible for a trader to calculate these signals manually (in the time required), and the trader's ability to evaluate a complete rule-based system is limited as well.

Computers can quickly achieve the "number crunching" necessary to recognize trading signals, and computer systems offer direction and suggestions about what to do in a given market and help limit the range of choices. This makes the trader's task less overwhelming, because the possibilities and opportunities become more clearly defined.

Trading systems approach the market consistently and objectively. Programs are designed logically. Rules are uniformly applied to defined market conditions. Trading systems are effective because rules are not the victims of trader judgment—which means that the whimsical nature of a trader is diminished.

The emotional aspect of trading can be significantly reduced as well because systems are devoid of emotion and judgment. Unfortunately, there is no computer to stop the emotional tendency of a trader to outguess the system—even when it is producing profitable trades! If a trader can discipline himself to follow a system with rigor, emotions will not rule the decision-making process. Trading systems are designed to "think," not to feel. Another positive feature of trading systems is that they generally include money management rules that facilitate trading discipline.

One of the more frequent arguments against computer-based trading systems is that they can become popular enough to influence the underlying price. This concern has been voiced both by the futures market federal regulatory agency (the Commodity Futures Trading Commission) and by individual traders.

The concern is that similarly (or identically) programmed computer-based systems used to manage large positions may cause large traders to respond in the same way at the same time, thereby causing distortion in the futures markets. The reality is, however, that although it is possible that two systems with the same philosophy and/or programming may react in similar ways, the chances of precisely similar signals occurring on the same day, at the same time, on the same side of the market are minimal.

An argument against the efficacy of trading systems is that markets are random and, therefore, cannot be interpreted based on pattern recognition. This argument further suggests that trading systems based on historical data cannot, therefore, be valid. While it is not guaranteed that past price patterns guarantee future price patterns, it is also *not* true that markets are random. The statistical reliability of many trading systems refutes the random argument.

Finally, the value of trading systems has been challenged on the basis that they define market behavior in limited ways when the market can, in fact, behave in an infinite number of ways. Systems are mathematically or mechanically defined, and it can be argued that this purely mechanistic approach to market analysis by definition diminishes the real-life complexity in relationships of events to mere percentage odds of future activity.

Although the criticism is valid in that systems do capture a very limited number of possibilities, this characteristic is also what makes systems useful. The ability to reduce information to observable patterns gives the trader manageable order and controllable direction. Without this, many traders feel overwhelmed and without bearing.

Trading systems give the trader a way to interpret, quantify, and classify market behavior. Because trading systems define potential opportunity and provide specific trading signals, following these signals can facilitate the development of trading skills as well as highly important and often-overlooked discipline.

Buying versus Developing a Trading System

Faced with the often-daunting task of finding and implementing an effective trading system, many newcomers to the futures markets are inclined to buy trading systems that have been developed expressly for the purpose of being sold to the public. In some cases such systems can actually help traders make money. Sadly, in most cases, such systems will, in the long run (and all too often in the short run), prove to be losing propositions. More often than not, traders are better off developing their own trading approaches. There are literally hundreds of trading systems. They can be bought, leased, or subscribed to at prices ranging from as low as $99 per month to the outright purchase price of $35,000. The ultimate question is, of course, whether they are worth the money, based on their effectiveness.

Since the early 1960s, the rapid growth of professionally managed money and multimillion-dollar futures funds has prompted the development and proliferation of numerous trading systems. In part, the popularity of trading systems has also been a function of public demand as well as public gullibility. Typically, the public gets what the public wants.

Unfortunately, what the public wants is not always beneficial. The decision to buy a trading system or to develop one's own independent system is often a difficult one for new traders. The lure of buying a turnkey system that has been developed by a professional (although not always) who can show promising historical results is often sufficient to overcome the cost of such trading systems. Yet the experience of developing a system on your own (which need not be computerized) often far outweighs the benefits of buying a system.

As noted earlier in this chapter, there are a number of software programs available that allow you to develop your own trading system (or systems). By using the rule writing and testing features of these programs, you can write and develop one or more of your own customized versions. You can back-test your trading systems, alter them, build in risk management methods and perfect the systems to your own needs and likes. In so doing, however, beware that you can fall victim to some of the same shortcomings that characterize many of the trading systems offered by system sellers.

In producing your own system you may be tempted to portray your systems in the best possible light, even though you may suspect, in your heart-of-hearts, that the results will not be capable of going forward in real time. I urge you to read the rest of this chapter carefully so that you do not become a victim of your own desire to produce or buy a system that looks wonderful on paper when viewed historically, but which cannot produce profits in the future.

Questionable Ethics and Questionable Results

Commercial developers of trading systems often make bold promises of profit and success for the systems they are peddling. Before the availability of low-cost computers, performance claims were often undocumented or poorly researched, as historical testing was, at one time, a tedious manual process.

The ability to more readily verify the claims of systems developers increased with the advent of advanced computer testing in the 1980s. Yet historical validation of system performance is not the *sine qua non* of futures trading results. Statistics can be manipulated and presented in a variety of ways that can enhance poor performance, exaggerate good performance, or mask bad performance.

In spite of the fact that virtually any system can be quickly back-tested by computer, provided its algorithms and money management rules can be programmed, the use of optimization can still yield results that are misleading. Optimization, simply stated, is the process by which literally hundreds or thousands of signals and combinations of signals can be tested in order to find the "best fit" in terms of largest potential profit and/or accuracy.

Any system expressed in operational (i.e., programmable) terms can be computer tested and optimized using the computer to test a variety of if-then scenarios. As a result, although fraudulent or erroneous claims can be debunked, clever marketers can present performance histories that are difficult to rebuke on the basis of accuracy. The good news is that optimization can help individuals identify trading systems whose back-tested results are stellar. The bad news is that the results will not be reproducible in real time because they were retrofitted to historical data.

Computerized trading and testing has led to new advances in system development. In this age of computerized everything, virtually every aspect of our lives is, in one way or another, regulated, dominated, determined, or otherwise affected by computers. Although some have hailed computers as the solution to all problems, their value is not entirely a *fait accompli*. The same conclusion applies to the use of computers in trading system research and development.

One would imagine that the use of a computer would eliminate all doubt about the efficacy of trading systems. If that is what you think, then you are dead wrong—and it may cost you big bucks before you learn you are wrong.

Let's examine a few of the common misconceptions and fallacies now prevalent in the field of computerized trading systems. Let's also dig more deeply into some of the methods that computerized trading system peddlers often use to enhance the appearance of their programs, thereby giving the perception of better results. Before doing so, however, here are several questions to consider about all systems:

1 *Does the system have "face validity?" Does it make sense?*
2 *Can the system adjust to changing market conditions in real time?*
3 *Does the system have too many variables? The more variables it has, the less successful it is likely to be in the future.*

These three general points are important to bear in mind as you review the many other performance criteria that can be used to evaluate a trading strategy during a test phase or under actual market time. One significant factor to be reviewed is the consistency of the trading strategy over a long period of time. Stability over time is critical. Be sure the test data is long enough to include changes in price level. Bull and bear markets should be covered as well as periods of extended low volatility.

It is important to understand the methods of optimization and to provide proper precautions regarding optimized trading systems. Performed properly, extensive testing can reveal a great deal. However, excessive optimizing can be misleading, deceptive, and costly.

Fallacy of the Vast Historical Database

Some trading systems assert their superiority as a result of testing on a vast historical database. The claim is meaningless. It's a tease and a smoke screen designed to distract attention from the real issues. A lengthy historical database, in and of itself, is meaningless. A vast historical database is only meaningful if used appropriately. Unfortunately, too many trading system developers use historical data to find the best system fit. They test and retest indicators, add to them, modify them, add rules, change rules, and combine rules until they have found a system that fits the back data perfectly.

Once the system is ready, they can market it to the public using the lengthy history as a promotional tool. What has the system developer created? Has anything of potential value been found? I've discovered that there is an inverse relationship between the complexity of a trading system and its future profitability: The simpler it works, the better it is. If you can find a few simple tools and test them under the appropriate conditions, then they will continue to work well for you.

The Selective Data/Selective Market Trick

Another trick some system developers have been known to use is the limited historical test. By testing a system in trending markets, you can create fabulous historical results. By testing systems for certain markets only, you also can show tremendous historical results. Virtually any trading system, no matter how intrinsically flawed, will work in trending markets.

Trends make systems right, and sideways markets make systems wrong. That's the way it has always been. Some markets are known for their "trendiness"—they establish long-lasting trends and, therefore, show good historical results. The yen, coffee, and cotton futures are markets that tend to move in stable long-lasting trends. Almost any system that follows trends will work in such markets. You don't need a $2,000 software program to make money with them.

What's the Drawdown?

Many traders lose money because they quit too soon. The urge to quit is greatest when things are worst. And things are the worst when the worst is almost over. It takes great discipline to persist when all appears lost. When it comes to trading systems, there are two variables that will destroy persistence and discipline—drawdown and consecutive losses.

Some systems can produce ten or more consecutive losing trades, which is enough to test the patience of any trader. But more than the number of consecutive losses is the aggregate dollar amount of those losses. And of even greater importance is the maximum drawdown.

Simply stated, maximum drawdown is the maximum decrease in account equity before a positive turn in equity. For example, you were ahead $25,000 on your system and you suffered a $3,000 loss on one trade. If the next trade is also a loser, say $1,200, then the drawdown now is $4,200. If the next trade is a $400 loser then your drawdown is now $4,600. If the next trade is a winner, then this drawdown period ends at $4,600. A new drawdown calculation begins when the next loss is suffered.

A drawdown of $1,000 in a $10,000 account is not unreasonable. However, a $1,000 drawdown in a $2,000 account is substantial in terms of percentage. What distinguishes winners from losers many times is the ability to sit through periods of drawdown and, above all, to avoid initiating a trading system during a period of rising equity inasmuch as one could be starting at a high point. Traders often begin to use a system when it is performing well. This is a natural tendency. After all, we all want to get on board when things are going well. All too often, however, traders begin to use a system when it is at its peak performance. They begin to use the system just before it enters a period of drawdown. Consequently, they lose money almost immediately. The best time to begin using a trading system that has demonstrated its profitability is after it has had drawdown.

If the historical drawdown has not been large, then you could enter at virtually any time. It is still best, however, to begin trading in a period of drawdown. Nevertheless, human instinct prompts traders to begin a new system when things look best, not worst. Systems developers will attract you to their systems when things look best and when performance has been on the upswing. As noted earlier, this can be dangerous since you may be enticed to begin using the system at the peak of its performance prior to a period of drawdown.

Stable versus Unstable Systems
Another thing to watch out for is a system that has experienced periods of significant volatility. To a certain extent this precaution relates to the issue of drawdown. While the best system you can have is one that has shown slow and steady growth through the years, this quality is, unfortunately, not what interests most traders.

Most traders are attracted to systems that boast hundreds or thousands of percent equity increase, not realizing that to achieve such gains it is necessary to risk a large amount of money. Stable, steady growth is by far superior to unstable and volatile performance—but traders too often fail to recognize the value of stability when assessing which trading system to purchase.

Dealing with Limit Moves
Because most trading systems are trend-following systems, their entry signals are triggered after bottoms or tops have been made. On occasion, such bottoms or tops are reached after important reports result in "limit up" or "limit down" price moves. A "limit move" is defined as follows: the maximum permissible price fluctuation for the day as determined from the close of trading the previous day. In other words, if live cattle closed at 52.50 yesterday and the daily limit is 1.50, then the highest price that could be attained today would be 52.50 + 1.50, or 54.00. The lowest possible price would be 52.50 − 1.50, or 51.00.

At times the limit moves will continue for several consecutive days. Some of the biggest moves in history have occurred on a series of limit moves. When a market is "locked" at the limit up, buying is often impossible because there are no sellers. Not all markets have trading limits, however. Since limits change from time to time, it is best to consult your broker for a list of current trading limits in the various markets.

Locked limit-down moves afford little or no opportunity to exit a long position or to enter a short position. Too many systems incorrectly purport in their back-testing that entry was made on limit days when, in fact, entry would not have been possible. This allows them to show very large profits on such trades when, in actuality, such trades would have been impossible. Unless a testing program is designed to test for such cases, the hypothetical performance results you would get are erroneous and misleading. Always ask how locked limit moves were treated in the test and ask for documentation.

Computerized Testing of Trading Systems

As noted previously, computer testing of mechanical trading systems has grown considerably since the early 1980s. Traders may easily verify the claims of system developers. The trading public need not be victimized by fallacious assertions regarding trading systems. Although the software to test systems is readily available, it is, however, necessary to know the essential ingredients that comprise a successful test.

Many traders today underestimate the ability of some promoters to manipulate statistics. Systems developers can "massage" statistics in order to show favorable results. Individual traders tend to deceive themselves in testing their own systems. Having high expectations and wishful thinking, they too fall prey to the fallacy of confusing past performance with future results.

In order to determine the validity of any system, it is crucial to remember that simply reporting highly favorable results does not guarantee success with that system in real-time trading. The basic assumption, "the better it worked in the past, the better it will work in the future," has been one of the more costly beliefs to traders.

Unfortunately, a misguided objective of many testing systems is to develop trading strategies that extract the greatest possible profit from historical data. Such "optimized" systems are not designed to portray the worst-case scenarios, but rather, are developed to demonstrate optimum past performance. This is not only naive; it is potentially dangerous.

Why Test a Trading System?

Why is it necessary to test a system? If testing a system gives you only hypothetical results with no guaranteed success in real-time trading, why bother? Although you will never really know for certain if a system will work in the future (in real time with real money), proper testing methods can allow you to learn the strong and weak aspects of your system. But I emphasize "proper" testing.

Traders have their different reasons for testing systems. Some traders test a system to "go through the motions," failing to take seriously the results. All too often, they disregard the results or rationalize poor results. They mistakenly believe that they can turn a mediocre system into a winner by managing the trades differently or by practicing different money management rules. Other traders develop systems in order to market them to the public. Their objective is to optimize the system in order to reflect best-case performance.

In effect, the "ultimate product" that they are trying to sell is a contrived system, curve fitted to an extreme degree. As attractive as they may seem, the odds of such systems working in real-time trading are slim indeed. Any statistician acquainted with the law of diminishing returns understands that the more variables and rules you add to a system, the less reliable the outcome will be.

The serious trader who tests systems with the rigor and discipline needed for success in the futures markets must have specific goals. Their reasons for testing systems are as follows:

1 *To determine whether a theoretical method is valid in historical testing.* How would the method have performed in the past? (Note that the method would be tested using historical data, not "fitted" to historical data.)
2 *To learn the assets and the liabilities of the system.*
3 *To identify how potentially different timing indicators combine with one another to produce a potentially effective trading system.*
4 *To examine the relationship of risk and reward variables within the system.* How do variables such as entry and exit methods using stops, position size, and so forth work in concert to produce the best overall performance with the smallest drawdown?

The time and expense of real-time testing a new trading system are considerable, so it follows that computer testing is the most efficient method for determining how a system would have performed in the past. The main purpose of testing systems is to learn what might work best in the future based on what has worked in the past.

Test for Key Results

Do not expect to find a 100 percent correlation between the past and the future. Nothing is definite in futures. There are, however, various important aspects that you should consider when you test any trading system:

1 *Length of the historical test.* It would seem logical to assume that the further back you test the system, the better the results will be. In fact, the opposite is true. Many trading systems and indicators do not withstand the test of time. The further back you test, the less effective most systems will be. Many system developers prefer a standard test of 10 years because it presents their systems best. The more important variable in testing systems is the number of trades rather than the number of years analyzed.

2 *Number of trades analyzed.* Analyzing data over the course of many years is not necessary if you have a large sample size of trades. I feel that at least 100 trades is required to produce statistically significant results, provided your system will generate this number of trades in back-testing. It is better to err on the side of more rather than less data.

It would not be wise to select a model based on just a few trades that occurred during a short period of time. Such a system would not work in market conditions distinctly different from those tested.

3 *Maximum drawdown.* A very important, but overlooked, statistic for testing purposes is percent equity drawdown. A system that generates a very high annualized percent return over a period of five years will be difficult to follow if it has drawdowns of 50 percent several times during that five-year period. It would take guts and a highly capitalized account to handle the equity swings. In my experience, a smooth equity curve is much more desirable.

This curve is important as it illustrates how practical your trading system will be with real money. It seems that most systems that offer the largest net profits have the largest drawdowns. Look at a large drawdown coupled with a string of losses and it is easy to see why most people may prematurely abandon a potentially good trading system. People generally should seek out trading systems that reflect steady growth and small drawdowns, rather than the "home runs" showing big short-term gains with large drawdowns.

4 *Maximum successive losses.* Although they can be painful, maximum consecutive losses can provide a useful metric. It gives you an idea of how much emotional pain you may have to endure while trading with your system. Few traders are willing to stick with their system after three or four consecutive losses. Often they discard a potentially good system. A forecast of the number of consecutive

losing trends can help prepare a trader for a worst-case scenario and prevent panic should it actually happen.

5 *Largest single losing trade.* This information is especially important if the loss exceeds your normal risk-control measure. There may a problem or contingency in the system you have overlooked. A natural tendency of traders is to overlook the biggest losing trades and to psychologically eliminate them. You will often see practices of "curve fitting" to compensate for the loss, which is deceptive, misleading, and potentially costly.

If you pay attention to the largest single losing trade, you can learn where to adjust the initial stop loss and manage the overall system with efficiency. You should also use this information to question why the largest single losing trade was bigger than the stop loss you had selected. The whole idea of testing a system is to avoid surprises that can negate your whole system.

6 *Largest single winning trade.* In some ways the largest winning trade is even more important to know than the maximum losing trade, because it can skew the net profit in an unreasonable way. One possible approach that avoids this potential imbalance is to eliminate the largest winning trade in each commodity and then reevaluate the net results. As I mentioned earlier, the quality you are looking for is consistency. An extremely large winning trade can misrepresent the overall results of the system's performance.

7 *Percentage of winning trades.* This statistic is not as important as you may think and can often be misleading. For example, most successful traders have 30 percent to 45 percent winners. Systems that reflect 80 percent winners can be bad systems if each loss is several times as large as each profit. When you actually do some testing, you will see that it is difficult to achieve much over 60 percent winners in a system. Note also the effect stops have on winning percentages.

8 *Slippage and commissions.* Do not trust any testing results that fail to include a liberal allowance for commissions and slippage, which is defined as the difference between the price you expected to be filled at and the actual price at which you were filled. Both can make a very big difference in your overall results. Many trading systems will make small steady profits when tested without slippage (i.e., in order fulfillment) and commissions, then turn into steady losers when transaction costs are factored in.

Pay particular attention to the transaction costs when the system operates on short-term trades or day trading. The more often trades are generated, the more critical transaction costs become.

Everyone has favorite numbers to factor in as transaction costs. I like to use

$75 for slippage and $50 for commission per round turn for a total of $125 per trade. This number may seem high, but I prefer to err on the conservative side and avoid unpleasant surprises. You may initially want to exclude the transaction costs to simplify the operation, but make sure you include them before you look at potential bottom-line results. Commission costs and slippage add up and can make an incredible difference in your testing results.

9 *Ratio of average win to average loss.* Traders tend to assume that they must have a proportionately high number of winners to losers in a system. Successful traders can have fewer winners than losers (30-45 percent winners as mentioned previously), but the average profit in each winning trade should be at least twice as much as the average loss on a losing trade. For example, say your system produces winners 40 percent of the time, and the ratio of the average loss is 2 to 1. Assuming the average win was $100 and the average loss was $50, after 10 trades, your profit from the four wins would be $400 and your loss from the six losses would only be $300. You have a net profit of $100.

Summary

Computer systems enable futures traders to analyze massive amounts of data in a matter of minutes. The net effect, however, has been minimized because the advantage is now available to virtually all traders, whether through their own computer systems or through the purchase of research performed by various services.

The advantages of computer systems for trading may, however, be illusory. Many traders, particularly novices, are convinced that they cannot achieve success in futures without relying on a computer in all aspects of their trading activity. This dependency is a myth. The fact that you have a computer, that you use your computer for trading, and that you use computerized charts and quotes does not mean, *ipso facto,* that you will make money in the futures trading game. Consider your goals before you conclude that a computer-centric system for trading is necessary for success. Remember that simplicity is an asset.

In regard to the testing of mechanical trading systems, the ability to verify claims of trading systems developers has increased due to the development of computerized testing systems. Today, however, systems developers use statistical manipulation to show optimum performance of a system. Often this practice distorts results and does not adequately reflect how a system will perform in real time. The trader should be aware that systems developers "massage" statistics to market their trading programs. Learning to evaluate the validity of testing systems is just as important as the actual testing.

With so many traders using computers to design and test trading systems, it is important to examine the testing process itself and to identify the common mistakes that can affect your bottom line. Always keep in mind, however, that testing is the means to an end, not an end in itself. In realizing this you will become aware that reporting highly favorable results does not in any way guarantee success in the future. The goal of testing is to learn the good and the bad about a system and to begin to know what to expect in the future. A good trading system will reflect slow, steady growth and consistent performance.

Part Two

Discipline and Trading

CHAPTER 8

Discipline: Your First Key to Success

All successful men have agreed in one thing—they were causationists. They believed that things went not by luck, but by law; that there was not a weak or a cracked link in the chain that joins the first and last of things.

— RALPH WALDO EMERSON

What separates winners from losers in the futures markets? Is it brain or brawn? Is it what you know? Is it age or maturity? Is it experience or longevity? Or is it self-discipline and persistence? When I am asked what is the single most important factor to success in futures trading, my response is not "trading systems," nor is it "the type of computer you have," nor is it "the type of inside information to which you might be privy." It is not "the amount of capital you have," or "the broker with whom you are trading." What ultimately separates winners from losers, commercial, speculative, short term, long term, or otherwise, is discipline in its many and varied facets.

Although there are literally hundreds of things I could tell you about different trading approaches and the lessons I have learned through long and hard experience, none of them would be more meaningful than the lessons I have learned about discipline. The advice I can give you about discipline is the most important knowledge I can impart. Discipline is the most essential determinant of success in futures trading. If I were to suggest that you read only one chapter in this book, this would be it!

What Is Discipline?

To most traders discipline is just another well-worn topic in futures trading. They have heard the word, they've studied the preaching, and they believe they have learned the lessons. My observations and experiences with futures markets and futures traders lead me to the irreversible conclusion that the lessons have not been learned!

The word "discipline" signifies something traders know they need and believe they have. In their heart of hearts, however, most traders know they are sorely lacking in discipline and that they will probably never have it.

Discipline is virtually impossible to teach or to learn from anyone else. It is complex, elusive, evasive, and often camouflaged. It is the *sine qua non* of success in virtually every form of human achievement, in every field and in every generation. Yet, to the best of my knowledge, there is no simple way to define discipline.

There are futures traders who have no objective trading system to speak of, but who, through the application and development of discipline, have achieved success. On the other hand, there are many futures traders with excellent trading systems, who for lack of discipline have remained unsuccessful, in spite of massive statistical evidence to suggest their techniques are indeed valid and capable of producing tremendous profits. In fact, I have found that in almost any form of investing or speculating the key element of success is discipline. I hope discipline has your attention.

The purpose of this chapter is twofold: first, to illustrate the importance of discipline; and second, to suggest a number of ways by which discipline can be developed and improved. First, let's look at the fashion in which discipline functions and at its ramifications in the successful trading approach.

Why Discipline Is Important in the Quest for Success

As you know, there are many different approaches to futures trading. Some are potentially more profitable than others. Some are simple, some are complex, some are logical, and some not so logical. Regardless of the trading approach you use, all trading systems and methods have certain elements in common:

1 Specific signals (rules) for entry and exit
2 Specific parameters, methods of calculating timing signals
3 Specific action(s) that must be taken as a function of 1 and 2

When systems and methods are tested by computer, they are not tested in real time, but rather in theoretical time, with perfect adherence to the trading rules that have been programmed into the computer in order to generate hypothetical or ideal results. A series of specific parameters are tested and what comes out is a listing of trades and hypothetical results based on the perfect execution of the rules that were programmed into the machine.

The output of the system test will yield many different types of information including such things as percentage of trades profitable, percentage of trades unprofitable, percentage of trades that break even, average winning trade in dollars, average losing trade in dollars, performance for given markets, and average length of time per trade. (Chapter 7 more thoroughly discusses how to test trading systems.)

All data derived from the computer test of a trading system is based upon perfect follow-up, implementation, and execution of trading signals according to the parameters programmed into the computer. This means the success of a system is based upon the trader implementing all the specific rules of the system. There is no room for error!

Neither is there room for lack of discipline! Some systems are profitable only 55 to 65 percent of the time. Other systems show higher percentages. I have rarely seen systems that are profitable more than 80 percent of the time. But such statistics can be misleading. Certainly you can imagine that a trading system that is correct 90 percent of the time, making a $100 profit on average each time and then losing $900 on the occasion that it is wrong would certainly not be very profitable. The individual trading the system would give back all profits made on nine trades on one losing trade.

Conversely, a trading system may show eight losers for every two winners. If the average profitable trade is much larger than the average losing trade, even a system having nine losers out of every ten trades could be profitable, if the bottom line per trade was higher on the winning side. Nevertheless, such a system would be thrown astray if lack of discipline resulted in much larger losses than expected for the eight losing trades. If lack of discipline interfered significantly with the profits on the two profitable trades, then the net results might be much worse than anticipated.

A third scenario would be a marginal trading system. Assume a trading system is profitable about 65 percent of the time. You can figure that approximately 65 out of every 100 trades are winners and 35 are losers. You can see that only 30 percent separates the winners from the losers. In other words, the trader must have sufficient discipline to keep the losses as small as possible and to maximize profits.

Discipline is the machinery that can make or break any trading system. There are some conditions under which discipline will not be the important variable. In most cases, however, it is the significant variable. All the glowing trading statistics for your trading system will be totally useless if you are not capable of duplicating the exact statistics generated by the computer test of your trading system.

In other words, you must stick as close to the averages as possible, or else one or two losses much larger than the average or one or two profits much smaller than the average will be sufficient to ruin your results. Sometimes this can occur strictly as a function of market behavior (for example, in the case of limit moves against you). More often than not, however, it is the trader who is responsible for maintaining the discipline of a system.

Doing Your Homework

It is uncanny how many times markets will begin major moves in line with the expectations of many advisors, analysts, and speculators without these various individuals being on board for the big move. Why do things like this happen? How often has this happened to you? I know from personal experience that many individuals have good records at predicting where prices will go. I also know that when it comes to doing their homework, they have especially poor records.

What do I mean by doing homework? I mean, very simply, keeping up to date on the signals generated by the system or systems you are following. In order to keep in touch with the markets according to your system, you must have a regular schedule for doing the technical or fundamental analysis your system requires. Whether this consists of simple charting that may take only five minutes per day, or complex mathematical calculations that may take considerably longer, the fact remains that the discipline of doing your homework is one of the prerequisites for successful trading.

If you have a system and fail to do the work that generates your trading signals, then you are guilty of poor discipline. If you have a system and do not follow it, you are just as guilty of lacking discipline. What good are all your work and calculations if you do not proceed where the signals point? Follow-through is not an option—it is the essence of discipline.

Can you identify strongly, or even partially, with some of the things I am saying? How often have you been in the situation of missing a move because your charts were not up-to-date? How many times has this frustrated you into making an unwarranted decision in an effort to compensate for your first error? If the truth were fully known, we know that many of us are guilty.

The sad fact about this situation is that its rectification is a very simple matter. In fact, the steps one must take in order to correct any problem resulting from lack of trading discipline are very specific, easily understood, and exceptionally elementary.

The discipline required to trade consistently and successfully is the same type of discipline required in virtually every aspect of human life. Whether it is the discipline required for losing weight, stopping smoking, or developing a successful business, the basics of all discipline are the same.

If you develop discipline in your trading, I am certain that it will spread to other areas of your life, including your personal affairs. Unfortunately, however, discipline in other aspects of your life may not necessarily spread very quickly to your trading. The nature of futures trading provides serious challenges to discipline developed in other areas of life. I will give suggestions for improving discipline later in this chapter.

How Lack of Discipline
Can Become a Chronic Problem

Lack of discipline is not confined to any one situation, any one trade, or any one trader. Lack of discipline is a way of life, albeit a bad one. Individuals who achieve success without adhering to certain disciplined practices do so as a stroke of good fortune and stand the chance of forfeiting their wealth through a lack of disciplined action. Lack of discipline is not a static part of the personality, but rather a cancerous growth that spreads through the trader's behavior.

This should come as no surprise to those who understand relationships, whether they are those between individuals or those between the individual and the marketplace. In an interpersonal relationship, lack of discipline and specificity can cause negative interaction. Negative interaction will then result in further tests of discipline and self-control. These tests will, in turn, result in other problems—failures and negative experiences—until the entire relationship is threatened. The same is true of one's trading.

Lack of discipline in instituting a trade may frustrate the trader into a further display of poor discipline. The net result is usually a succession of errors, each compounding the other, and each likely far worse than the previous. Frequently it can grow at an exponential rate. It is for this reason that you must take great care to avoid making even the first mistake due to a lack of discipline: "Pluck the weed by the root."

How to Improve Your Discipline

I certainly don't have all the answers for improving your discipline. However, I do have a number of very cogent, time-tested techniques to help you improve. All of the suggestions will require action and thorough implementation if they are to have a beneficial effect.

1 *Make a schedule.* In order to help you keep your trading signals up to date, set aside a given time of the day or week during which you will do the necessary calculations, charts, or other market work. Doing the same work every day of the week will help you get into a specific routine, which in turn will eliminate (or greatly reduce) the possibility of not being prepared when a major move develops.

2 *Don't try to do too much.* Attempt to specialize in one particular trading approach. If you try to trade in too many markets at one time or with too many systems at one time, your work will become a burden, you will not look forward to it, and you will be more prone to let your studies fall behind.

Ideally, seek to work in no more than three to five markets at any given time, and attempt to specialize in only one specific system.

3 *Use a checklist.* One of my favorite analogies is the similarity between the trader and the airplane pilot. Before take-off a good airplane pilot goes through a pre-flight checklist. I certainly would not want to fly in a plane with a pilot who was sloppy in this procedure—would you?

The trader who wishes to eliminate trading errors should also maintain such a checklist and consult it regularly, preferably before making each trade. Of all of my suggestions, the checklist is probably the best one for all traders. I would suggest that even after your checklist has become automatic, you still maintain it, because lack of discipline is likely to attack you at almost any time. It can strike without notice and often does.

4 *Reject third party input once your decision has been made.* I have come to respect the fact that good traders are usually loners. They must do their work in isolation, and they must implement their decisions in isolation. A pushy or talkative broker, a well-intentioned friend, or a very persuasive newsletter can often sway you from a decision that only you should make.

There are times when your decision will be wrong, but these are part of the learning experience, and you alone must make your decisions based on the facts as you see them.

If you have decided to follow your own trading system, then by all means follow it and forget about other input. If your system is based on input from other sources, however, then try to implement your decisions without being swayed from them once you have made up your mind. The benefits of deciding on your own far outweigh the potential benefits of having too much input.

5 *Evaluate your progress.* Feedback is a very important part of the learning process. Keep track of how you are doing with your trading not only in terms of dollars and cents, but also in terms of specific signals, behavior, and techniques. This will give you an idea of how closely you are sticking to the rules, which rules you are breaking, and how often you may be breaking them.

A record of mistakes soon becomes a guideline of how to avoid them.

6 *Learn from every loss.* Losses are tuition. They are expensive, and they must be good for something. Learn from each loss, and do your very best to avoid taking the same loss twice or more for the same reason. Do not repeat the same errors. To do so indicates that your discipline is not improving.

So remember, temper your losses with acknowledgement and wisdom.

7 *Understand yourself.* This is certainly a big job and not one easily accomplished. It is extremely important that you understand your motivation and your true reasons for trading the markets. Frequently individuals do poorly in the markets because their objectives and goals are not well established.

Self-understanding helps clarify your personal goals and thereby makes the process of attaining your goals more specific.

8 *Work with your trading system and remain dedicated to it.* If you are like most traders, you will have done considerable research on a trading method or system. Some traders, however, become quickly disenchanted with their systems and hop from one technique to another. This is one of the worst forms of poor discipline. It does not allow sufficient time for a system to perform. In so doing, the speculator takes considerably more overall risk than he or she should.

9 *Evaluate and verify your objectives.* At times, poor training discipline can be a function of unclear objectives. If you have decided that you want to trade for the short term only, then you have a very clear objective. However, if you are not certain about the time frame of your trading, about the trading system you plan to use as your vehicle, about the relationship you wish to have with your broker, about the quotation equipment you plan to use (if any), then you will be prone to make mistakes.

My suggestion is to make all major trading decisions before you even get started with your trading. You can make some corrections along the way, but you should make the majority of decisions before any serious trading.

10 *Know when to quit.* In order to improve your trading discipline, it is important to have an objective measure of when you will terminate a given trade, profitably or unprofitably. Whether you terminate at a particular price or a particular dollar amount is of no consequence. The fact remains that you must know when you have had enough.

11 *Make commitments and keep them.* In trading it is important to make and keep commitments in the markets just as it is in every phase of human endeavor and interaction. If you do not make a commitment or if the commitment you make is not clear, then you stand the chance of not following through on an important phase of your trading.

For this reason, I encourage all traders to make specific commitments, not only in terms of such things as trading systems, trading approach, available capital, or maximum risk, but also in terms of each and every trade they make.

Do not make a trade unless you are fully committed to it. What does this mean? It means that many individuals are prone to establish a position in the market based on what "looks like" a good signal or when it "looks like the market wants to turn higher." In other words, they make commitments on the basis of vague indications.

In order to make a commitment that will serve you well, do not make decisions based on sketchy information. The uneasy feeling you get when you make such a decision will be enough to let you know that you are not making a commitment based on correct procedures.

One good way in which to determine how, where, when, and what type of commitment you wish to make is to examine yourself using a checklist or questionnaire designed to ascertain the precise nature of your situation. Although this checklist requires only a brief amount of thought, it offers an abundance of insight.

Depending on your individual situation, there are many more ways to improve your discipline. Take the time to learn them; it is the wisest of investments.

The Self-Evaluation Checklist

If you are concerned about your self-discipline, then here is a brief self-assessment checklist that may help you focus on any potential difficulties. Simply answer the following questions honestly and then read the directions that follow the questionnaire.

❑ I am very decisive. Once a trading decision has been made I follow through with few exceptions.

❑ I tend to ignore input from any sources other than my trading system.

❑ I use stop losses in all my trades.

❑ I have a trading system and I use it consistently.

❑ I always avoid taking tips from other traders as well as from my broker.

❑ I tend to ignore the news even if it is contrary to my position(s) in the market.

❑ I follow a specific set of rules in my trading.

❑ My trading results have been slowly but steadily improving.

❑ I often evaluate my trading results in order to assess my progress.

❑ I am familiar with my strengths and weaknesses as a trader.

❑ I rarely concern myself about trades and trading in my family life or personal relationships.

❑ I feel comfortable with my trading decisions.

❑ Although I know that there are many traders who are more skilled than I am, I believe that my methods work and that I can apply them consistently.

❑ I am interested in slow and steady profits and improved performance.

❑ I tend not to get caught up in emotionally based trading decisions.

Your answers to all of the above should be "yes." If you answered "no" to more than five of the above statements then you might want to evaluate your self-discipline, because you are likely to have difficulty with this important aspect of trading.

Summary

Discipline is the single most important quality a trader can possess. It means staying up-to-date on the signals your system generates. This includes developing a consistent schedule—and then following through on it. In any trading program, discipline must be practiced day in and day out.

Lack of discipline can become a way of life, but it is a learned way of life. This need not be so if you are constantly evaluating and reevaluating yourself as a whole. Without discipline even the most potentially profitable system will lose money. Any system or method of trading requires discipline or losses will follow. Anything less will lead to losses, an ever-compounding number of mistakes, and ever-increasing frustration. These will, in turn, lead to more problems. Improve your self-discipline and your profits will improve dramatically.

CHAPTER 9

The Art of Contrary Thinking

If a man does not keep pace with his companions, perhaps it is because he hears a different drummer. Let him step to the music which he hears, however measured or far away.

— RALPH WALDO EMERSON

In the 1600s buyers and sellers of tulip bulbs congregated in Holland to participate in what was to become known, many years later, as the Dutch tulip mania. Although inherently worth only a few pennies (or a few dollars at most), supposedly rare tulip bulbs were bought and sold for as much as thousands of times their value. Greedy buyers and sellers supported inflated tulip bulb prices. Each bulb trader practiced the "greater fool theory." They all felt that they could buy low and sell high or buy high and sell higher to someone who was a greater fool than they were. There was panic buying of a commodity that was in great demand, but that had no value other than what people were willing to pay for it.

There are many lessons to be learned from the tulip mania, not the least of which is that fear and pessimism tend to correlate strongly with market lows, while greed and optimism tend to correlate strongly with market tops. The tulip mania was an event that marked a dark but exemplary period in the psychological and economic history of humankind.

Today we look back in amazement on those times, shaking our heads and saying, "How could something like this have happened?" Yet we need not look too far back in our own recent history to see countless examples of similar manias sweeping our markets. Whether these manias occurred in the areas of land, real estate, precious metals, sugar, or the stock market is irrelevant. The fact remains that panic and mania are still very much a part of our modern society. Emotion still closely governs speculators in all walks of life and in all markets.

Reality, Economics, and Prices

In our often troubled and volatile economic times, no single market sector is as subject to emotional fluctuations as is the futures market. The slightest rumor or news can send the markets skyrocketing or plummeting precipitously with no seeming end in sight as the frenzy feeds upon itself. Similar behavior has been seen in world stock markets since the early 1990s, although to a lesser degree.

Although prices can surge or plunge out of proportion to the reality of fundamentals, ultimately, economic realities take hold, eventually returning prices to their proper levels. In the interim, however, emotion and psychology rule the pits. To understand the psychology of the mob is to understand the psychology of the speculator. Understand how to use these psychologies to your advantage, and you'll understand the power and the art of contrary thinking.

Although the power of contrary thinking is well documented and well understood, it has not been quantified or organized into a cohesive trading system or method. Trading on the basis of mob psychology is somewhat elusive methodology in spite of its immense conceptual value. An idea that cannot be quantified is, unfortunately, one that will be difficult to employ in a scientific or even quasi-scientific setting—which is the reason why the concepts advanced by proponents of contrary thinking do not necessarily correspond with the performance of contrary opinion techniques. Let's examine precisely what I mean by contrary thinking in order to see how it can be of practical value to the speculator.

What Is Contrary Thinking?

Contrary thinking is the art of thinking and interpreting reality in a different way from how the majority of individuals think and interpret reality. Contrary thinking is possible in every form of human endeavor. Millions of individuals are contrary thinkers, often expressing their views in contrary ways. Hopefully their contrarian views will lead to contrary actions that are profitable.

Thought, however, does not necessarily lead to action. There is a vast difference between contrary thinkers and contrary doers. Contrary thinkers want to "zig" while everyone else is "zagging." They expect higher prices while most people expect lower prices and then watch for prices to fall when most people watch for prices to rise. Contrary thinking is not necessarily a measure of stubbornness, but rather the ability to avoid being caught up in the sentiment of the "crowd."

Some people are swayed by the direction of a major trend and, moreover, they are strongly influenced by the opinions of others. Therefore, market movement in a particular direction, if strong enough and long enough, tends to arouse public interest. Traders and investors develop tunnel vision. They see only what they have been told to see or what they want to see.

The important facts, the ones that will lead to an eventual change in trend, are often ignored. Even when markets begin to change direction, those who have been mesmerized into fervently believing that the trend has not ended will continue to cling desperately to their beliefs. In the meantime, the contrary thinker has suspected all along that the direction of the trend was due to change and that the opportunity for profit lay just around the corner.

There are literally hundreds of classic examples in the economic history of the world to support the theory that a strong consensus of opinion often suggests an eventual opposite price movement. I could probably turn this chapter into several by citing some examples of contrary opinion in contemporary times. My job, however, is not to function as a history teacher; rather, it is to familiarize you with valuable concepts that should be added to your trading repertoire. Therefore, for specific examples please refer to the reading list and the bibliography at the end of this book. My point is that, despite the many investment fads and financial fallacies in modern times, most investors and traders have not learned anything about their own emotional makeup.

The writings of traders such as Jesse Livermore, Arthur Cutten, and W. D. Gann clearly underscore the importance of being a contrarian. To act and think contrary to the crowd is a valuable personal quality in every walk of life. It is important that the contrary thoughts and actions be selective, however. It is also important that contrarian thinking be employed at crucial turning points in our lives and in the markets.

Quantification

There have been a number of attempts throughout the history of the markets to quantify various measures of contrary opinion. These attempts have, however, been only sporadically successful. The concept of odd-lot short sales in the stock market is one application of contrary opinion. It is a measure, essentially, of how bearish small investors are at any given time. One would expect, on the basis of contrary opinion, that the more bearish small investors are, the more likely prices are to continue rising. Odd-lot short sales are a measure of actual short selling by small investors as an expression of their bullish or bearish sentiment.

The explanation of this phenomenon is very simple. Essentially it says that the small trader cannot afford to sell short a round lot (100-share blocks) of stock. Furthermore, the odd-lotter is typically unsophisticated and relatively uninformed. Therefore, a high bearish consensus of action among odd-lot short sellers often indicates that the opposite is about to happen.

Historically, the odd-lot short sales indicator has translated into a very good tool. On occasion, the odd-lot short sellers have been right, but rarely for long, and rarely for much of a move. More often than not, they are incorrect at critical turning points in the stock market.

Market commentator and analyst R. E. Hadady has advanced the notion that contrary opinion in the futures markets can be measured quantitatively by conducting a survey of sentiment among brokers and advisors on a weekly basis. Hadady was one of the first analysts in the futures markets to promote the ideas of contrary opinion.

The Hadady theory is a most interesting one and its concepts are valid, yet

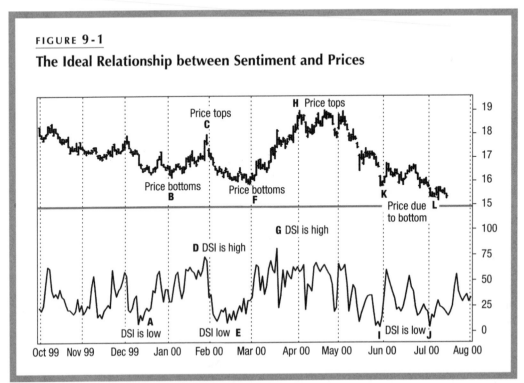

FIGURE 9-1

The Ideal Relationship between Sentiment and Prices

Source: MBH Commodity Advisors, Inc.

Source: MBH Commodity Advisors, Inc.

FIGURE 9-2

Example of the Daily Sentiment Index (DSI)
S&P 500 Futures (February 12, 2001–August 10, 2001, daily)

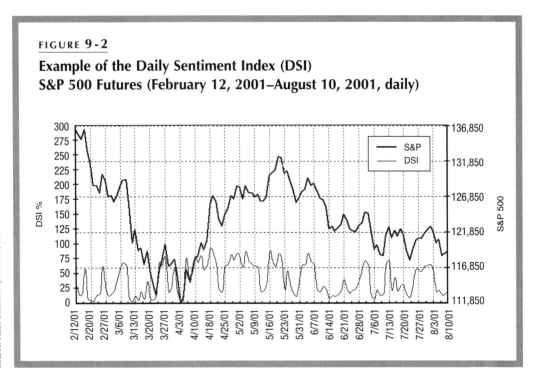

there is still the nagging question about its inability to be more precise in timing the market turns. Hadady has developed a number of techniques for making timing more precise, yet it would seem to me that there must be a better way to employ contrary opinion in the futures markets.

My main objection is that most contrary opinion surveys merely reflect opinion and not action, and that there is a large disparity between market opinion and market action. Although a market may rise and opinions may continue to become exceptionally bullish, if extremely persistent buying by the public does not back up these bullish opinions, then the opinions are not especially valid. Contrary opinion works because opinions lead to action. If there is contemplation but no action, then opinions may not be so valid.

The techniques developed by Hadady and other followers of contrary opinion have great potential in the markets, but good timing must back them up. If you plan to use bullish consensus or contrary opinion indicators, be certain you use them in conjunction with timing indicators such as those described in this book, or with other traditional but effective tools.

FIGURE 9-3

The Daily Sentiment Index (DSI) Report

DSI MARKET	12-21-2001					12-20-2001				
	RAW %UP	3MA %UP	5MA %UP	9MA %UP	18MA %UP	RAW %UP	3MA %UP	5MA %UP	9MA %UP	18MA %UP
T-bonds	60	61	45	33	34	61	52	35	28	31
T-notes	60	61	46	35	36	61	53	37	30	33
Euro Dollar	61	60	58	62	59	60	58	57	63	58
S&P Index	63	61	61	45	53	59	61	52	42	54
Nasdaq Index	59	59	58	46	54	56	59	50	44	55
Swiss Franc	22	49	56	55	42	64	64	67	55	42
Euro FX	18	48	53	52	46	63	62	62	53	46
Japanese Yen	5	8	7	10	14	10	9	7	11	14
British Pound	33	54	65	68	52	64	69	74	71	51
Canadian Dollar	31	45	52	54	51	48	54	61	53	51
Dollar Index	77	65	53	56	62	63	53	44	56	63
Crude Light	51	52	53	43	48	45	54	54	40	48
Heating Oil	45	50	52	46	49	43	55	55	44	50
Unleaded Gas	45	51	51	48	51	45	53	55	45	52
Natural Gas	60	38	32	39	31	33	25	32	37	30
Gold	33	27	43	44	41	25	39	49	44	40
Silver	77	59	66	66	59	56	60	66	64	56
Platinum	79	63	62	61	64	55	57	58	60	62
Copper	45	38	41	39	47	34	41	40	38	49
Corn	13	16	17	22	32	15	17	20	25	32
Wheat	47	52	49	43	38	44	51	48	42	37
Oats	62	52	59	71	78	49	51	63	74	78
Soybean	25	24	22	20	24	25	21	21	21	23
Soybean Oil	29	21	19	22	36	15	16	18	25	37
Soybean Meal	34	29	25	24	22	33	22	24	22	21
Orange Juice	56	54	48	39	40	61	50	43	36	41
Coffee	19	33	27	27	21	60	32	28	28	21
Cocoa	63	64	69	73	71	63	67	73	70	71
Sugar	47	42	43	49	61	45	38	45	50	63
Lumber	88	81	81	72	61	79	80	78	70	59
Cotton	64	64	68	65	67	61	67	71	65	67

12-19-2001					12-18-2001					12-17-2001				
RAW %UP	3MA %UP	5MA %UP	9MA %UP	18MA %UP	RAW %UP	3MA %UP	5MA %UP	9MA %UP	18MA %UP	RAW %UP	3MA %UP	5MA %UP	9MA %UP	18MA %UP
63	34	27	22	28	31	18	19	16	25	9	14	17	14	24
62	37	30	24	30	35	21	23	19	27	13	17	20	16	26
60	56	57	64	56	55	54	60	62	55	53	56	64	61	54
62	60	44	44	55	61	47	39	46	56	58	32	33	49	56
61	58	42	46	56	60	44	39	49	57	53	30	35	52	57
62	65	65	50	40	65	70	65	48	37	68	66	57	43	35
62	61	60	48	44	62	61	60	48	41	60	58	53	43	39
9	7	9	11	14	8	6	11	11	14	5	10	12	12	14
65	75	75	71	48	77	81	76	70	45	84	77	74	64	41
55	60	64	51	49	58	67	65	50	47	66	69	58	51	45
56	42	46	58	64	39	34	47	59	66	30	45	54	62	69
60	57	50	40	47	58	55	43	36	47	53	44	35	36	47
63	58	54	43	49	60	57	48	39	49	51	49	41	39	49
63	56	55	46	51	50	55	52	42	50	54	54	46	43	51
22	23	34	36	31	21	35	38	37	33	25	42	43	36	35
24	52	52	46	40	68	65	56	48	39	63	57	49	46	36
45	66	68	65	54	78	77	71	67	52	75	72	68	65	49
56	59	59	63	61	60	60	60	65	61	61	60	59	65	61
34	43	40	37	52	55	43	39	38	54	39	37	36	36	55
19	19	22	29	32	18	21	21	30	33	21	24	27	35	35
65	51	45	40	35	44	44	39	36	35	43	39	38	36	37
44	61	71	78	78	61	74	80	82	78	77	84	85	86	78
23	20	20	22	23	15	20	18	23	25	22	20	19	24	28
19	17	19	30	40	13	19	20	35	43	18	22	24	40	46
20	20	22	21	21	13	22	22	21	22	27	26	23	22	24
45	42	36	31	41	44	36	32	27	42	36	31	28	28	42
19	18	21	24	20	17	20	23	24	21	18	24	26	24	21
66	73	75	70	73	73	78	78	69	73	79	79	79	68	74
33	41	47	54	64	36	48	52	59	67	53	56	55	63	69
75	79	74	69	58	86	79	69	69	57	77	69	64	64	55
68	71	69	64	67	71	75	66	64	67	75	68	65	62	66

Source: MBH Commodity Advisors, Inc.

FIGURE **9-3** (continued)

The Daily Sentiment Index (DSI) Report

DSI	12-21-2001					12-20-2001				
	RAW	3MA	5MA	9MA	18MA	RAW	3MA	5MA	9MA	18MA
MARKET	%UP	%UP	%UP	%UP	%UP	%UP	%UP	%UP	%UP	%UP
Live Cattle	79	71	69	56	61	62	71	58	53	61
Live Hogs	86	69	67	56	47	62	62	63	49	46
Pork Bellies	88	55	60	53	49	35	49	55	46	48
CRB Index	61	57	58	56	57	57	56	58	55	56
Nikkei Index	59	49	47	45	49	42	45	45	42	50

Daily Sentiment Index

The Daily Sentiment Index (DSI) is an informational tool I developed based on ideas of contrary opinion. It is created from surveys taken of the opinions of futures traders on a daily basis, recording their opinions as either bullish, bearish, or no comment. When compiled, the data reflects the percentage of bullish sentiment by market, providing traders with a timely assessment of market sentiment. **Figure 9-1** illustrates the ideal relationship between market sentiment in percentage of bullish traders and market trends, tops, and bottoms. When prices are relatively high, market sentiment is very high. Market sentiment is low when prices are low. Note how price tops C and H correlate with DSI tops D and G. Note also how DSI lows A, E, I, and J correlate with price lows B, F, K, and L.

Theory of DSI

DSI theory is based on the hypothesis that market sentiment tends to peak and trough with prices. The central aspect of DSI theory is that on any given day, a high level of bullish or bearish sentiment, as determined by my survey, will generally indicate an opposite move in the direction of the market. Oftentimes, the move will arrive sooner rather than later.

For example, when my survey indicates 80 percent or more bullish sentiment, I usually interpret this as an indication that the market is topping and is likely to move lower. On the other hand, if my survey indicates that traders are highly bearish, (in other words, 80 percent or more agree a decline will occur), then I expect prices to move higher.

12-19-2001					12-18-2001					12-17-2001				
RAW %UP	3MA %UP	5MA %UP	9MA %UP	18MA %UP	RAW %UP	3MA %UP	5MA %UP	9MA %UP	18MA %UP	RAW %UP	3MA %UP	5MA %UP	9MA %UP	18MA %UP
73	68	51	53	62	77	52	46	51	63	53	35	43	50	64
58	63	62	44	46	65	64	55	40	47	65	63	47	35	47
43	59	61	47	50	68	66	57	47	52	65	65	49	41	51
53	58	56	55	55	59	61	54	55	56	61	56	54	55	55
45	45	43	44	53	47	45	45	46	54	44	42	42	48	55

Source: MBH Commodity Advisors, Inc.

Contrary opinion is, by definition, an opinion that is opposite to the view held by the majority of market participants. If the majority expects prices to rise, a contrarian would be bearish, expecting prices to decline. Many different techniques may be used to detect prevailing market opinions. There are different ways to gather the data as well. Central to any contrary opinion methodology is the idea that strong agreement that anticipates market direction generally indicates that price trend is likely to turn in the direction opposite the consensus.

Guidelines for Using DSI

In order to make effective use of DSI, traders need to

1 Keep track of the daily percentages.
2 Take particular note of the high (80 percent and over) and low (20 percent and under) percentages.
3 Watch the direction of prices on the day after and for several days thereafter.
4 Watch for price moves that are opposite from the extreme sentiment readings. When DSI is 80 percent or over, expect prices to move lower. If DSI is 20 percent or under, expect prices to move higher.
5 Develop your own method of application. I suggest using technical timing indicators to trigger market entry when sentiment is extreme.

DSI and other contrary opinion systems do not guarantee success in trading futures markets. DSI is a tool for interpreting "overbought" and "oversold" market conditions.

When used in conjunction with other indicators and your own timing techniques, DSI application can help you anticipate potential changes in market trend. It can also serve as a warning signal that will help you avoid buying tops and selling bottoms. Examples of the DSI are shown in **Figures 9-2** and **9-3**.

Commitments of Traders Reports

Another way to determine the bullish or bearish attitudes of the traders is by studying the monthly CFTC (Commodity Futures Trading Commission) Commitments of Traders Reports. These reports contain valuable information on the composition of longs and shorts in the marketplace by percentages and groups, showing increases and/or decreases from previous monthly levels. Unfortunately, the reports are monthly, and by the time the news is available to most traders it is likely that a change in the numbers has already occurred. If these figures could be obtained weekly, they would be an invaluable source of information to all speculators. You can visit the reports on the CFTC website (www.cftc.gov).

For those who are seriously interested in studying contrary opinion and bullish consensus relationships in the markets, this type of information is essential. The individual or organization who can develop a reporting system that studies similar distribution or that arrives at the heart of bullish/bearish consensus in a more specific and, in particular, more frequent fashion, will truly have an exceptionally valuable market tool.

Summary

Contrary thinking is an important skill that allows you to develop an opinion that is often opposite of the view held by the majority of market participants. You can use this opinion to your advantage to monitor the consensus of bullish opinion and anticipate changes in the market trends. The Daily Sentiment Index is a contrary opinion tool that, when used in conjunction with timing indicators, can help you anticipate changes in this process. This and various other indicators of market sentiment can serve as warning signals that will help you avoid buying tops and selling bottoms.

CHAPTER 10

How to Trade Like a Pro

The love of money and the love of learning rarely meet.

— GEORGE HERBERT

During my years as a futures trader, investor, market analyst, author, and trading coach, I have seen many investors prosper, but I have watched many more fail. What separates winners from losers is not, at first blush, easily discernible. There are many things that we do not know about the markets and many things we do not know about traders. There are, however, some important things that we have learned over time.

We know that certain traits, characteristics, and techniques correlate highly with success in the markets. Moreover, I believe (as do many traders) that these highly important characteristics can be learned. The first hurdle we encounter on the road to success is that of defining the actual behavior of a winner. This can be a daunting and elusive task.

Attitudes and Behavior

Attitudes often influence behavior. I have found that the attitudes and behaviors of winners are markedly different from those of losers. A winner will have flexible thinking, admit to being wrong, and will often be willing to learn from mistakes. A loser, on the other hand, all too frequently sabotages trading with self-defeating attitudes, stubborn beliefs, and an unwillingness to learn from errors, no matter how costly they have been.

My work has led me to conclude that futures trading is similar to most other businesses. Whether a person is involved in sports, medicine, sales, or trading, attitudes and behaviors will determine the degree of success. Although some clear-cut differences exist between trading and other fields, there are more similarities than there are differences. Let's take a look at some of the common traits shared by most successful individuals, regardless of their specific profession or vocation:

1 *Discipline.* Whether you're a football quarterback, a retail salesperson, or

149

futures account manager, you must learn how to manage your emotions and be mentally fit to be successful at any game. Learning to be in control of your emotions will enable you to be more objective in any environment in which you choose to participate. Objectivity will enhance your capacity to recognize an opportunity and will help you to know when not to take action.

Oftentimes, traders feel they must always be involved in the market. Discipline offers the self-control to know when to stay out of the market as well as the ability to take advantage of an opportunity at the right time. Discipline is also required in attending to the day-to-day details of your business.

If trading is your business, then the day-to-day operations must necessarily include your chart work, calculations, system evaluation signals, and bookkeeping. If you skipped Chapter 9 on discipline, go back and read it again. It is extremely important!

2 *Persistence*. In every form of business, persistence pays off. Persistence means you hang in even if you have experienced rejection or defeat. A successful salesperson does not give up if he experiences a dry spell when no one is buying. Similarly, a good trader does not take a string of losses personally. A good trader will attempt to learn from prior mistakes and persist in developing winning trades.

There is, however, a fine line between persistence and bullheadedness. In futures trading, as in other businesses, it may take quite a few successive losses before a large victory can be attained. Although it is important to know when not to quit, it is also important to learn from mistakes and admit when you are wrong. Persistence is also vital in finding a trading system or method that is best suited to your needs.

3 *Patience*. It is often necessary to wait for the right opportunities, rather than acting on the wrong ones. Because there are always many incorrect actions you can take in the market, it is important to wait for the right opportunities. Many traders are anxious and fear they are missing something if they are not always participating in the market.

The patient trader has confidence in waiting for the correct opportunity to present itself.

4 *Independence*. Most successful people in any business have taught themselves independent thinking. This often requires going against the norm and establishing a perspective that is different from the crowd's. Independent thinking can be uncomfortable for many people. As a trader, it is often necessary to ignore well-intentioned input from friends, associates, and brokers.

Trading ideas, trading systems, and implementation of trades involve single-ness of purpose and firm resolution. Therefore, it is necessary for a successful trader to develop independent thinking and avoid the "herd" mentality.

5 *Contrary thinking.* If contrary thinking is not one of your traits, you must work toward developing it. A common quandary of most traders is the fear of going against the crowd. Cultivating the art of contrary thinking allows a trader to take actions that oppose the majority. This is important, as generally the majority is wrong and public losses are commonplace.

It is crucial to learn how to assess what the crowd is thinking and develop the courage to take an independent trading approach in the market. Contrary think-ing will also help the trader avoid being trapped when the public takes hold of a market and panics. An astute trader can take advantage of the emotional extremes in the market and step in when severe moves are about over, taking appropriate positions accordingly.

6 *Honesty with yourself.* This trait requires you to make a rigorous assess-ment of your strengths and weaknesses and may be difficult to develop. This is not often easy, and it is seldom done. Human beings are more inclined to blame other people and situations for their failures in life. Assuming total responsi-bility for your actions is a difficult task, but it is absolutely required for achieving success as a trader or in other business endeavors.

Developing the skills of responsibility demands a hard and honest look at where you are competent and where you are incompetent. One thing is sure: The market will show you! It is in your best interest, therefore, to engage in a continuous process of self-reflection. Learning to take an honest inventory of yourself will enable you to accentuate your strengths and work on the weakness-es that make you vulnerable in the market.

7 *The ability to act quickly.* There is a clear and important distinction be-tween developing a sense of urgency and acting impulsively. A good trader wants to pay constant attention and be ready to take action without being too sponta-neous or whimsical.

As indicated in previous chapters, the futures markets are fast. They do not wait. A trader cannot feel overwhelmed by indecision and fear. These feelings will foster a sense of paralysis and lead to inaction. It is not enough just to be in the right place at the right time—you must also act. There are ways in which you can develop this skill, so if you do not possess it now, you should learn the per-ceptual tools to improve your capacity to act quickly.

Why Traders Fail

As you can plainly see, the qualities required for success in futures trading are just as important as, if not more important than, the system you decide to use. The analogy I like to use in discussing the trader and the system is that of the car and the driver.

In order to win a race, you may spend millions on perfecting the ultimate vehicle. Yet, if you have a poor driver or one who cannot effectively manipulate the powerful vehicle through competition, traffic, danger, and adverse weather, you will not win the race and your investment in the ultimate vehicle will be a waste! This discrepancy between trader and system is the reason why so many people fail in the futures market or, for that matter, in every form of investment.

Taking the car and driver analogy one step further, you can see that a good driver, in an average vehicle, can actually win the race. Car and driver are inseparable, just as system and trader are. There is a strong, subtle, and pervasive interaction of the two, where one influences the other. You cannot have one without the other. I maintain, therefore, that in the investment and speculation worlds, too much attention has been given to the car and very little attention to the driver.

The world is full of investors and traders who, were it not for their blindness to their own shortcomings and subsequent trading habits, could be very successful. I have found that the system is not nearly as important as the trader. In answer to the question, "Why do so many people fail?" I say simply that they have not learned the necessary skills to become winners. Winners are created, not born.

How to Identify Incompetence

At the risk of offending my readers, I will say that you probably know where you are lacking in confidence. If you don't, take a bit of time to examine some of the traits I've outlined in the checklist below.

The hardest part of starting on the road to success is getting off the road to failure. Doing so requires you to recognize what road you are on. You need to make sure that your map fits the territory. The car-and-driver analogy is applicable here as well. If you're driving from point A to point B and you get lost, you may eventually find your way through luck. This, however, is unlikely. The only effective and prompt way to find the proper direction (before you run out of gas) is by asking someone who knows and then following the directions.

A "reality check" is also essential in futures trading. You must be able to assess your character limitations honestly. The checklist, if answered honestly, will help you admit to problems you may now have. In recognizing them you will have won half the battle.

☒ I have trouble getting and staying organized.
❏ I have difficulty planning the future.
☒ I have been accused of acting on impulse.
❏ I have limited time to work on the markets.
☒ I am impatient with others and myself.
☒ I tend to think too much and overanalyze.
❏ I have been told that I give up too easily.
❏ I feel insecure when I disagree with the majority.
❏ I feel good when my broker agrees with my trading decisions.
❏ It is more important to be lucky than good.
☒ Most of my business ventures have met with failure.
❏ I need a top trading system to win in the futures markets.
☒ I tend to get frustrated quickly.
❏ Many times I get overwhelmed and cannot act.
❏ I do not like making decisions.
❏ I tend to make poor decisions under pressure.
☒ I feel depressed and resigned when I am wrong.
❏ My self-esteem is dependent on what others think of me.
☒ I tend to procrastinate.
❏ I look to blame others for my mistakes.
❏ I feel sorry for myself when things are not working out.
☒ I often experience extreme emotional swings.
☒ I have trouble with commitments.
❏ I do not respect other people.
❏ I idolize other people and their ideas.
❏ I have too much pride and cannot readily admit when I am wrong.
❏ I manage money poorly. I am overly wasteful or miserly.
☒ I am not good at making or keeping promises.
☒ I do not manage stress well.
☒ I tend to be prejudiced and stubborn in my views.
❏ I do not like learning new things.
❏ I cannot afford to lose too much money in futures trading.

Though by no means exhaustive, the above list will act as a very quick screening test for success. I have found that if you identify strongly with a number of these traits and cannot honestly eliminate most of these items from your self-assessment, then you have much to work on before you can begin trading. The best thing this book can do for you, beyond explaining the simple mechanics of trading, is to let you know whether or not you are ready to begin trading.

Regardless of how ready you think you will be, the acid test of trading with your own money always creates pressures that you have not previously experienced. Preparation, planning, personality change, and perseverance are the 4Ps of trading that must be learned by all who seek success in futures or, for that matter, in any business venture.

How to Overcome Weaknesses

Now that you've been honest with yourself and confessed to some of your shortcomings in life and in the marketplace, you can begin some preliminary work on how to improve and trade like a professional. Assuming you have a system that is correct at least 60 percent of the time, you can now begin the following practices in order to improve your eventual trading success.

1 *Be organized.* Organization is vital to the success of any venture. This is especially true in the world of futures trading. It is important to know where you are headed, when you expect to get there, and which vehicles you will use to reach your destination. Without organization, these tools can often be misplaced. Your charts, books, formulae, trading rules, and telephone numbers must be readily available and organized.

There are many details to think about while trading. Creating an organized environment can free your concentration for the important things.

2 *Develop and practice discipline.* There are many ways to develop your discipline. One of them is to take a course on self-improvement, such as those offered by the Dale Carnegie Institute. You will learn that success requires discipline and that discipline can be learned. Discipline can often be improved through the simple application of behavioral learning techniques.

My book *The Investor's Quotient*, 2nd Edition (John Wiley & Sons, 2000), gives specific suggestions and techniques designed to help you improve your discipline. In addition, there are many simple exercises that you can use.

Remember, discipline from one area of your life tends to be reflected in all others. Therefore, if you lack self-discipline when it comes to changing such negative habits as excessive drinking, eating, or smoking, then you will probably lack the discipline required for successful trading. You may need to overcome these bad habits first, or you may need to conquer all lack of discipline at once.

Finally, remember that discipline is not synonymous with rigidity. Being rigid in following rules is not necessarily a form of discipline. Being a disciplined trader also means being flexible enough to change course as soon as you see that the action you have taken is not working. The rigid trader will believe too strongly in his trading rules, which can prove destructive. Trading is a game of probability, and there is no room for rigidity when it comes to probability.

3 *Develop a simple but effective trading system.* One of the greatest limitations on success in trading is that systems become too complicated, too burdensome, or too time-consuming to use. If you build a boat, make certain you can get your boat into the water. Once in the water, make certain you can move.

Too many traders spend too much time developing complicated, sophisticated trading systems that are too difficult to implement. My knowledge of top-ranking, successful futures traders shows that most of them use simple methods. Simple is often best, and less is often more.

Think about simplicity when developing your trading system. If you keep it simple you will be less consumed with details, less troubled with self-discipline, and you will shorten your market response time (which alone will prove very valuable).

4 *Learn to isolate and monitor impulsive behavior.* There's a great deal to be said for isolationism in trading. In order to keep free of impulse, it is often best not to know the news. Then you can "keep your head while all those around you are losing theirs." You will, in so doing, avoid the costly errors that are so often the result of impulsive behavior rather than following your system.

I favor isolation. I prefer not to listen to the radio or television financial news. I do not read the financial newspapers or listen to the financial opinions of others. In particular, I do not discuss the markets, even with other professionals. I isolate myself because I know that I may be influenced by the information. In order to be strong and to avoid impulsive actions motivated by the emotions of fear and/or greed, I must limit my exposure to extraneous information and concentrate instead on selected information sources such as prices, charts, trading systems, and timing indicators.

5 *Plan your trades and trade your plans.* This market cliché is just as true today as when it was coined. It is the best way to avoid virtually all of the losing inputs. If you are prepared, and if you act according to your plan, you will have taken the first and most important step toward practicing self-discipline.

6 *Keep your objectives clearly in mind.* Chapter 17 provides specific guid-

ance on setting trading objectives. Note that you must first define your goals and then keep them always in mind. If you are a short-term trader, then you must think and act like one. This means maintaining a consistent, short-term time horizon in all your futures trading. If you are a long-term trader, then your perception of the markets and your corresponding actions must be consistent with long-term time horizons.

Set your main objectives, organize your goals in a way that supports your objectives, and develop a system that checks for consistency. It is easy to get sidetracked from your original intentions. Maintaining consistency by asking yourself if the day-to-day actions reinforce your goals will help keep you on track. I have found it best to have a list of objectives and goals handy for quick reference during times of need.

7 Manage stress—don't take the markets home with you. In order to improve market decisions, it is necessary to deal effectively with stress. There are many ways to cope with stress. Exercise, for example, can help you vent frustrations and give you a chance to get your mind off the markets.

It is also helpful to manage your psychological stress when you experience losses. Undoubtedly, you as a futures trader can expect to experience a number of losses; you must learn not to take these losses personally. If you do not learn this, stress will build and your confidence will falter.

Leave the markets at the office. If you plan to trade as your profession, then this rule is vital. If you plan to trade in your spare time, then have certain hours set aside for this activity and do not become addicted to the market.

8 Keep commission costs low. The overhead of futures trading consists of losses and commissions. Commissions comprise a built-in loss factor. Poor order execution comprises another aspect of the built-in cost of doing business. Between poor order fills and commissions, about 25 percent of profits can be eaten up before your very eyes. Because the futures markets move so quickly, poor price executions are common and costly. Furthermore, the fast, often large short-term moves in futures prompt traders to act more frequently. This can often prove quite costly since it encourages traders to trade too often.

Many traders are shocked when they see how much they have paid out in commissions every year. Some traders who want and need the advice of brokers must do business with a "full-service house." They will, therefore, pay higher commissions. There is nothing wrong with this, provided it is cost-effective. If you deal with a full-service house and pay higher commissions, it does not necessarily mean you will fail.

However, you must get some return for what you are paying in higher costs. If you do not get a return, then you are not making a sound business decision. If you trade frequently without needing advice or information, then you are entitled to lower commissions. You can ask your full-service broker for a discount. Be informed about the broker's discount policies. Do not be afraid to ask how much trading you must do in order to benefit from the commission break. Some brokerage firms, for example, provide special research reports, courses, charts, and/or consultation with their market analysts, none of which you may want or need. If you don't use these services than you should qualify for lower commission rates.

Finally, if you find that you are not using any of the information provided by the brokerage house you are dealing with, take the time to investigate another house that offers discount commissions. But first, ask your current broker to determine if she can lower her rates, because a good broker/trader relationship is very important. Chapter 11 covers these issues in detail.

9 *Avoid overtrading—be conservative.* One of the greatest secrets to success in trading is to avoid "overtrading." There is no substance or truth to the belief that you must be in every market at all times. As a matter of fact, market professionals like to concentrate on certain markets and only on certain types of moves.

Many traders overtrade in order to feel involved. They become addicted to the excitement of big positions and constant action. They live by the motto, "If you are not afraid, you are not paying attention." The futures market is a dangerous place to play this type of game.

You cannot and should not be in all markets at all times. And you are risking too much when you overtrade in terms of volume. Therefore, be conservative and trade manageably, with only the best signals and the most reasonable risk-to-reward ratios. Generally, a portfolio of 10–15 unduplicated or uncorrelated markets is best.

10 *Avoid wishful thinking.* Most unsuccessful traders get stuck in trades that are going against them and begin to hope things will change. They lose all concepts of discipline, rigor, and rules. Wishful thinking is, in essence, rationalization, a distorted view of reality and, most often, will lead to failure. Anytime traders allow their thinking to be guided by hope, they are resorting to fantasy rather than reality.

In futures as in other financial arenas, markets have their own logic, fleeting as it may be at times. Chances are, the market is not listening or responding to your internal messages of hope. You are better off checking in with reality, your equity. Decide to shift your thinking away from hopes and wishes and back toward the market.

11 *If you trade online, make certain considerations.* If you have opted to trade futures via your computer, entering orders online, then follow these important guidelines:

(a) Online trading tends to foster overtrading. Monitor your activity in the markets to make sure you are not trading too much.

(b) When you enter online orders, there is no one on the other end of the telephone to check your orders, quantities, and prices for accuracy. Too many traders make costly errors when using online order entry.

(c) Select a broker that offers true online trading as opposed to those who route their orders manually after they have obtained your orders electronically.

(d) Be cautious about trading in the "after-hours" markets when volume is often thin and liquidity as well as price executions can cause major (and costly) problems.

Tools for Successful Trading

The student of futures trading has a very clear and concise goal. This goal is not primarily to beat the market or to become skillful for the sake of skill alone. The true speculator is, first and foremost, interested in profits.

As you can tell from your own trading experience, from other aspects of life, and from the many caveats in this book, there is no surefire or simple road to success in the markets. With so many techniques to choose from, with so many different orientations, and with so many trading systems available to speculators, what you ultimately develop will be an individual, tailor-made approach designed specifically to suit your purposes. Whether you end up with a purely mechanical approach based on the research of others or a primarily subjective approach based on your own interpretations and studies, the fact remains that the ultimate decision making is yours and yours alone.

Yet, regardless of what techniques you select or how you select them, you can readily see from what you have already read in this book and from what you may already know that there are some common threads that weave through every approach to futures trading. These commonalities influence and regulate the success or failure of virtually every trader.

Although it may be true that some individuals achieve success by breaking all the rules, it is also true that such individuals are clearly in the minority and that their success is the exception rather than the rule. Unless you are blessed with fantastic luck, you will need to achieve success in the futures markets the good old-fashioned way: You will have to earn it. The only way to earn lasting success is through the diligent and disciplined application of specific techniques and methods, few of which are directly related to systems and most of which are clearly the function of attitudes, psychology, and discipline.

You may not want to hear this, but the fact is that it matters little what system or systems you select, how tremendous their hypothetical performance may be, or how well others may have done with these systems. What ultimately matters is how you apply the systems and the consistency with which you can put the techniques into operation.

The human being is not a computer. The trader cannot achieve the level of perfection that may be required to institute a trading system in complete accordance with the ideal conditions under which it was tested. The degree of slippage, drawdown, and trader error is often significant. Furthermore, it frequently seems that real-time market conditions deteriorate the performance of most systems. In fact, no system based on hypothetical or computer-simulated results is worthwhile unless it can replicate these results with reasonable similarity in real time.

For these reasons, the steps toward trading success do not rest exclusively or even heavily upon selection of a trading system. Although the selection of a system is important, too often a system's value may have been overstated by those with a vested interest in selling systems or in managing a fund based on such systems. In order to achieve success, you must follow what I consider the time-tested rules of profitable trading.

Although I will begin my list of these tips with items related to system selection, you will observe that these items do not dominate the list. Remember, also, that variations on each item in the list are certainly possible in order to adapt them to your particular situation.

1 *Find or develop a trading system that has a real-time record (or computer-tested record) of 60 percent or more winning trades.* An additional essential criterion for this system is a ratio of approximately 2 to 1 in terms of dollars made versus dollars lost per trade (including commissions and slippage as losses). In the absence of real-time results, computer results are acceptable, provided you have made provisions for their limitations as discussed previously in this book. Though the figures just given need not be replicated exactly, attempt to come close.

2 *The system you find or develop should be consistent with your time limitations or availability (with or without a computer system).* If the signals are generated by an advisory service, then make certain you have familiarized yourself with the basics of the system, its trading approach, and other details of the system as described earlier in the text.

3 *Select a brokerage firm that will be compatible with your needs.* If you are an independent trader and need no input whatsoever, then select a discount firm that gives good service and prompt order executions. If, however, you are a novice trader requiring a full-service firm, then be willing to pay higher commissions in order to have your needs fulfilled.

4 *Select a specific broker within the firm, or specify your needs to the firm if you will not be working with one particular broker.* Make certain that both you and the broker are aware of each other's needs and keep the lines of communication clear.

5 *Make certain you have sufficient risk capital to trade using the system you have selected.* Be certain that your risk capital is truly risk capital and not funds that you are otherwise counting on for some future purpose.

6 *Develop and formulate your trading philosophy.* As you know, your perceptions of trading, your expectations, your goals, and your market orientation (in other words, either long term or short term) are all factors that contribute either to success or to failure.

7 *Plan your trades and follow through on your plans.* Try to avoid trading on a whim. Rather, work from a trading plan *every day* so you will avoid the temptation of making spur-of-the-moment decisions that are not based on any system or method you are using.

8 *Be an isolationist.* As noted earlier in this chapter, there is great value in being a loner when it comes to speculation. You don't necessarily want anyone else's input. You don't necessarily want anyone else's opinions. As time goes on and the lessons you learn begin to accumulate, you will realize that your own good opinion is just as valuable, perhaps more so, than the opinions of any others—experts or novices.

9 *Make a commitment: Take the plunge!* Make a commitment to trading. The commitment should consist of rules, organizational procedures, goals, and expectations. Delineate these carefully, with consideration and with forethought. By making your plans, you will avoid costly errors that are not consistent with your strategy.

10 *Once you've decided, act!* Do not hesitate a moment once you've made a trading decision (whether the decision is to enter a trade or to exit a trade). It matters not whether you are taking a profit or closing out a loss. As soon as you have a clear-cut signal to act, don't hesitate. Act as soon as your system says you must act—no sooner, no later.

11 ***Limit risk and preserve capital.*** The best way to limit risk is to trade in only three to six markets at once and to avoid trading markets that have swings much too large for your account size. Once you have decided to limit risk to a certain dollar amount or to limit risk using a specific technique, make certain you take your losses as soon as they should be taken. Do this on time—do not delay.

12 ***Don't anticipate.*** Many traders go astray when they anticipate signals from their trading systems. The trading system is your traffic light. The traffic is always heavy. Stop on the red, go on the green, be cautious on yellow. If you anticipate trading signals from your system instead of waiting for them, you might as well not have a system at all.

13 ***Recognize that the market is the master; you are the slave.*** Like it or not, you cannot tell the market what to do. It will always follow its own course, and it is your job to figure out where it is going. Once you've done so, you must follow the market through its many twists and turns. If it is zigging and zagging, then you must zig and zag. If it is trending higher, you must trade from the long side. If it is trending lower, you must trade from the short side.

It may be instructive for you to review, from time to time, which side of the market most of your trades were on. If you find that you have been bucking the trend of the market, then you must review either your system or your discipline. One of the two (perhaps both) is not functioning properly. Many traders have gone astray by failing to follow the market, thinking that it is their job to forecast the market. The job of the trader is to follow, not to forecast. Let's leave forecasting to the economists.

14 ***Do your homework.*** Whether you are using a computer or pen and paper, or whether you are a novice or a seasoned veteran, you must keep your research current. Futures markets move so fast that there is precious little time to update your trading signals once a move has occurred. You must be there at the very inception of a move or shortly thereafter, otherwise you will have difficulty getting aboard for the bigger move. The only way to do so is to keep your homework up-to-date. You can program your computer so that it will automatically update your signals or system every day at a certain time. Regardless, discipline is always involved in keeping current.

15 ***Avoid extremes in emotion.*** The greatest friend of the speculator is the emotion of others; emotion within the speculator is one of his greatest enemies.

When trading, you must keep your emotions under control and ignore them. Regardless of the trend of emotions, their consequences can be exceptionally dangerous to the speculator because they can result in unwarranted actions. I have commented on this throughout the book with good reason. Systems are not tested with emotions.

16 *Assume responsibility for all your of trading activity.* Accepting that you alone are responsible for the outcome of your trading is a major step toward achieving success. Many traders are unaware that they put a psychological barrier between the actions they take and the results of these actions. They tend to blame other people, the market, or anything else that will remove the focus of responsibility from them. Becoming rigorously honest and "owning" your actions will lead to consistency and success in the markets.

17 *Recognize that hope and fear limit your attention to the market.* Both attitudes turn a trader into a passive player. When you hope a position will go your way or fear that it will go against you, you abandon your ability to think and take action. Hope and fear are similar in that both will produce behavior that is paralyzing for the trader. Inability to respond to changing market conditions will destroy a trader's confidence and lead to substantial losses.

18 *Avoid overconfidence—it will breed complacency.* I have often heard of traders who have a string of good trades, which invariably is followed by a big loss. Why does this happen? The emotional "high" of achieving success in the market can lead to such a feeling of satisfaction that the trader actually becomes lazy. Realize that the market is oblivious to your experience of success or failure and therefore demands that you always pay attention when you are involved. Allowing your judgment to be impaired by any overconfidence will precipitate hazardous trading.

19 *Monitor your performance and pay attention to results.* The rate and frequency of change that takes place within futures markets are unlike those of most other environments. The opportunity for a trader to receive constant and instantaneous feedback is always present. How much feedback and how often a trader wants to study it and learn from her actions is another question. It has been said that trading the markets is similar to getting a report card every day. The ability to take advantage of this feedback and learn from it will lead to increased confidence and success in the markets.

20 *Develop positive relationships.* People influence how we look at the world and how we think about ourselves. Friends often act as a mirror of our own reality. Consequently, it is important to surround ourselves with people who have a healthy and positive sense of themselves. If we associate with people who complain, blame, gossip, or just plain quit, we will be influenced by their behavior. Moods are contagious, and, if we surround ourselves with negative people, we will eventually become negative. As traders, therefore, it is critical to be aware of the company we keep and to be with those who maintain a healthy and winning attitude.

21 *Do not trade on tips, "sure things," or inside information.* The temptation in all of us is to find the easy way. But you know the easy way is rarely the best way. There will always be lottery winners, but your odds of winning any lottery are slim. Therefore, avoid the temptation of taking tips, following inside information, listening to the opinions of other traders, or believing that the person you are listening to or talking to knows more than you do. Sometimes they do, but most of the time they do not. Collective opinions are, of course, helpful in the case of contrary opinion studies, but individual opinions or tips are basically useless to the trader.

22 *When you make money, take some of it away from the market.* When you have been doing well, remember to remove money from your account systematically. Whether you do this on a profitable trade basis or on a time basis (for instance, daily, weekly, or monthly) is not important. What is important is to do it.

Traders have winning and losing periods. During the winning times, profits will accumulate rapidly, and before you know it you may become impressed with your success. You will examine ways to expand your trading in view of your tremendous profits. You will look at how much money is in your account, and you will be tempted to trade larger positions.

Although there will be a time for this, it is usually not right to do so when you are feeling exceptionally euphoric about your performance. One way to reduce euphoria and put profits away for a rainy day is by having a systematic method of withdrawing profits.

23 *Develop winning attitudes and behaviors.* You can do this by reading the writings of the great traders. Spend more time developing yourself than you do developing your systems. The key variable in the trading success equation is the trader and not the system. I maintain that a good trader can make virtually any system work.

24 *Remember that "the trend is your friend."* This old expression is known to all, but used by few. Whether you allow the major trend to filter signals from your system as the final deciding factor or whether you use a system that is based entirely on trend-following principles, always be cautious when your trades are not consistent with the existing trend. Naturally, there will be times when your signals are against the trend. There will be times when the trend is apt to change. However, you should always be careful about trades and signals against the trend because they will most often be wrong.

25 *Do not try to trade too many markets.* There are many different markets, but most move together. There are only a few major market groups. They are as follows: meats, metals, grains, currencies, stock indices, tropicals, interest rate futures, and energy futures. Take one market from each group, preferably the most active, and focus on it. Few traders can be involved in all markets at once.

26 *Do not take the market home with you.* Futures trading can be a consuming business and whether you are trading well or not, it is advisable to get into the habit of leaving the markets at the office. As discussed earlier in this chapter, do not carry the effects of your trading into other aspects of your life. If you are trading well you may become complacent in areas where you need to work. Conversely, trading poorly can often lead you to feel depressed and not motivated to take care of other concerns in your life. Try to keep work separate from other areas and reserve time to take vacations and get away from the trading environment.

27 *Do not lose sight of the main goal.* Your goal in futures trading is to make money. There is no goal greater than this in futures trading. Although there may be other benefits such as self-satisfaction, the thrill of trading, and the sublimation of hostility and competitive instincts, they are all secondary. If you seek revenge against the market or other traders, or if you wish merely to compete for the sake of competition or to trade only for the thrill of trading, then the primary goal of speculation will be lost and so will your money!

28 *If you trade online, be on guard for errors.* If you execute your orders via computer using an online brokerage house, remember to double- and even triple-check your orders. Once you press the "send" button your order will be out of your hands. It will usually be filled within seconds. You must, therefore, be extremely careful, because one wrong digit or symbol could cost you big bucks. This threat of careless, costly error is as an ever-increasing problem.

29 *If you trade online, have a backup.* All too often an online trader will either be the victim of a computer failure or be unable to connect with the brokerage firm. Be prepared for such eventualities by having handy the appropriate telephone numbers to call in orders. If your online connection fails or if your online broker cannot be accessed, you may not be able to locate your current positions. In such cases a hard copy (paper) backup will be very helpful.

Summary

Success in the futures market will require you to cultivate new behaviors and to eliminate others. Evaluate yourself with the checklist provided in the beginning of this chapter, and identify your strengths and weaknesses. Use your self-evaluation in conjunction with the successful practices I have listed so that you develop the winning attitude and character that is such an integral part of successful trading and speculation in futures and options.

The tips for successful trading presented in the latter part of this chapter are based on my personal experiences and observations in futures trading since 1968. Although some tips may be more important to you than others, I know that at one time or another, all of these rules will be important to all traders. Employ these rules in your trading program by studying them. Keep them at your disposal and review them regularly. They will help keep you on the right track, and they will help keep you honest with yourself.

Perhaps one of the greatest errors a speculator can commit is self-deception. The markets are brutal, and the pain of losses is omnipresent. No trader or speculator is immune to losses. What ultimately separates the winners from the losers is the ability to be honest with oneself. From this rare quality arises clear perception. A clear perception of reality grants us the ability to use only what is effective and to discard all that is not.

Part Three

The Mechanics of Trading

CHAPTER 11

What You Should Know about Market Information Services and Brokers

If we could first know where we are, and whither we are tending, we could better judge what to do, and how to do it.

— ABRAHAM LINCOLN

You have many decisions to make when you first begin trading. One important decision is which information service you will use. The right information service will not only save you considerable time and effort, it will also help you to make money. Another decision you need to make is choosing the proper broker, suitable for your style of trading. This chapter seeks to inform you of the types of services available and what aspects you need to be aware of in selecting a broker.

Why Use a Service?

The first consideration in purchasing any type of service connected with futures trading is its ability to help save you time. If you can purchase a service for several hundred dollars a year, then you are practicing good business sense. A good information service will save you time and energy in learning about the markets.

Today there are many active markets, with many different contract months, futures options, and so on. Individual speculators can purchase considerable market information on a regular basis at a reasonable cost, thereby avoiding the time, expense, and effort involved in producing the information manually or with their own computer system.

That said, remember that many times you may wish to do your own homework, because this is frequently a very good way to keep in touch with the markets. In particular, individuals whose main method of trading is charting should spend at least their early months of trading doing their own charts, because they can learn much from observing how the basic chart patterns develop.

These basic understandings and skills will build the foundation to group advanced level concepts down the road. This is why I strongly recommend that each speculator spend some time manually calculating, if possible, some of his indicators. I have had many insights about the market while manually computing indicators and signals. For the chartist, the benefits of a service may be enhanced after an initial period of manual updates.

Types of Market Information Services Available to Futures Traders

I categorize futures market information services into two basic groups: (1) informal services that provide strictly factual information, such as charts and statistics, and (2) advisory services that provide interpretive market information. It is interesting to note that many services that do not consider themselves interpretive in nature are just that.

Information Services

There are essentially three types of factual information services:

1 *Statistical services*. Essentially, statistical services do nothing but report statistics. The statistics may be technical or fundamental, but the key element here is that they do not offer any interpretation of the statistics; they merely report them as they have occurred. This category includes both fundamentally and technically oriented statistical services.

Statistical services available to futures markets followers may include such things as government reports, government statistics, Commitments of Traders Reports, shipping information, crop reports, and planting intentions. Any report that provides merely factual information is considered informational and not interpretative. Be aware that many services that provide such data also offer their own interpretation of the data. This kind of service I consider to be somewhat advisory in nature, depending upon the fashion in which the information has been reported. You will likely find that specialized services tend to provide the most consistently profitable recommendations because the vendors of such services can often devote more attention and study to these markets. Services that try to cover too many markets may give good quantity but less quality.

2 *Chart services.* The area of chart services covers a wide variety of publications. There is, however, a very clear distinction between chart services that merely report factual information and chart services that interpret and advise based on the chart information. The distinction is important because the independent futures trader does not wish to clutter her mind with opinions or analyses prepared by others.

It is interesting to note that some services that in the past were purely informational have slowly become more advisory. However, they still separate their chart analyses physically from their charts. The independent trader can simply separate the recommendations and opinions from the charts and dispose of the recommendations in order to avoid being influenced by them.

Ideally, however, I recommend that the trader who wishes to make decisions totally uninfluenced by the input of other analysts subscribe to a chart service that is purely informational, containing no chart analyses whatsoever.

An interesting sidelight of chart services has developed in recent years. It is becoming more fashionable for them also to include various market indicators, such as moving averages, momentum, stochastics, MACD, volume, and open interest, among others, in chart form along with the charts. These indicators may be helpful to some traders. However, as is the case with market opinions that supplement the offerings of factual information services, I find that the truly independent speculator avoids them. Indicators of such a nature can influence you in both subtle and overt ways.

Please understand that I am not deeming these indicators useless, nor do I advise all traders to avoid them. I am, however, alerting you to the fact that many traders may not wish to have such input. If you feel the need for additional information, or are interested in supplementing your market analyses with the input provided by indicators that you feel have good potential, use them. Make sure, however, that you have made your decision based on your needs and recognize the indicators' inherent influence.

Other considerations in subscribing to a chart service are equally important. Perhaps the single greatest feature of any chart service is the user's ability to update charts manually. The chart service should allow sufficient room to project cycles and trendlines into the future, as well as room on which to update the charts. The price scales should be easy to work with and the paper should be thick enough to permit manual updates. Within reasonable limits, the larger the charts the better they are.

An important consideration that many traders have overlooked is the availability of opening prices on a daily price chart. Opening prices are important to the speculator, perhaps more important than many analysts believe them to be. My preference is for a chart service containing them. Unfortunately, in today's chart service market, this narrows the available choices quite significantly, because most services do not plot opening prices. Certainly, their use is a matter of individual preference, but I suggest you give it strong consideration after reviewing available advisory work and techniques using opening prices.

3 News services. In some respects, news services are similar to chart services. Some report the news and some report and interpret the news. The caveats in this case are similar to those I outlined earlier for the two different types of chart services. Again, an independent trader must evaluate the relevance of the information based on his or her specific needs. Many traders, in fact, prefer not to know the news because their approach is primarily technical.

Advisory Services

The real issue is do you want or do you need an advisory service? Remember that there are assets and liabilities regardless of which decision you may make. The benefits of having an advisory service are essentially threefold:

1   Many advisory services do full-time work on indicators and techniques that may be consistent with your orientation to the market. Consequently, you may save yourself considerable time by subscribing.
2   Many advisory services have good performance records that can help you profit in the markets. Just keep in mind, though, that all services have their good times as well as bad, just as traders do.
3   Advisory services may help you maintain your discipline. It is easier for some traders to follow the advice of another than it is for them to take their own good advice.

On the other hand, there are a number of points to consider on the negative side of advisory services.

1 Dependency. Many traders do not look favorably upon the possibility of becoming dependent on an advisory service. Although the particular advisor or newsletter may be doing well at present, performance could change markedly over time. This is, of course, the risk one takes in depending upon someone else's advice.

2 Lack of teaching. Individuals who subscribe to a service that does nothing more than make recommendations and provide minimal analyses or justifications for these recommendations may find they are not learning anything from the service. Those in the futures markets in order to further their understanding, and who plan at some point to develop an independent approach, will not benefit from such services.

3 Results. It can often be difficult to duplicate the results of some advisory services. This could be due to a number of factors, including trader discipline or inaccurate/misrepresented reporting of results. Before considering an advisory service, verify performance claims through an independent evaluating service (if one is available for the service you are considering). Be certain that slippage and commissions are counted as part of the losses.

4 Methodological considerations. In deciding to commit to a given advisory service or services, carefully consider the systems or methods they plan to employ in their trading. In some cases, the methodology of the services is clearly stated for potential and current subscribers. In other instances, however, the service may wish to keep confidential most aspects of its approach, giving nothing but advice as to when to buy and sell. There is nothing wrong with either procedure.

The secretive approach, however, may not satisfy some individuals who feel they must know why they are committing their money. Furthermore, the secretive approach does not provide any educational benefits to the subscriber. You may also want to know the overall risk management philosophy; therefore, you would want to know the specifics of the trading.

Evaluating an Advisory Service

With so many services available to today's futures trader, I recommend that you follow a number of specific steps and procedures before selecting a service. Although I have a vested interest because I publish several advisory services for speculators, I am attempting to give you a totally unbiased point of view.

Remember that the basic question is "Do you really want to subscribe to an advisory service?" The answer is strictly an individual one that must take into consideration your own needs, assets, strengths, and weaknesses. My purpose is to provide you with a truthful answer, and not one that will serve my purposes. I am certain that I speak for a majority of trading advisors who publish newsletters when I say that we do not want to entice subscribers to our service unless they can truly employ it either as part of their own research or trade exclusively with our recommendations.

The ultimate goal is for everyone to profit, subscribers and newsletter writers alike. None of us want unhappy subscribers who feel that they have purchased a service without benefit. This is why I would rather discourage someone at the start, as opposed to enticing individuals who are really not ready for an advisory service.

Given the fact that many individuals want to trade futures but have limited time they can devote to futures analysis, the need arises for an advisory-type service. Individuals who cannot make the time commitment are, therefore, drawn to services that are akin to their market orientations. Those who follow cycles, for example, may be attracted to one type of service, whereas individuals who are more interested in fundamentals may be attracted to a different type. There is a market advisory service available for virtually every type of market orientation covering everything from fundamentals to astrological systems.

With this background in mind, and with the full realization that advisory services are not for all speculators, consider the following points when selecting a service.

1 *Specificity*. Some advisory services claim fantastic performance records that, upon closer examination, are discovered to be based on very general recommendations that leave too much of the decision-making process to the reader.

Vague recommendations can be interpreted in many different ways, and the individual making these recommendations can make virtually any claim with 20/20 hindsight. Therefore, when considering a service, make certain that its recommendations are specific regarding entry, exit, and follow-up. Such specificity can be in the form of specific price orders or in specific market instructions (for example, buy on Monday's open).

2 *Timeliness*. Some advisory services are not sufficiently timely to permit real-time implementation. Either subscribers receive their advice too late, or their recommendations are made too late to permit real-time implementation.

Ideally, you should either be able to maintain close touch with your advisory service on a daily basis or the recommendations provided in its newsletter should be so specific and with such close follow-up that telephone contact would be unnecessary.

3 *Objectives, stops, alternatives*. A good advisory service should provide you with all three of these highly specific forms of guidance. Ideally you should have price or time objectives, stops, and specific follow-up procedures that will leave you with alternatives, regardless of market conditions. For example, "take your profit Tuesday on the close of trading."

If you are going to pay an advisor, then make sure you are paying for a complete package. Some services are wonderful at getting you into the market, but vague and nonspecific when it comes to getting you out.

4 *Cost*. The cost of some services may be prohibitive in terms of what you receive. Although each service is unique in the information it provides, the cost of what you get may not turn out to be effective in terms of how you use the information, or of the extent to which the information proves profitable.

Unfortunately, it is impossible to know this in advance. Rather, you must make this evaluation at regular intervals once you have found a service that suits your needs.

5 *Portfolio size.* Some advisory services with excellent performance records have achieved their hypothetical results in a fashion that most speculators cannot duplicate. In some cases, they have taken on extremely large positions, scaled into the market holding losing positions, hypothetically purchased or sold extremely large numbers of contracts, or added more and more margin to their hypothetical account until they have weathered most storms.

Because this is not a realistic way for the average trader to approach the market, you should not follow the work of a service such as this. I'm aware of several services that have practiced such procedures in one form or another (sometimes in all forms). Without naming names, I recommend you be aware.

Realistically, most futures portfolios should not contain more than five to ten positions at any time. That's just my orientation, but I think you'll find this approach makes sense for most speculators.

6 *Hot line.* Does the service have a hot line you can call at least daily in order to obtain the latest recommendations, updates, and follow-ups? The recorder is a good way to keep in touch with your service and its recommendations; however, a hot line is not necessary if the service can maintain a thorough follow-up in its newsletter.

Note that some recorder hot lines are essentially useless because they do not provide specific recommendations. Rather, they provide nothing but general comments. Many advisory and statistical services are available either via e-mail and/or through Internet access. This saves time and money while bringing you timely information very quickly.

7 *Performance record.* You will observe that the performance record is not one of the major items on my list, yet it is important. Provided the performance record is honestly reported and truly representative of the service's record, you should consider its history carefully. The would-be subscriber who looks merely at the bottom line may be in for a rude awakening when he actually subscribes to the service.

You must examine in close detail such items as the largest single loss, the largest single profit, the average loss, the average profit, and the win/lose percentage ratio. The reasons for this are abundantly clear and have been discussed earlier in this book, in Chapter 7. Remember that a service that makes most of its profits on a few highly profitable trades may not be the best service for you.

The rule of thumb in assessing the potential of any service in your program is whether you can duplicate its results. If you can, then the service is for you. If, however, the results would be difficult for you to replicate, then you are best advised to look elsewhere.

8 *Deduction for commissions.* Read the fine print! Some services deduct only small commission charges from their performance records. Other services do not deduct any commissions at all from their performance records. Commissions could end up eating all the profits their records showed.

9 *Price fills.* In assessing realistic representation of recommendations, be sure to look for hypothetical price fills. Some services claim recommendations being filled on entry and/or exit when, in fact, such fills may not have been possible at the stated price (for reasons discussed in Chapter 12). This is an important point to consider when evaluating a service because your trading will be very real, not hypothetical.

10 *Which markets are traded?* Some services specialize in only certain markets. The markets that are the specialty of a certain service may be either too risky or too volatile for you. You can determine a service's specialty from examining the performance record and from studying the service's promotional literature.

Also bear in mind that the service may give recommendations in particularly thin markets, which also may not be to your liking. Advisory service recommendations to a large audience in a thin market can often result in exceptionally bad price executions on entry and exit. Do not subscribe to a service that is not consistent with your needs, general expectations, and orientation regarding specific markets covered.

Although this list is not exhaustive, the above ten points should offer you a foundation upon which to evaluate your service(s). Although a good information service can be helpful, as has been noted, realize that, ultimately, you need to trust your own judgment. Whether you subscribe to a good service, have a good system, or have a good broker, nothing will help if you cannot trust your own decisions.

What Type of Trader Are You?

Determine not only what type of trader you are but also what kind of trader you would like to be and where you plan to go with your trading. There are several types of traders. The following is a list of their characteristics:

1 ***The novice.*** This trader has little or no experience; feels nervous, uncertain, and insecure; and is probably lacking in knowledge. This individual needs a broker who "holds his hand," and who is patient and familiar with the concerns of the beginner trader.

2 ***Experienced short-term or day trader.*** This individual has considerable experience and is primarily interested in quick trading (usually intraday or over a period of several days). Such an individual would require no input from a broker and may require only quotes and good execution.

3 ***The long-term trader.*** This individual does not trade often and may require specialized services from a broker such as statistical and/or fundamental information.

4 ***The independent trader.*** Regardless of market orientation, many traders prefer to be totally independent and seek no input from their broker. Such individuals should select a broker for order-taking purposes only.

Essentially, these are the four types of traders common in today's markets. Some traders seek to have broker input, and some traders are not interested in any information from their broker. The broker who provides information, quotes, ideas, and so on, should be reimbursed for these additional services, whereas the broker who provides nothing but price fills should be able to provide lower commissions. Hence, the distinction between "full-service brokers" and "discount brokers."

Finding a Broker

From my observation, one of the most misunderstood things about futures trading, aside from the placement of orders, is the relationship between broker and client. In order to fully understand this relationship, it is important to understand your aspirations as a trader. Returning to the question posed in the preceding section, what type of trader are you? With this question in mind, you can find the broker who best works for you.

Your relationship with a broker can prove to be your greatest asset or greatest liability. This is why I strongly suggest that you do not take the issue of selecting a broker lightly. Many decisions must be made, and they must be made correctly as early in the game as possible; having the right broker for you early on makes this achievable.

The most important element to establish in your relationship with your broker is trust. Without trust, you may sabotage your own trading. It is necessary, therefore, to be clear and up-front about your needs and expectations. The more specific you can be about your style of trading, the services you require, and the commission you are willing to pay, the better chance you will have of developing an effective relationship with your broker.

Full-Service Brokers

Full-service brokerage firms pride themselves on producing worthwhile research, providing quotes to clients through their individual brokers, and frequently maintaining one or more managed account programs.

Discretionary Accounts

The discretionary or managed account takes all decision-making functions and controls away from the customer and puts them into the hands of a pro. This may be a group or an individual who will exercise control over the account. This group or individual manages the trades and, with the exception of when to add or take money from the account, they control the decisions.

Discount Brokers

Discount brokers, both in stocks and futures, charge significantly lower commission rates than do full-service firms. Although most discount firms do not provide research, some have recently moved to a sliding scale under which they provide additional services such as research and broker input. Similarly, many full-service firms are now discounting their commissions to customers who do not require additional services.

The commission price war has gone about as far as it can go, but it still is in the trader's best interest to explore and ask questions concerning the type of broker she needs. In addition to the factors mentioned, pay particular attention to (1) the financial stability of the firm, (2) the commission structure, and (3) the different services you need.

Online Brokers

As communications technology has advanced, so has the system of electronic order entry and execution. Some futures exchanges (such as LIFFE, the London International Financial Futures Exchange) are fully electronic. In other words, they do not have trading pits, a trading floor, or floor traders who participate in the traditional "open outcry" system.

When you trade through an online broker you do not deal with any one individual for order placement; rather, you place your orders directly through your computer. In many cases the orders go to the exchange where your order is matched with opposite orders. In other words, if you have an order to buy at the market, your order will be matched by an order to sell at the market.

In some cases trading online is not fully electronic trading. Your order may go to your brokerage firm electronically, but it will end up in the hands of a floor broker where it is executed in a trading pit and then confirmed to you electronically. When all markets are fully electronic your order will be executed by electronic means.

Online brokers offer different services and different commission rates. The rates and services offered can vary markedly. Furthermore, the speed of order execution can also vary substantially. Before you open an online brokerage account, make certain that you research the services you will get at no charge as well as the speed of order execution.

Summary

There are many different types of advisory, chart, and data services. There are hundreds of brokerage firms. Your choice of an advisory service and/or broker should be a function of your trading goals, your style of trading, cost, reputation, and speed of order execution. An honest self-assessment of your goals will allow you to make the selection process more accurately and will also facilitate the development of a functional working relationship with your broker.

This aspect of futures trading may seem either rudimentary or mundane to you, but it is, nonetheless, an integral aspect of the trading process. It is impossible to overstate the importance of carefully and frugally selecting your market information sources as well as your broker and brokerage firm. Simply stated, the correct advisory service can help you select winning trades, and the correct broker can help you implement your trading decisions flawlessly and consistently.

CHAPTER 12

What You Should Know about Order Placement

Beauty from order springs.

— WILLIAM KING

I am always amazed by the number of newcomers to futures trading who attempt to place orders without understanding the meaning of different types of orders and their correct usage. I urge you not to trade until you have achieved a complete understanding of the following:

❑ *The different types of orders that can be used in futures trading*
❑ *When and why certain types of orders are used*
❑ *The different rules that apply at different exchanges*

It is sad but true that one of the most critical but least understood aspects of futures trading is the use of orders. Trader misunderstanding of orders often leads to unnecessary disputes with a broker. Many new traders, upon receiving a bad order fill, tend to blame their brokers. A thorough knowledge of order placement can prevent much aggravation, as well as many poor price fills. Using the wrong order can cost you dearly. Using the right order at the right time is critical to the success of any trading method.

Following an order from inception to completion offers a useful illustration of the process and thereby of the logic underlying certain order types. Remember that there are two broad categories of order placement, traditional and online. Let's first consider traditional order entry.

Traditional Order Entry and Execution

Assume you call your broker and place an order to buy one contract of March Treasury Bond (T-bond) futures "at the market." Specifically, this means you want to buy March Treasury Bonds at whatever price can be obtained for you when your order reaches the floor of the exchange or the trading pit (the difference to be explained later).

The order-entry process begins when you contact your broker either by the phone or via computer. Let's presume you telephone the broker and say, "Buy one March T-bond at the market." Depending on the type of trading you do and the type of broker you have, you will either hang up the phone or you will hold for your price fill.

When your broker receives the order, he will fill out a numbered order form (ticket) containing your account number and your specific order. The ticket will then be time-stamped. Your broker will call the order to the trading floor of the exchange. A clerk at the order desk for your brokerage firm will take the order from your broker and write a similar ticket. The order will be handed to a runner (messenger).

The runner will take your order ticket to the pit broker who will then execute the order by finding a seller to match your buy order. The floor broker will write down the price at which your order was filled, and hand it back to the runner. The runner will take the order ticket back to the order desk on the trading floor. The floor desk will report the price back to your broker, who will in turn give you your price fill, either while you are waiting on the telephone or by calling you. The entire process for a market order, as described above, can be completed in a matter of minutes or even seconds.

If you do business with a broker who can fill your order using so-called arbitrage methods, the transactions just described will be somewhat different. Once your broker has taken the order from you and given it to the floor clerk, an individual at the order desk on the floor will hand-signal the pit trader to execute your order. The pit trader will then execute the order and, by hand signal, report the fill back to the order desk. In this way you can very frequently have your order filled and reported back to you often in less than one minute. Arbitrage techniques are becoming more common in active markets such as stock index futures and interest rate and currency futures.

The procedure described above was for a market order. Because market orders are executed at the prevailing price without bargaining they are the fastest orders to be filled. You will get filled at the prevailing price in an actively traded market. The use of market orders in futures contracts that do not trade actively is clearly discouraged for reasons that will be clarified later.

Other types of orders, called conditional orders, are executed in essentially the same way, but depending on type of orders involved, they may not be filled immediately. Rather, they are brought into the pit and given to the pit broker who keeps them in his "deck." The deck consists of small cards, on which the pit broker keeps track of orders he has filled and the orders he needs to fill. Some exchanges now use electronic decks in order to track and record orders more quickly and accurately.

Online and Electronic Order Entry

Since the late 1990s electronic order entry and online trading in stocks and futures has been gaining in popularity. In stocks it is no longer necessary to speak with a broker in order to buy or sell most issues. Orders placed via computer directly to the brokerage firm execute within a matter of seconds. Futures trading has also taken this direction, although not as quickly. A number of exchanges throughout the world are fully electronic and permit electronic order entry, such as the LIFFE (London International Financial Futures Exchange), Frankfurt's EUREX, and the SIMEX in Singapore, among scores of others. The electronic exchanges do not have pit brokers or trading pits; rather, all of their transactions are handled by computers that match buyers and sellers via orders. This type of order entry is indeed the wave of the future. Within a few years it is likely that most floor brokers will be gone and that most trading pits will exist only within the memory and disk drives of computers. The pit broker will become part of a colorful past. However, even though online order entry in all markets is inevitable, traders will still need to know how to place orders and how these orders are executed. Here is a review of order types and their usage.

Market Order

A market order does exactly what it says. Placing an order to buy or sell at the market means that your order will be executed at the best possible price as soon as the pit broker has received it. In an active market, such orders are safe to use and very common, but it is not prudent to use a market order in a less actively traded market (currently, orange juice, palladium, or oats) and you should use it only if you need a fill immediately.

In a slow market where the bids and offers are less frequent, a market order stands the chance of being filled far away from the last trade. If, for example, you place an order to buy at the market, but there are no price offers close to the last trade, the floor trader or pit broker will continue to bid higher and higher until your market order has been filled. In a thin or inactive market this could be at virtually any price. Therefore, your order will frequently not get filled at a very good price compared to what you think you should have gotten.

Be very careful when using market orders in thin markets. In fact, as noted above it is best not to use market orders at all in such cases, unless it is imperative that you make a trade.

Market-on-Close (MOC) Order

A market-on-close order is an instruction to the pit broker to execute an order for you, to buy or to sell, at or near the close of trading. Your order is frequently executed during the last few seconds of trading and, in most cases, is not too much different from the closing price. Very frequently such orders are filled in the closing price range. On occasion, MOC orders do not result in particularly good fills. It has been my experience, however, that MOC orders in most active markets, such as S&P 500, T-bonds, and crude oil, do not result in terribly bad price fills. But several ticks difference between what you expected and what you received can occur.

On occasion, an MOC order will work to your advantage, particularly when a market is near limit up or limit down. Assume, for example, that you would like to buy at the end of the day. Assume that the market is weak. In such a case, the market will often drop even lower on the close, as those who were buying during the day have MOC orders to sell. If you are short and have a MOC order to buy, or if you want to go net long, chances are you will get a reasonably good fill, often at or close to limit down.

The reverse often holds true with MOC orders to sell. In other words, if the market is sharply higher and you have a long position you want to liquidate by the close or a short you want to establish, this could be an ideal situation. Frequently, in a market that has been strong all day there will be a rush to the upside, bringing prices close to or possibly limit up. This happens because those who were short for the day rush in to cover their short positions. There will be buying, which runs the price up. Because you will be selling, you may get a better price fill than you expected. MOC orders should also be avoided in thin markets.

Market-on-the-Open Order

This is a very simple, self-explanatory order, entered before the opening to buy at the market as soon as the market opens. Typically, there is a great deal of activity on market opens, but in thin markets this could result in a reasonably bad price fill. Some market analysts and advisors have strong sentiment against buying on the open. They feel that the opening is not necessarily a good reflection of market activity. Indeed, on many occasions in the past, traders have witnessed significant reversals after a strong opening in a given direction.

Certainly, as an example, if our market entry was on the buy side on a sharply higher opening during one of the reversal-type days, then we would indeed be in jeopardy, or vice versa, during a sharply lower opening. Some traders consider the opening price of a market to be very important and have developed specific techniques for using opening prices as a means of predicting significant levels of support and resistance as well as timing signals.

Market-If-Touched (MIT) Order

A market-if-touched order is an order to buy or sell at the market if a specific price is touched. For example, an order to buy June hogs at 54.10 MIT would become a market order as soon as 54.10 is hit. The actual price at which you would get filled could be at 54.10 exactly, at more than 54.10, or even a lower price than 54.10.

Stop Orders

There are a number of variant forms of stop orders. Stop orders are buy or sell orders at prices that are generally either above or below the market.

Buy Stop

This is an order to buy at a given price above the market. When the indicated price is hit, your order becomes a market order that is filled at the best price possible thereafter. Such orders are used to exit a short position or to enter a long position on market strength.

Sell Stop

This is an order to sell at a price below the market. Once the price is hit, your order is filled at that price or at the best price possible. Such orders are used to exit a long position or to enter a short position on market weakness.

Stop Loss

The term stop loss is applied to a position that offsets an existing position. Such an order is designed to limit a loss, hence the name *stop loss*. Orders are not entered as stop-loss orders, but rather in the variety of ways described below. Hence, the term *stop loss* is a generic term that could be applied to orders above or below the market.

Stop Limit

The stop limit order is a specific type of stop order used either above or below the market. A sell stop limit means that you want to sell below the market, but at no lower than the price of your limit. In other words, you must be filled at your price or not at all. This is a good way to guarantee a fill at a certain price, but if the market goes through your price and does not trade at it, or the order cannot be filled even at the limit price, you will not be filled. You may not get the protection you want if you are using this order as a stop loss. The reverse holds true for stop limit orders above the market.

You should use stop limits when you want to avoid a bad fill, or when you are working with a precise technical level. I do not recommend using stop limits for the purpose of stop losses.

Stop Close Only

This is an instruction to sell or buy within the closing minute of trading. A sell stop close only order will be executed at or below the given price during the closing minute. A buy stop close will be executed only at or above the given price during the last minute of trading. Many times the fill price will not be in agreement with the last tick or settlement price due to the time span during which a stop close only order can be filled.

Fill or Kill Order

This order is not used very frequently, but it has its merits. A fill or kill order is essentially an instruction to the pit broker to fill your order at a given price within a matter of minutes or to cancel your order. It is a way of placing a price order close to the market in an effort to obtain close to an immediate feedback on disposition of your order.

Such an order is best used when you wish to enter or exit a position quickly, but rather than doing so at the market you want to do so at a given price in order to avoid the possibility of a poor price fill. Fill or kill orders can be used in thin markets, or in markets that have been hovering around a certain price level but for some reason will not come to the price level at which you are seeking to enter or exit a position.

Good-Till-Canceled (GTC) Order/Open Order

A good-till-canceled order means exactly what it says. This order type is also known as an open order. A GTC order remains in the market until you cancel it. As a matter of procedure, most brokerage firms clear the books of orders at the end of every day's trading unless these orders are specified as good-till-canceled orders or open orders.

Most short-term traders do not find it necessary to use good-till-canceled orders. They can be used when you will be out of touch with the market, but I strongly suggest against trading when you are not in touch with the markets. Such orders are much more common in the stock market.

Different Rules at Different Exchanges

Different futures exchanges in the same country often have slightly different rules. In some cases the rules are markedly different. Trading rules also vary from country to country. At times the variations can be substantial. For example, some U.S. exchanges accept predetermined market price orders known as market-if-touched (MIT) orders whereas others do not. Some U.S. exchanges accept MOC orders while others do not. Some exchanges will not guarantee a price execution on orders that are placed later than fifteen minutes before the close of trading. Some orders that can be used in open outcry markets cannot be used in fully electronic markets. Furthermore, some brokerage firms have their own specific trading rules based on their particular needs and trading floor situations. Be aware of these rule differences before you trade. Some brokers firms have a preprinted sheet that lists the different orders accepted by different exchanges. Ask your broker to send you one, or see if the information is available at your broker's website.

Things Change

At times exchanges and/or the regulatory officials who oversee futures trading may impose certain temporary limitations and/or rule changes on the markets as a result of underlying conditions either within a given market, domestically, or internationally. Some rule changes may, on occasion, be necessitated by technical problems at the exchanges. In any event, your broker should advise you of such conditions. You are strongly advised to follow the rules. If you do not follow the rules, even though you may not like them, then any errors you make will be your own responsibility.

Summary

Order placements are very important because they will affect the price at which you buy or sell—which in turn will affect your bottom line. One thing to remember with regard to order placement is that you must be specific and decisive. Don't get a bad reputation with your broker for being unclear—saying one thing, but meaning another.

Finally, remember that in many cases existing orders must be found in the pit broker's deck before you can replace them with another order! This could markedly affect your price fill. Therefore, if you have an existing order that must be canceled and replaced with a market order, remember that your existing order must be found and removed so that there is no duplication. This takes time. The result could be a poor price fill. Therefore, if you suspect you will need to cancel and replace, cancel as soon as you can. Then enter your market order when ready. This will ensure your order is filled immediately, and your resulting price fill could be better. Carefully follow the proper cancel procedure. It could save you much grief and much money as well.

Remember also that different futures exchanges in different countries often have their unique rules and regulations. Some U.S. exchanges have different rules. It behooves you, therefore, to know what orders can be used at the various exchanges. You can get this information from your broker. If you are uncertain as to which orders can or cannot be used, then find out well ahead of time. Don't wait until the last minute to find out. The delay may cause you to miss a trading opportunity.

Advanced Trading Strategies
and Techniques

CHAPTER 13

Advanced Concepts in Moving Averages

He who dares, wins.

— ANONYMOUS

I have already familiarized you with the basic methods of using timing indicators with a simple moving average of closing prices (see Chapter 5). The availability of high-powered computers at reasonably low prices has spawned many variations on the theme of moving averages. Having worked extensively with different types of moving averages, I have found the use of moving averages of highs and lows to be exceptionally good for determining technical support and resistance levels as well as potential turning points in the futures and stock markets.

For those who wish to pursue more advanced applications of the moving average techniques, this chapter explains specific approaches. Although both high and low moving averages and moving averages of closing prices appear to have good potential for use as full-blown trading systems in futures markets, they are not offered here as such because specific money-management rules and stop-loss procedures would need to be added to the basic timing signals. Those who wish to develop these two moving average techniques as trading systems should do more research on stop and risk procedures appropriate to their individual trading situation.

Moving Average Methods

There are many different types of moving averages that can be used for the purpose of generating buy and sell signals. Each type of moving average has its advantages as well as its drawbacks. The discussion below explains the differences between the different types of moving averages as well as their assets and liabilities for the speculator. Here is a review of the different types of moving averages.

Simple Moving Average

To calculate the simple moving average, add and then average a set of prices or other data, spanning a specific amount of time. The calculation normally involves closing prices, but you may also use highs, lows, an average of all three, or even other numerical data. You drop the oldest data point when a new one is added. Hence, the average "moves" following the market. A line graph of the daily averages appears as a smoothed version of the raw data.

Longer moving averages smooth out all minor fluctuations and show only longer-term trends. Conversely, shorter-term moving averages accentuate the short-term trends at the expense of long-term trends.

Long-term and short-term moving averages each offer certain advantages and disadvantages depending on how they are used. In general, using a longer-term moving average will allow you to enter and exit the market less frequently. Shorter-term averages are used to quickly enter and exit the markets and do not capture the major trend of a market. Longer term moving averages tend to produce larger profits but also require that trades be held for longer periods of time.

Weighted Moving Average

A weighted moving average places greater emphasis on more recent data by weighing each day's data differently. Whereas the simple moving average gives equal weight to each data point, the weighted moving average assigns more importance to recent data. Some traders are of the opinion that recent prices are more important than older prices and prefer to use the weighted moving average because it tends to react quickly to recent data. A weighted MA can often get you into and out of trades more quickly. The drawback of a weighted MA is that it tends to downplay events and price changes in the more distant past.

Exponential Moving Average

The exponential moving average is also weighted (i.e., assigns greater importance to more recent data), but it does so by using an exponential formula for each price in the series. However, the exponential moving average gives all the data points equal weight. Both exponential and weighted moving averages tend to generate more trades in narrow trading range markets—which can result in costly whipsaws (in other words, numerous false signals).

Triangular Moving Average

The triangular moving average (TMA) assigns greater importance to the midpoint of the data series. Consequently, it is less affected by old prices and new prices. Research indicates that triangular moving averages are more stable than either weighted or exponential moving averages. In other words, the TMA tends to produce fewer incorrect signals but in doing so it also tends to overlook some winning trades.

Best Performing Moving Averages

In order to test the performance of moving averages, I conducted an exhaustive test of numerous dual- and triple-moving averages. Some MA combinations were considerably more profitable than others, but all moving averages were subject to large drawdowns and required large risk.

The Moving Average Channel (MAC)

The Moving Average Channel (MAC) is a concept market technician Richard Donchian developed in the 1950s. Instead of plotting only the moving average of closing prices, or for that matter, of several closing prices, Donchian suggested plotting the moving averages of high and low prices of each time frame (i.e., day, week, month). The result was a price channel or band containing two moving averages, one of highs and one of lows.

I have found the technique to be especially promising as a trading tool and have researched its possible applications. I have found, for example, that the channel can work very well for the purpose of finding support and resistance. The MAC acts as support when prices decline in a bull market and as resistance when prices rally in a bear market. **Figure 13-1** shows the channel for December Treasury bonds futures over a three-month period. **Figure 13-2** shows the same channel with price and various rallies to resistance and declines to support. **Figure 13-3** shows how the channel indicates support for December Japanese Yen futures.

The application of this technique is straightforward in terms of finding support and resistance. My work strongly suggests, however, that more specific applications can be developed in terms of timing. Note the following characteristics of the moving average channel:

1   The moving average channel of ten units of the high and eight units of the low appears to be the most practical. Other time units are either too short or too long to provide meaningful indicators. In other words, using a moving

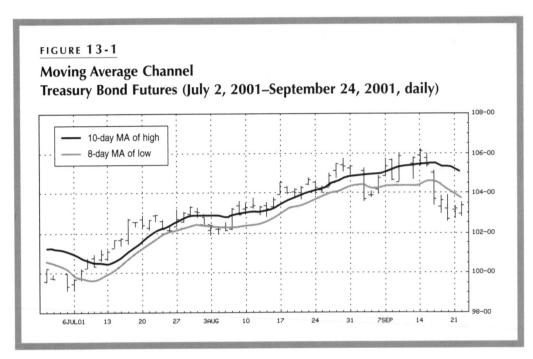

FIGURE **13-1**

Moving Average Channel
Treasury Bond Futures (July 2, 2001–September 24, 2001, daily)

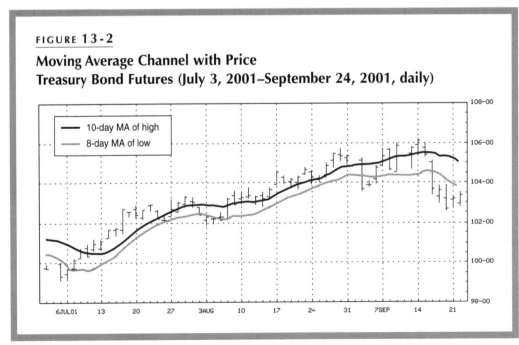

FIGURE **13-2**

Moving Average Channel with Price
Treasury Bond Futures (July 3, 2001–September 24, 2001, daily)

Source: Bloomberg

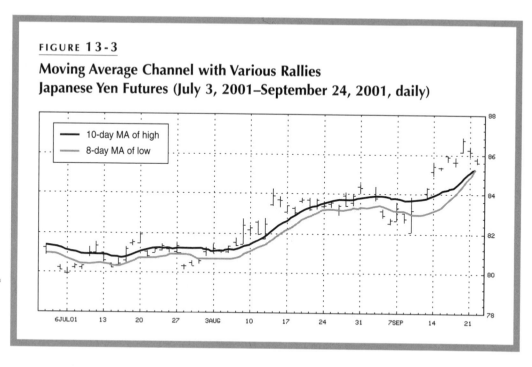

FIGURE 13-3

**Moving Average Channel with Various Rallies
Japanese Yen Futures (July 3, 2001–September 24, 2001, daily)**

Source: Bloomberg

average of too few days or too many days fails to provide useful information.

2 When a market has started a bullish move, corrections within that move tend to find support at either extreme of the channel or within the channel.

3 In a bearish move, rallies tend to find resistance at either extreme of the channel or within the channel itself (in other words, the price below the channel).

4 Once price bars begin to appear fully outside of the channel on the upside, it is probable that a bullish move has started.

5 Once price bars begin to appear fully outside the bottom of the channel, it is probable that a downside move has started.

These basic applications of MAC I believe offer potential value for the futures speculator. They help him to form an opinion as to whether prices have changed trend or if they remain in a previously established trend.

If we take one more step with the moving average channel technique, adding to it a three-period moving average of closing prices, we arrive at a technique that appears to have great potential as a trading system. Essentially, the addition of the three-period moving average of closing prices allows you to determine numerically when prices have seemingly lost their momentum within the existing channel and are likely to change direction. This technique is a way of deter-

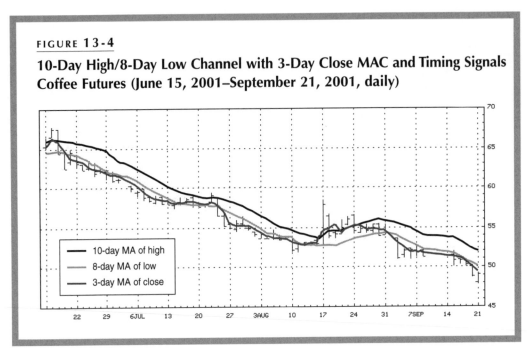

FIGURE 13-4

10-Day High/8-Day Low Channel with 3-Day Close MAC and Timing Signals Coffee Futures (June 15, 2001–September 21, 2001, daily)

mining when the market has run out of gas on the upside or downside.

Figure 13-4 illustrates this technique, showing the potential buy and sell signals using the indicator and relating them to an actual price chart showing the hypothetical buy and sell points. Because the technique determines when prices have probably turned higher or lower, the speculator capable of assuming larger risk can follow every signal, being in the market at all times, and thereby employing this technique for money management purposes.

The drawback is that losses could sometimes get very large. Yet, profits would, at times, also be very large. **Figures 13-5, 13-6,** and **13-7** offer some further illustrations of this technique.

The 3 High/3 Low Moving Average Channel for Short-Term Trading

Another interesting application of the moving average is its use as a shorter-term trading approach. The concept is a very simple one, indeed. When prices are in an up trend, there is a good probability that declines will be supported at

FIGURE **13-5**

10-Day High/8-Day Low/3-Day Close MAC Signals
Silver Futures (June 16, 2001–September 21, 2001, daily)

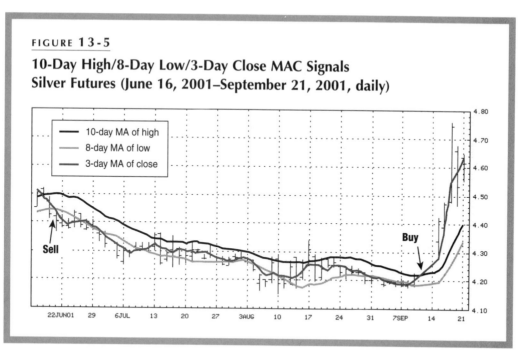

FIGURE **13-6**

10-Day High/8-Day Low/3-Day Close MAC Signals
Swiss Franc Futures (June 18, 2001–September 21, 2001, daily)

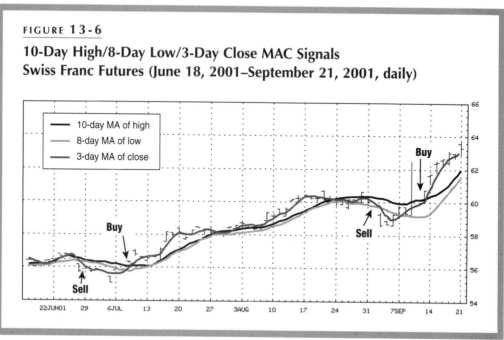

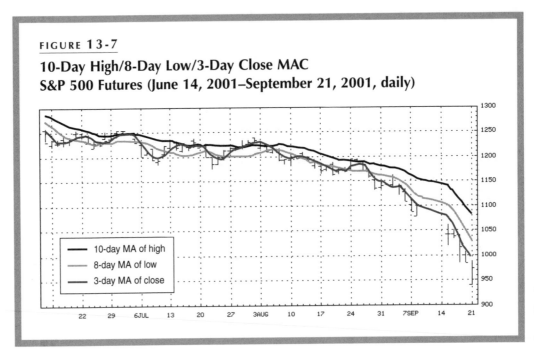

FIGURE 13-7

10-Day High/8-Day Low/3-Day Close MAC
S&P 500 Futures (June 14, 2001–September 21, 2001, daily)

Source: Bloomberg

the three-day MA of the low. When prices are in a downtrend, there is a good probability that rallies will stop, or find resistance, at the three-day MA of the high. If you are able to determine the trend of a market with reasonably good accuracy, then you can use the 3/3 method for short-term trading. **Figures 13-8** and **13-9** illustrate this approach.

Here are guidelines for using this technique:

❑ Determine the trend of a market. Various tools exist that can assist you in accomplishing this task with fairly good accuracy. Among them is the use of momentum as a trend indicator.

❑ If the trend is up, then you buy at the three-day MA of the lows and you take profit at the three-day MA of the highs.

❑ If the trend is down then you sell short at the three-day MA of the highs, and you buy back your short position at the three-day MA of the lows.

Figures 13-10 and **13-11** show how this technique is applied. **Figures 13-12** and **13-13** show how the technique is applied with the use of a fourteen-day momentum indicator. (The momentum indicator also called "rate of change," is available on most trading software.)

Note, that when using the 3/3 method you will be entering based on the MA

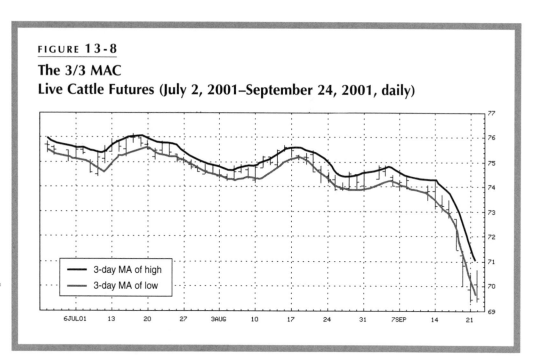

FIGURE **13-8**

The 3/3 MAC
Live Cattle Futures (July 2, 2001–September 24, 2001, daily)

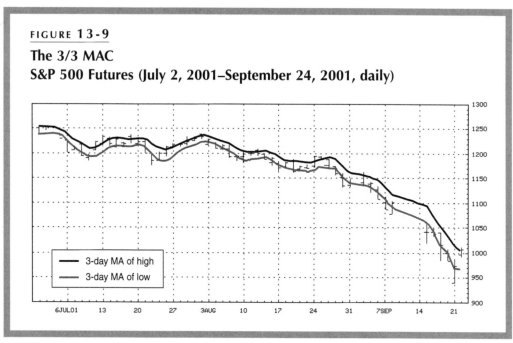

FIGURE **13-9**

The 3/3 MAC
S&P 500 Futures (July 2, 2001–September 24, 2001, daily)

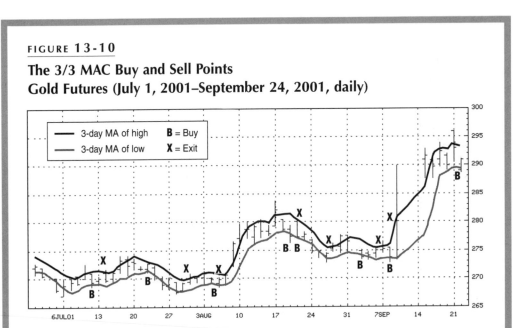

FIGURE 13-10

The 3/3 MAC Buy and Sell Points
Gold Futures (July 1, 2001–September 24, 2001, daily)

Source: Bloomberg

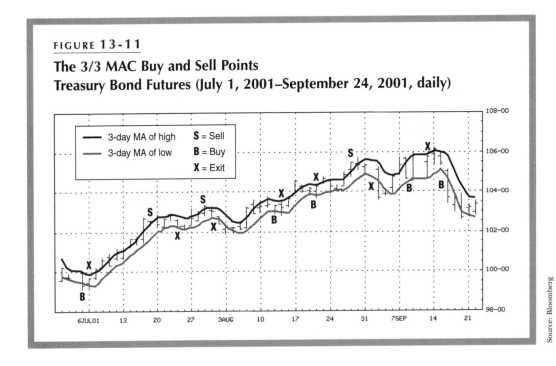

FIGURE 13-11

The 3/3 MAC Buy and Sell Points
Treasury Bond Futures (July 1, 2001–September 24, 2001, daily)

Source: Bloomberg

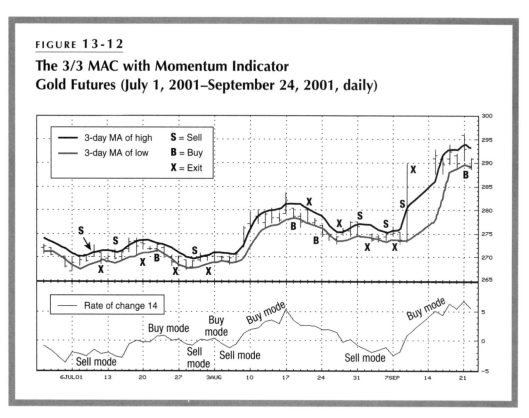

FIGURE 13-12

The 3/3 MAC with Momentum Indicator
Gold Futures (July 1, 2001–September 24, 2001, daily)

values of the previous day. These values may not be touched during the day, but at the end of the day when the new MA value is posted it will appear as if a trade was filled. The illustrations in Figures 13-8 through 13-13 show only trades that could have been filled (but in fact were not) based on these rules. Please take some time to grasp what I am telling you. Although the concept is a simple one, its application can be complicated if you fail to grasp the rules. The best way to use this method is as follows:

- If the momentum indicator is in an upward trend, then place an order to buy at the three day MA of the low.
- If the momentum indicator is in a downward trend, then place an order to go short at the three day MA of the high.

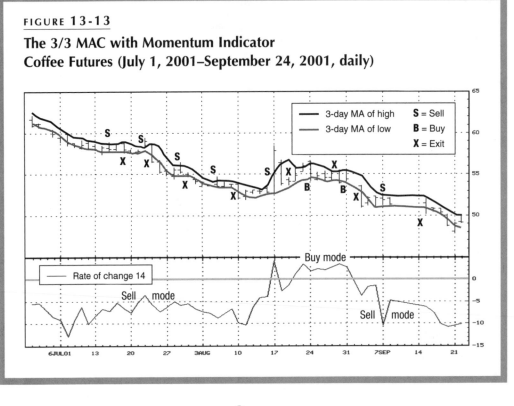

FIGURE 13-13

The 3/3 MAC with Momentum Indicator
Coffee Futures (July 1, 2001–September 24, 2001, daily)

Source: Bloomberg

Summary

There are several basic moving averages, all with different methods, advantages, and limitations. While the MAC seems to offer help in finding support and resistance, the addition of a three-period moving average can offer even more insight to the approaching end of an upside or a downside trend. Combining the use of open, high, low, and closing prices in an MA-based system can often produce substantially better results than the use of traditional moving averages.

CHAPTER 14

Aspects of Intraday Trading

Nothing ever grows in the shade of a big tree.

— CONSTANTIN

For many years, veteran futures traders and aspiring futures traders were systematically cautioned against the "evils of day trading." The public was led to believe that profitable day trading was impossible unless you were a financial markets professional such as a floor trader, or a speculator who had found a way to pay minimal commissions. Though it may have been true in the past that day trading was a venture reserved only for the select few, in recent years, a number of substantive changes within the futures industry, as well as in the area of market technology have made day trading a feasible venture for many traders.

The most important of these changes was discount brokerage, which became popular in the 1980s. The ensuing price war caused brokerage commissions to fall precipitously. Although competition has been fierce within the futures industry, it has been highly beneficial to the consumer. Competition has brought with it consolidation as well as better, faster, and lower-priced service. The services provided by many discount brokers are often equal to or better than what many full-service firms offer. In view of the trend toward lower commission rates, increased computer power, and the rapid communications possible between the individual trader and the exchanges, intraday trading has become a more viable prospect for all types of traders. Some of the dangers of intraday trading are no longer present today. In fact, it may be fruitful to consider the possible benefits that you may derive from day trading.

Advantages of Intraday Trading

The following list of advantages of intraday trading is not designed to influence you into making short-term or intraday trading your main focus, but rather to offer a different perspective from what you may have been exposed to in the past.

1   Intraday trading allows more efficient use of margin money.

2   Intraday trading allows you ability to test trading systems more rapidly, in real time.

3   Intraday traders need to do less market analysis. This is so because they are not concerned with major price trends.

4   Intraday traders generally do not need to know the news. Any intraday news events will have an immediate impact on the market, thereby changing technical indicators, which, if reasonably good, will permit traders to capitalize on the trend change.

5   Intraday traders will be out of their positions at the end of the day. Win, lose, or draw, if you do not exit your position daily, you are not an intraday trader. Intraday traders therefore are forced to take their losses quickly, overcoming an obstacle that proves to be the undoing of many position traders—riding losses.

6   There are many good intraday price swings. Such swings occur regularly, particularly in the more active markets. This means there is profit potential.

7   Intraday trading forces you to have discipline. Intraday trading in fact *requires* the utmost discipline. It will be a good proving ground for you. Even if you choose not to do intraday trading consistently, the experience and the lessons you learn will be valuable in all types of trading and investing.

8   Intraday traders get a fresh start each day. By starting fresh each day you will not be concerned about a loss or profit you may be riding from the previous day. The start of each new day is the start of a new relationship with the market, and with it a new opportunity.

9   Intraday traders need not trade every day. Intraday traders can call it quits at the end of each day. Consequently, they can leave for trips, vacations, or other business any time they choose. They do not need to be concerned about a position they may have, and they will not need to be concerned about positions they may want to take.

There are probably many other potential advantages to intraday trading. Although this book is not intended to be a treatise in support of intraday trading, you may want to consider some of these advantages in your overall decision regarding the futures markets.

Prerequisites to Intraday Trading

Certainly you must meet some prerequisites concerning major issues, both practical and technical, before making a decision to trade on an intraday basis. Some of these prerequisites reflect trading considerations that have been discussed earlier in this book. If you have any doubts about fulfilling all the following prerequisites, then you ought to reconsider intraday trading.

1 *Time.* You cannot do other things while trading intraday. You must make a time commitment because you must watch the market actively all day or until your positions have been closed out. You need not trade intraday every day of the week, but for those days that you do trade intraday, your total attention will be required.

2 *Quotes.* Some individuals believe they can trade intraday using quotations obtained from television shows, talk radio commodity futures programs, or quotes from their broker. Although it is possible to trade short term with limited information, intraday trading is either difficult or impossible if you do not have constant access to reliable price quotation sources. A computer may not be necessary, but you must have a method that is simple to calculate, permitting prompt decision making.

Note that a quotation system is not absolutely necessary with certain trading systems. Some systems generate buy and sell points based on the previous day's trading range, and then enter on buy or sell stops the next day. These systems also use specific stop losses and, therefore, allow all orders to be entered before the market opens. Hence, a quotation system is not necessary in such cases.

3 *Low commissions.* Use a broker who charges you reasonably low commissions. As explained in earlier chapters, the cost of commissions is a major one for the day trader. You must keep this cost as low as possible while retaining good price fills.

4 *Prompt order executions.* Frequently, you may be in and out of intraday positions within a matter of minutes. If you want to exit a position within a matter of minutes after you entered it, you must know the price at which you entered. If you do not know, then the delay in obtaining this information may prove costly. For this reason, it is very important to trade with a brokerage firm that can provide you with prompt reporting of order fills.

5 *Discipline.* I have already discussed the issue of discipline in Chapter 8, yet it is impossible to overemphasize its importance in a day-trading program. I refer you to previous chapters and sections that deal with the subject.

6 *A trading system or method.* You will need a system with the capacity to alert you to intraday moves very early in their inceptions.

If you are currently day trading and find that your results are not what they should be, or if you are considering day trading, I strongly urge you to consider the above points carefully.

Using Price Objectives and Stop Losses

An important issue to consider with intraday trading is the aspect of price objectives versus stop losses. The day trader must make decisions about whether to close out a position once it reaches a certain profit objective or whether to use a stop loss in the event that the position turns against the trader.

It is not an uncommon experience to have a position work in your favor for a period of time, and then turn against you without a concomitant trading signal to indicate the change. In such cases, you may lose profit, or the profit might actually turn into a loss. This situation is unacceptable for the day trader, who must closely guard profits in order to preserve trading profitability on the bottom line. You can use two approaches to solve this dilemma, each with its positive and negative aspects.

Using Price Objectives

One approach is to employ specific price objectives for each market. In Treasury bonds, for instance, you might set an objective of 10 points. (This is merely an illustration. The 10-point objective is not something I have determined through research.) Every time the market allows you the opportunity to take a 10-point profit or greater, you will take it.

Unfortunately, the speculator who practices this approach may leave considerable profit in the market, should the position continue to move in the anticipated direction. When the market makes very large intraday moves, the practice of taking a 10-point profit will not only limit profits, but will also cause the speculator to lose her position. There may not be an opportunity to re-enter the market later in the day for participation in continued moves.

On the other hand, the market may reverse direction, and the speculator would be thankful that she took the 10-point profit. Unfortunately, there is no definitive way to know in advance what to do and when to do it. Therefore, the alternative procedure of using a trailing stop might be advisable.

Using Trailing Stops

There have been ongoing arguments both in favor of and opposed to trailing stops. Most of these discussions have been related to the use of stops for position trades. Although a trailing stop for position trades might not be an effective procedure, I maintain that a trailing stop should, indeed, be used for a day trade once a given profit objective has been attained.

In other words, I recommend that once you have reached a certain profit level for each day trade (in dollar terms), you enter a stop loss that will pay your commissions and eliminate or greatly reduce the possibility of your profit turning into a loss—one of the worst situations for a day trader.

Furthermore, by a series of predetermined steps, the stop loss should be continually raised, closer and closer to the existing market price, so that as the day's end approaches, the possibility of locking in a profit is increased. Naturally, the progression will reach a level where it is irrational to place a stop loss and more advantageous to simply liquidate the position at the market.

Systems for Intraday Trading

The seemingly vast number of short-term trading systems that are available for sale to the public illustrates the popularity of day trading and short-term trading. Some of these systems are so-called black-box systems whose exotic methodology is not known to the user. Still other systems are less computerized or not computerized at all.

It is difficult to say which type of system or systems are best suited for use by any particular individual, because there are so many from which to choose and traders have so many different objectives and expectations when it comes to intraday trading. Here are some suggestions for a few viable techniques.

"The Old Standbys"

Some of the traditional technical methods such as moving averages, support, resistance, oscillators, and trend methods are applicable to intraday trading. Except for the fact that all positions must be closed out by the end of the day's trading, the entry techniques that have been discussed in this book are all reasonable methods. For example, in addition to the exit indicators that moving averages and moving average channel methods provide, traditional trendline and timing signal analysis also yield viable exit indicators. Futures traders, however, like all consumers, are always searching for the new and better, and in this search day traders are constantly being introduced to new products.

Stop and consider, however, that the professional day trader on the floor of the exchange does not generally have access to a computer and must keep track of most technical work mentally or must trade on the basis of gut feelings. I certainly have nothing against trading on the basis of gut feelings or intuition, as long as it is successful. Most individuals, however, cannot do so with consistent success and, therefore, even trading in the pit requires some sort of a systematic approach, even if it is not as mechanical as might be desired.

In addition to the standard techniques already described here, let me suggest an approach that, until recently, has not been especially practical because it requires the constant monitoring of prices. It is, however, an approach suitable for any individual who is in close touch with the markets.

The Tick Chart Method

The so-called tick chart employs a very elementary concept. The tick chart is, very simply, a price chart that records in dot fashion all prices at which a market trades during a given period of time. In other words, if you were recording a tick chart on gold futures using five-minute increments of time, you would place a dot (or some other distinguishing mark) at the appropriate coordinates on the chart to illustrate that the market had traded at that price. It is as simple to use as it is to maintain.

The price, whatever it might have been, has already been "ticked at" and will not be recorded again. If the market were to continue to trade at that price, or if the market did not trade at all subsequent to this for the remainder of the five minutes, no other marks would be recorded in the five-minute time segment. When the five-minute segment ends, the next five-minute segment begins and a mark is placed at the next price tick. Assume that the market then ticks at a higher price. A tick is placed at that price. Assume further that the market ticks up again. A tick is placed in that price, and so on.

The method sounds simple enough, but even though its exterior exudes simplicity, it is highly complex because it represents a number of significant technical aspects of the market. The tick chart allows the trader to determine levels of support, resistance, accumulation, distribution, breaks of resistance, and breaks of support.

By letting the trader know where and when considerable trading took place, the trader can have a good idea of where and when prices could find support on declines or resistance on rallies. The assumption is that if prices traded for a relatively long time within a given price range, then this level will probably serve as support when prices ultimately decline. Some of the other technical ramifications are illustrated in **Figures 14-1** to **14-3**.

The tick chart can be maintained on time frames of the user's choice. The shorter the time frame, the more active the trading signals generated by the tick chart will be. Furthermore, certain forms of traditional analysis can be applied to the tick chart as means of generating additional signals. Among these are trendlines, chart formations, support, and resistance.

In addition to the techniques described in this book, there are many other trading approaches, systems, methods, and techniques pertinent to day trading. There are probably hundreds of different approaches, all of which may have potential application, provided you adhere to the basic rules of money management.

I can certainly say that, with respect to intraday trading, discipline is more important than it is with any other approach. Yet day trading has a built in disciplinarian, if you will, in the sense that the day trader ought to be out of his position at the end of the day if truly committed to day trading.

With very few exceptions (probably fewer than five in one hundred) positions

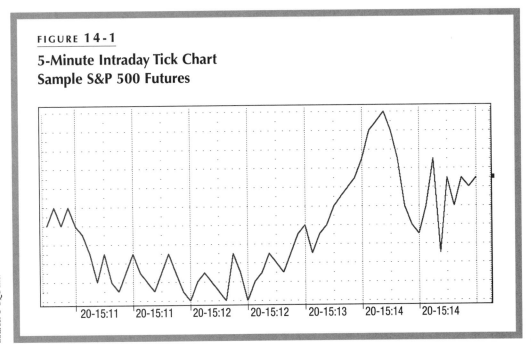

FIGURE **14-1**

5-Minute Intraday Tick Chart
Sample S&P 500 Futures

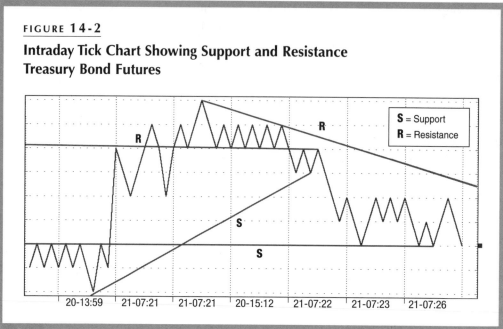

FIGURE 14-2

**Intraday Tick Chart Showing Support and Resistance
Treasury Bond Futures**

Source: © CQC Inc.

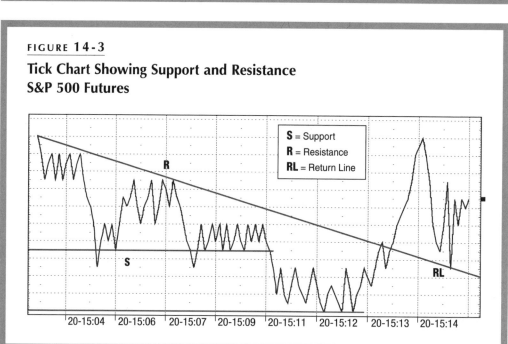

FIGURE 14-3

**Tick Chart Showing Support and Resistance
S&P 500 Futures**

Source: © CQC Inc.

should never be kept overnight. Among such exceptions would be the infrequent occasion when a trader may not be able to exit a trade if it has locked at the daily limit. Furthermore, if a very large move in favor of the position occurs, some traders may hold part of their position until the next day in anticipation of a larger profit. All too often, those who do keep day trades overnight are disappointed they did so when the next day's trading begins. This is not to say that maintaining a position overnight, particularly in recent years when opening price gaps have been particularly large, cannot make significant amounts of money. At times, traders who have made a large profit during the day may opt to keep some of their position overnight with the expectation that more profits will accrue the next day. Another reason for holding on to a day trade is to exit at a possibly better price in the twenty-four–hour market. However, the name of the day-trading game is reduced risk, so why increase it by holding positions overnight?

Books and Seminars

Many books have been written about day trading in the futures markets. As the author of several books devoted to this topic, I frequently receive letters and e-mail from new traders inquiring whether they need to buy my books on day trading in order to be successful. My answer is always the same: I tell them that although you can glean considerable knowledge from books, no knowledge will be useful unless you can translate what you learn into disciplined action. The good news is that there are some excellent day trading books available to new and experienced traders. The bad news is that very few individuals actually have the self-discipline to follow the rules and methods of successful day trading.

The same conclusion holds true for seminars and courses. Many new traders are lured into attending high-cost seminars or buying high-priced video courses. None of these will help you if you are an undisciplined trader. In some cases you may even lose more money because you have applied the methods and/or systems inconsistently.

Do yourself a favor: Unless you make the commitment to follow through on the knowledge you get from seminars, video courses, books, tapes, or online courses, don't even bother spending your money on any of them. The best information in the world will be useless if you don't use it. The best information in the world will help you lose money if you don't use the information consistently and correctly.

Websites and Chat Rooms

Some of you may be lured into participating in online day trading chat rooms or advisory websites. If you have not already discovered them on your own, know that most chat rooms are breeding grounds for the uninformed, the insecure, braggarts, liars, bashers, and rumormongers. There is very little (if any) useful information that can be obtained from chat rooms. This also holds true for many online message boards where traders post questions and answers.

Outright lies and so much incorrect information posted in these places, which I have seen myself, render them useless, even counterproductive for traders. Do not let yourself get dragged into that abyss. This is not to say that there are no worthwhile places for day traders online. I have not discovered any as yet, but in time I may. Rumors are plentiful, but solid trading information is scarce.

The only potentially good use for chat rooms is to take the consensus of market opinion in them as a contrarian indicator. If you don't believe me, then visit some chat rooms daily for a few weeks. If you can tolerate the immaturity and squabbles long enough, you'll find that the prevailing opinion of chat room visitors is usually the opposite of what will happen in the markets.

Some websites, on the other hand, do provide day traders with useful technical information. In many cases these websites are not free. If you want to find good technical trading information using an online resource, then take the time to investigate your alternatives. Don't just sign up for the first service you see. Find a website that gives you information you might otherwise have to spend your time collecting, and then decide if the price you need to pay is worth the savings in effort and the profits you can generate.

Summary

With lower brokerage commissions and less market analysis required, intraday trading might not necessarily be the evil that so many industry commentators for so many years reported it to be. Intraday trading carries with it many prerequisites but offers a built-in discipline for traders. Although each trader must decide whether to use stop losses or price objectives for existing positions, procedures such as trailing stops offer ways to reduce the chances of your profit turning into a loss.

Finally, use of a tick chart can provide a simple and useful strategy for the trader. It can serve as a first step into the complexity of viewing technical aspects of the market, applicable not only in intraday trading but in all trading approaches.

CHAPTER 15

Are Futures Options Right for You?

The optimist proclaims that we live in the best of all possible worlds, and the pessimist fears this is true.

— JAMES BRANCH CABELL

A relatively recent addition to the world of speculation is the futures option contract. Just as traders were beginning to understand stock indices, interest rate futures, and currency futures, the futures options market added to public confusion. It was rather ironic that futures options were unleashed upon the public during a period (1985–1986) that was very difficult for many traders. Perhaps the people who devised futures options believed they would provide a vehicle for the public with which maximum loss would be the cost of the option plus commission, thereby bringing more traders into the markets and increasing liquidity. In essence, this is just what happened.

To fully understand how options can be used and abused in futures trading, let's examine some very simple definitions of the futures options contract, as well as some elementary applications of the vehicle. Let me stress at the outset that this chapter cannot provide a comprehensive analysis and explanation of the literally hundreds of possible uses of futures options. Interested parties should consult some of the recent texts on this subject, such as *McMillan on Options* by Larry McMillan (Wiley and Sons, 1996) and *Option Volatility and Pricing* by Sheldon Natenberg (McGraw-Hill, 1994).

Twice Removed

Stock options are simple to understand because they relate to an underlying security or a relatively tangible asset (in other words, shares of stock, which represent ownership of an entity). Futures options are very difficult for the average individual to understand because they deal with a "twice-removed" abstract concept.

An option on a future is, in effect, an intangible on top of an intangible. Because a futures contract often represents something that has not yet been produced or manufactured, an option to buy or sell something that is not yet real is even more abstract to the general public.

Yet the concept should not be so unfamiliar, because many areas of the investor's world currently deal in fairly similar abstracts. Options on new construction are a good example. A builder begins to develop a piece of property for apartments or condominiums. In order to sell the units, the builder sells options to buy units that have not yet been constructed.

The option gives a buyer the right to purchase one of the units by a certain date. Sale of the option raises cash for the builder and locks in the buyer's right to purchase a unit (usually at a fixed price) at some point in the future, regardless of what prices may have risen to or fallen to by that time. The buyer of the real estate option can apply the option price toward the purchase of the unit before the option's expiration. If the buyer decides not to purchase the unit, he can sell the option or lose the money he spent to buy it.

In many ways, the futures option is similar, but the buyer won't necessarily get his money back when the option expires. A futures option gives its buyer the right to buy or sell the underlying futures contract at a given price at some time in the future, regardless of what the actual price may be. Therefore, if a buyer of an option is fortunate, or better yet, has done good technical research or exercised good judgment, and the underlying market moves in his favor, the option will increase in value, because the underlying futures contract will increase in value.

The creators of futures options, in their great wisdom and foresight, have given us two types of options. The call option gives the buyer the right to buy the underlying futures contract by a certain date at a certain price regardless of the actual price. The put option gives its buyer the right to sell the futures contract at a certain price at some point in the future regardless of what the actual price may be.

You can readily see that if you buy a call option and the price of the underlying commodity goes up, you make money. If you buy a put option and the price of the underlying commodity goes down, you also make money. There is certainly no more mystery to this than there is to being long or short the market.

Many Ways to Go

Imagine the myriad possibilities that are feasible when futures and options are employed in conjunction. The many different combinations or strategies include such things as buying a call option and selling a call option of a different month, buying a call option and buying a put option at the same time, buying the underlying commodity and buying the put option to protect yourself, buying call options instead of the underlying commodity to minimize risk, buying put options instead of the underlying commodity to minimize risk, and so on.

Is it no wonder, then, that options and option strategies have proven overwhelming to most speculators? Due to such complexities, the reception of options into the world of futures trading since the mid 1980s has not been an especially smooth one, with the exception of options on Treasury bond futures. Primarily this poor reception has been a function of ignorance on the part of the public and its consequent unwillingness to accept futures options as a viable means of limiting risk.

Advantages of Futures Options

The advertised advantage of futures options is the fact that their buyers have limited risk. Risk is limited to the cost of the option plus commission. In other words, a futures options contract costs you $600, then the absolute maximum you can lose will be the commission plus $600. Such a limited loss factor has great potential appeal to the public and constitutes the primary marketing tool used to interest speculators in futures options.

A secondary benefit of options is the fact that they can increase tremendously on a percentage basis over a very short period of time. Couple this with specific limited loss and tremendous upside potential, and you have an almost ideal situation on which to sell a speculator.

Another benefit of futures options is that, up to a certain point, they will continue to hold their value and, as a consequence, they will buy you time without forcing you out of the market. If, for example, you expect gold to make a major move down, but you do not know for certain when the move will occur, you could buy a put option without being concerned that you must have precise timing on your entry. The put will buy you time and, within a reasonable time frame, you will be able to withstand moves in the market against you, knowing that your maximum loss is specifically limited. The only way you can lose is if the market continues to go against you or if the market goes nowhere.

This "buying time" feature is especially beneficial to an agricultural producer who may want to protect against price decline by purchasing the appropriate put options. Because the market for many options is large and liquid, he could close out the option at any time. Naturally, however, the worst thing that can happen is that the option will become worthless, losing its entire value. Because options expire on a given date, the closer the expiration date, the less will be the value of the option unless the market is moving strongly in favor of the option. Options have a limited life span. If they are not exercised, they lose all their value at expiration.

An option does not represent anything other than an opportunity. An option is neither a share of stock nor a commodity contract. It is merely an opportunity which, like many opportunities in life, if not taken then is lost. Yet opportunities must be taken at the right time or they will not be productive. Options work in the same way.

Another feature of options is that their value can be very accurately predicted at any time. Each option's value is clearly related to the underlying value of the futures contract it represents and its time to expiration. A considerable number of statistical computer programs are available in the field of options evaluation. These programs allow you to evaluate various strategies over a specific period of time, using possible price objectives. They give you the potential value of your option, given the outcome of each scenario.

Institutional money managers, stock fund managers, and pension fund managers can employ options in stock index futures and Treasury bond futures in programs to hedge against their holdings either in the cash markets and/or in stocks and mutual funds. Virtually all futures markets have options, although the most active options are in currencies, stock indices, energies, and interest rate futures. Speculators and investors use options as a defined risk alternative to futures.

Liabilities and Limitations of Futures Options

The single greatest liability of futures options is that they provide speculators with a false sense of security. Whereas the producer may certainly benefit, the trading public or individual speculator frequently feels that there is less risk in entering an options position than might be the case in a futures contract. The speculator may be enticed out of making a trade in the futures market, because she feels that an option will cost less and could yield more.

Although the option may indeed cost less and could yield more, it appears just as difficult to make money speculating in options as it does speculating in futures. The logic of options seems to be irrefutable, but understand that time is of the essence. The speculator reasons, "Why should I risk losing $1,600 on a futures contract in gold when I can buy a gold call option for $850, with the possibility that gold may rally several thousand dollars per contract?"

The speculator hopes that she will have sufficient time to participate in at least a portion of the move. Had she taken a position in nothing but the futures contract, she may not have been able to withstand a move in the opposite direction. But the option also had limited time.

The use of a limited-risk futures options strategy in conjunction with seasonal price tendencies is a very sensible strategy. Although options will limit your risk, you may take many more total losses due to deterioration of time value (called "time decay"). On the other hand, if you have a very well-defined price target and holding time, then you can use options to your advantage. For example, if you wanted to buy a gold futures contract that had a risk of $1,000, you might be able to buy a call option with only $500 risk but which could expire worthless if not exercised.

The attractiveness of futures options due to their limited risk and high profit potential can be illusory. The speculator should not only see the limited risk and high potential, but she should also be aware of the downside. If 20 option positions are taken with a loss of $400 on most, then the few winners must be large ones if the overall result is to be positive. Although you may be enamored of the obvious benefits of options, you must remember that 90 percent of options expire worthless because the traders who buy them often hold them for too long, and, as a result, time decay takes its toll. If you are making your first venture into the futures trading area and if you have very limited capital, then options may not be the right thing for you.

Strategies for Using Options

The specific manner in which you use futures options strategies is significantly more important than the underlying limited risk. As in the case of futures market transactions, you must attempt to use options in the same way that professionals do. This is not especially simple, but there are very specific methods and procedures for doing so.

Here are some very elementary strategies that are feasible, but that, as you will see, have different applications. I suggest you consult a more thorough text for complete strategic methodology if you have a serious interest in futures options implementation.

1 *Buy a call option instead of going long.* Assume that you have good reason to believe that a market is going higher. You wish to limit your risk by using an option instead of buying the underlying futures contract. What should you do? Here are a few questions to consider: Do you expect a large move or a small one? Do you expect a short- or a long-term move? How much time should it take before the trend higher begins?

Generally, if you expect a large short-term move, then you might consider buying an in-the-money option or an option that is near the money. (An in-the-money option is one that trades above the strike price, whereas a near-the-money option is one that trades close to the strike price.) Such options will be higher priced, but they will move up more than the underlying market.

An alternate procedure that involves lower risk would be to buy options that are farther from the money by virtue of their nearer expiration or larger distance from the strike price. Such options may be selling at much lower prices, but may move only one-third as quickly as the underlying contract. A gold futures contract, for example, may gain $500 in a few weeks whereas the option for that futures contract might only increase $100 in value.

In order to answer these types of questions, it is best to use an options evaluation program, either one provided by a software service or one maintained by your brokerage house. You can get some very specific answers to these questions by running one of these programs.

2 *Buy put options in expectation of a down move.* The procedure here would be essentially similar to what has been described for call options above, but you would buy puts instead of calls, expecting prices to move lower and the puts to move up. The same general rules would apply. If, for example, the risk on a short Swiss franc trade might be $2,500, you might opt to take less risk by buying a put for $800. Although you stand to make less profit on the put, your maximum loss would be $800 plus commission.

3 *In expectation of a large up-move, buy futures and buy put options for protection.* To a certain extent, this is a spread strategy. Assume that you expect a market to move much higher and you plan on purchasing, or you have already purchased, a net long position in the futures market. Assume also that you wish to protect yourself from having a naked long position (that is, from being long the market with no risk protection). You could get some protection by buying a put option that would be limited in cost, but, in the event of a decline in your underlying long position, would protect you from significant loss.

Naturally, you would be liable for commissions on each, and if your net long position goes in your favor, the put option position would decrease in value. This strategy, however, is not an especially bad one, because there is no limit to how high the long futures contract may go, but the put option can only decrease to zero.

For example, assume you establish a long position in soybeans expecting a fifty cent rise that would be worth $2,500 per contract, and you establish a long put option position that costs you $700. Your profit potential would be $2,500 minus $700 worth of "insurance."

Assuming that the long soybeans went against you, your put option would increase in value, although not necessarily on a par with the decrease of your long position. The right combination of long futures and long put options is necessary to give you complete protection. Remember that "time decay" is your enemy. Every day that passes without a rise in the price of soybeans means that the option will lose a little value.

4 ***Sell futures short and buy a call for protection.*** This procedure works exactly the opposite way from the one just described. Again, the right fit or match of call options and short futures contracts is important for complete protection. The right fit is, simply stated, an option whose strike price is very close to the current price of the market.

5 ***Buy a put and a call when you expect a major move, but you don't know which way.*** Some markets are notorious for making big moves. Treasury bond futures, for example, have made some major moves throughout the years. Yet there are times when you are not certain which way the move will go.

Underlying market conditions such as bullish consensus, trading volume, economic factors, chart patterns, and cycles all suggest that the market is likely to make a large move. Still, you are not certain in which direction. You could purchase a put and a call on the same market, which would mean the only way you would come out at a loss is if the market fails to make a big move during the life span of your options.

6 ***Buy covered options to limit risk.*** In a "covered" option strategy, you become the seller of a call or put option, taking in the money from the buyer and protecting yourself with a futures position that will cover you in the event of a move against you. These strategies are considerably safer, yet they may not yield as much as "naked" options sales.

7 *Buy option spreads to exploit the differences among long-term, short-term, and intermediate-term moves.* Many times, the market will move differently based on near-term and far-term expectations. A prime example is short-term and long-term interest rates. Although there are times when short-term interest rates will decline while long-term interest rates hold steady, there may also be times when long-term interest rates will decline and short-term rates will actually rise. Such situations are ideal for spreading two ends against this middle or various combinations of spreads (i.e., being long the nearby option and the distant option while being short the middle options).

Such spreads using futures options are numerous, and an entire science of spreading with its own lingo and methodology has evolved in recent years. The simple act of spreading near-term vs. long-term vs. mid-term rates is called a butterfly spread. In such an instance, a speculator might buy a nearby option, buy a deferred option, and sell two options in the middle.

Such spreads can combine exceptionally low risk with tremendous profit potential, provided your timing and interpretation of market conditions are correct. For those wishing to dig more deeply into this subject, many good references are available.

Summary

Once you penetrate the doubly intangible nature of futures options, many distinct strategies surface, especially those of value in limiting speculators' and producers' risks. This being said, the same characteristics of futures options may also offer limited profit potential as compared to the underlying futures contracts.

In particular, time decay, the rapid time deterioration of the options premium, is a negative factor that you must acknowledge at all times. As you can see, futures options can be advantageous if you can use them correctly. If, however, you are looking to make a killing by trading extremely low priced ("out of the money") futures options, then your odds are not especially good.

Before you embrace futures options as your savior, remember that in practice most futures options expire worthless. Most options buyers lose money, while most options sellers make the money that the options buyers lose. If you plan to use options profitably, you must have a specific strategy that takes into consideration their time decay aspect.

CHAPTER 16

Artificial Intelligence and Neural Networks: Myth or Messiah?

I see no reason why intelligence might not be instantaneously transmitted by electricity to any distance.

— SAMUEL MORSE

The application of neural network technology to computerized futures trading systems has become very popular. Neural networks differ from other standardized programs in that they have "thinking" ability. They also have adaptable processing capabilities that enable a system to recognize price patterns to a degree that has heretofore been impossible. For trading purposes, the ability of neural networks to learn from trial and error may prove to be one of the most significant advances ever in trading systems.

With the rapid progress in neural network technology it is easy to fall into the trap of thinking that neural networks may be the "perfect" systems. Although they do offer efficient ways to perceive market opportunities, the role of risk management and trader discipline cannot be ignored. As I have already pointed out, and cannot emphasize enough, emotions gone astray will continue to limit the potential of all trading systems, no matter how promising their back-tested results may be.

Artificial Intelligence

Historically, the approach to designing computerized systems has been based on rules and symbols. While symbol processing enables computers to perform thinking tasks such as math and logic problems faster and more accurately than our brains can, they are limited in their ability to generate new thinking. Traditionally, computers are given a list of instructions to follow and therefore are unable to create new patterns, which fall outside of the limits of predetermined programs.

Until relatively recently, computer systems were based on simulations of human decision-making processes. This model has been both a help as well as a hindrance. Computer scientists who view the working of the human mind as a metaphor by which to explain the operation of the computer, however, have developed artificial intelligence (AI).

While this rule-based model of the mind has been appealing to AI researchers and psychologists, it has been limiting in its ability to explain common sense–type thinking and generative thinking. More recently, however, researchers have been replacing the rule-driven description of our thinking processes with a new model that attempts to duplicate the circuitry of the brain. The shift toward considering the complex interaction of the brain's billions of neurons is now being reflected in the structure of neural networks.

Characteristics of Neural Networks

Neural networks differ from AI and standard programming practices in a number of significant ways. Neural nets are built with components modeled after the neuron and grouped in interconnected nets.

Unlike digital computers, neural nets don't have a "central processor" that operates on a few bits of data at a time. Instead, like our brains, the neurons act on data all at once, bringing the entire system to bear on a problem. Also, similar to our brains, memories in a neural net are spread throughout the network; they are not isolated in a separate memory bank.

Neural nets process information differently than do traditional programs. Each neuron evaluates signals from other neuron-like components and then "decides" on the basis of the answer whether it should send out a signal of its own.

Furthermore, standard programming practices rely on a list of instructions. A neural network, however, is "taught" through a series of examples. After being exposed to specific patterns as examples, the machine eventually "learns" to make the judgments on its own, even on patterns it has not seen before. This is, of course, the theory that is yet to be developed into practice.

Neural networks have the ability to produce answers quickly due to their more flexible style of information processing. Like our brains, neural nets can draw inferences form categories and make associations. In his book, *Neural Network Design and the Complexity of Learning* (MIT Press, 1990), J. Stephen Judd comments on the thinking process of neural networks:

... aside from generalizing, neural networks seem to extrapolate their learned knowledge to other parts of their domain that they have not had access to, thereby performing something of great value beyond mere storage.

Neural Networks and Trading

The risks, complexity, and volatile nature of futures markets require sophisticated methods of viewing and interpreting market data. Neural networks can be helpful in evaluating technical indicators through their ability to recognize patterns. Neural networks also appear to improve their performance with experience.

While neural networks hold great promise for futures and equity traders, caution is advised. There is no ultimate tool for winning the trading game. At times any technology, no matter how promising, may fail. At times the technology is poorly managed. Some traders, although encouraged by the potential of a sophisticated neural network program, cannot discipline themselves to take orders from a machine, and eventually sabotage the program. The emotional limitations of traders must never be underestimated. It can undo all constructive inputs in short order.

Neural networks' ability to match patterns, form generalizations, merge new situations into old, mirror existing structures, and find the best fit among many scenarios are all promising attributes. Coupled with sound trading rules and disciplined risk management, neural networks can provide traders with great potential for success. I stress, however, that the potential cannot be fulfilled unless accompanied by an effective program of risk management and trading discipline.

Summary

Neural networks have come upon the futures trading scene showing great promise. Unlike older computer systems and even artificial intelligence, neural networks closely mirror the brain and solve problems by learning from a series of patterns and examples and seem to become more successful with time. Although the ability of neural networks to learn from trial and error may prove to be a significant advance in trading systems, no technology will be the ultimate instrument for traders. As good as any system can be, the management, emotions, and discipline of the trader will always temper it. You, the trader, are the ultimate trading system.

Part Five

Putting It All Together

CHAPTER 17

Developing Your Own Trading Plan

Each man is the architect of his own fate.

— APPIUS CAECUS

A common complaint I hear from many futures traders, both in the public and professional sectors, is that there is too much information to digest. There are numerous computerized trading systems, perhaps thousands of different trading techniques, and a wide variety of computer software programs and hardware combinations, in addition to countless newsletter services, chart services, advisors, consultants, brokers, managed-account programs, guided-account programs, and pools.

Also, additional new futures contracts continue to evolve along with futures options. For example, single stock futures have burst onto the scene recently, first in the United Kingdom and other overseas markets and now in the United States as well. Adding to the confusion, more and more attention is focused on overseas markets and their direct influence on the U.S. futures markets. These include stock index futures and interest rate futures in virtually all major European and Asian capitals as well as exchanges in Africa, Australia, South America, New Zealand, Mexico, and Canada. It is easy to see how a trader can feel lost or overwhelmed.

Many of us are beginning to question our basic understanding of markets and the value of time-tested approaches. We have seen trading volume in the agricultural futures markets decline while volume in the financially related markets has soared. Preference has switched from the basic, or "tangible," commodities to the "intangible" commodities (such as interest rates, stock indices, and currencies). This is, no doubt, an expression of the current state of world affairs, as well as a reality with which all traders, veteran and novice, must contend.

Given the oversupply of information and the difficulty many traders encounter in formulating an overall trading plan, this chapter attempts to simplify the process for you by pointing out some factors that will naturally limit your choices. The term "trading plan" does not refer to a specific system, method, or technique. It refers to an overall approach that covers virtually every aspect of trading in the market from psychology to finances.

The term "trading plan" is a global term. When you are done with this chapter, you should be able to take the many different aspects of the entire book and turn them into a workable program that will help you accomplish many of your goals and objectives in an efficient, enjoyable, and relatively painless fashion.

Begin by Listing Your Limitations

The problem most aspiring traders encounter when initiating a trading plan is that they attempt to reach for heights that are, in reality, unattainable due to their own personal limitations. It is unrealistic, for example, to expect that you might continue your present occupation full time while also attempting to day trade the futures markets successfully.

We have been told for many years that we must set our sights high if we wish to achieve great things. This may very well be true. Yet, to set goals high without building the foundation to achieve the goals guarantees frustration and failure. I would, therefore, suggest that in forming a trading plan your number one task should be to list your specific limitations, as opposed to listing your specific goals. Your goals will be directly determined and limited by the amount of input you can give toward fulfilling these goals.

To list your limitations, answer the following questions:

1 Do you want to spend time each day watching the market, or actively trading a specific system? If so, how much time can you devote to do so?
2 If you can devote time each day, what percentage of time will you give to market hours and what percentage to after-market hours?
3 Do you want to buy a computerized trading system and other specialized hardware/software components in connection with futures trading?
4 What type of quote service do you want?
5 Do you need a full-commission house broker or a discount firm to execute trades only?
6 What source of information or advisory service do you need?
7 How much of the cost of the items you've chosen in questions 3 through 6 is covered by the money you have allocated to trading?
8 Do you want to be a short-term, intermediate-term or long-term trader?

9 Are you willing and able to take the pressure of intraday trading?

10 Are you willing to ride large losses, or are you willing to take small but more frequent losses at worst?

You may wish to consider adding many other factors, some general, and some individual, to your list. The value of the list is that the answers you provide will limit what you can realistically attempt. This is why all trading plans must begin with your limitations.

List Your Goals

Most traders' goals are financial. If your goals are financial, then list them in terms of dollars, or in terms of percent return on starting capital. Once you have listed them, reexamine them in light of your limitations. If you realize now that your expectations cannot become realities within the limits of your time, finances, and so forth, then change your goals to be in closer accord with your limitations.

You may need to go through this process several times until you have finally arrived at a workable combination. Direct your efforts toward setting goals that are attainable. Also, make certain that you set a practical time period within which you can achieve the goals.

Be Realistic

I cannot emphasize enough the importance of being realistic in all of your dealings with the markets. There are many stories of fabulous success in the marketplace; the speculator is often tempted to believe that such success may be achieved without doing the necessary work. Although some individuals acquire vast fortunes in futures trading beginning with virtually nothing and within a very limited time, this story is clearly the exception rather than the rule.

In fact, those few traders who have amassed fortunes in brief periods of time tend to give it back to the market just as quickly. To believe that you can achieve quick fortunes is not realistic. Your chances are about as good as those of winning one of the state lotteries. If you plan to begin trading with minimal capital and limited time input, then you are most certainly fooling yourself. Although it is not my intent to discourage creative and motivating dreams, I do want to discourage virtually all traces of unrealistic thinking when it comes to success in futures trading.

If you begin (or maintain) your relationship with the market by dealing in irrational fantasies and expectations, then hopeful thinking will take over in other areas of the relationship as well. For example, consider the wishful thinking that prompts traders to hold onto a losing position well past their stop loss point. Consider also the wishful thinking that prompts traders to hold onto winning positions well past their objectives, often watching a good profit turn into a loss. This wishful thinking is born of unrealistic goals. Your relationship with the market must be the single most honest relationship of your life. It requires being honest with yourself. You cannot fool the market; you can fool only yourself.

Virtually every unrealistic fantasy-based action in the markets will come back to haunt you, perhaps for a long time. Hence, my severe caution is to avoid all unrealistic expectations and fantasies not only when you create your trading plan, but, more difficult, when you put it into action!

Choose Your Trading System

The different trading approaches, methods, and systems presented in this book are very general. Once you've decided that a given approach is best suited to you within the constraints already outlined in this chapter, then begin acquiring more information about that system.

If you're an experienced trader already employing a particular approach, then take the time to reevaluate it in terms of the guidelines provided in this chapter. You may find that what you've been doing for a long time is really not for you! You may find that a totally different approach will better suit your needs and limitations.

The system you use need not be complicated, sophisticated, computer generated, or mystical. All you need is a method by which you can generate the following:

1 ***Entry and exit signals that have a record of accuracy in excess of 60 percent.*** A method that is correct 30 percent of the time can make money, but you will need to accept the fact that consecutive losses and drawdown may be large.

2 ***A specific method of entry and exit, once signals have been generated.***

3 ***A specific objective or reversing point for new signals.***

4 ***A specific scheme for money management of signals such as a stop loss, and dollar risk amount for current trades.***

5 ***A system that does not have periods of severe drawdown.*** This last

issue, drawdown, is an important one to consider in evaluating any trading system and is discussed in Chapter 7. However, because it bears so heavily on potential success or failure, note the following additional points in conducting your evaluation.

The hypothetical trading results of many systems appear extraordinary when taken over a period of many years and when examined on the bottom line. Yet when studied in detail, the reality emerges: some of these systems would in fact have had to experience historical periods of severe reversals in total profit. If you had started trading such a system near a peak or just prior to a period of severe drawdown, you would have had to suffer through a period of persistent losses.

Such losses might not only cause you personal and emotional anguish, but they could easily deplete all of your risk capital, knocking you out of the game before your system recouped its losses and went on to attain major gains. Since your market entry is, in some respects, a random event, you may not be astute enough to enter the market at the most favorable time, thereby opening yourself to the possibility of a severe drawdown. There are, however, a few significant strategies for avoiding extremes of drawdown.

- *Select a trading system that has shown minimal drawdown.* You may have to sacrifice total performance for minimal drawdown, but it's a good trade-off. It is true that a good record of limited drawdown in the past is no guarantee of minimal drawdown in the future, but as a promising sign it can help you decide between your options.
- *Begin trading a given system only after a period of drawdown.* This strategy may require you to wait a while before you begin trading the system you've chosen, but you will be less apt to be starting at the wrong time and thus avoid the possibility of having to sit through a market move that works against you.

The latter point is particularly important. To wait and act only after a period of drawdown would be similar to waiting for a good investment to decline in value so that you can enter on a setback, thereby reducing overall risk.

In formulating your trading plan, you obviously need to select or create a system or method that best suits your needs. One of the key considerations is the performance history of the system or method under evaluation. The hypothetical (and even real-time) trading record is one of the most misunderstood things in the world of futures trading. This all-important topic is discussed at length in Chapter 5. However, some points I consider exceptionally important to all who are considering a system, whether you are buying a trading system or have created your own, and they bear repeating. The following issues I deem vital!

1 *Determine the maximum margin required to follow all trades and calculate this amount in addition to the drawdown of the system.* It may take some time to figure, but it will be well worthwhile. By knowing the absolute worst-case historical scenario, you will have, at the very minimum, an idea of how bad things have gotten or might get.

2 *Take commission costs into consideration.* Some hypothetical performance records do not account for commission costs. The cost of commissions can certainly add up. Don't forget to take these into consideration or to recalculate the results to reflect the commissions you are paying.

3 *Determine whether the performance record bases profits on the purchase and sale of multiple contracts in different contract months for the same market.* In other words, a system may buy or sell several different contract months in a given market at the same time. This tends to weight the profitable side of the record, often quite substantially. Be aware of this when you evaluate a record.

4 *Beware of track records that have a limited history.* You can prove virtually anything if your statistics are manipulated in the right way. Some trading systems show fantastic results over the past five years, yet, prior to this, the systems did not work well at all.

Some systems work exceptionally well in bull or bear markets, but fail miserably in sideways markets. A thorough system test should include samples of performance in all markets—classic bull markets, bear markets, and sideways markets.

5 *Spot-check hypothetical price fills.* System performance records may assume a much better price fill than might have been possible in real time. Ideally, a system test should give the worst possible alternatives, not the best.

6 *Determine how money management is used as part of the system.* Is the system a reversing one, or are specific stops used with each trade? This information will give you an indication of how trades are closed out. While evaluating stops and risks, take into consideration your personal expertise and financial abilities.

Plan Your Time and Make a Schedule

Once you've made all of the major decisions, it will be time to put these decisions into practice. The best way to ruin a good trading system and good intentions is to implement your decisions in an inconsistent or disorganized fashion. In order to use your time, money, and systems in the most efficient and effective way possible, you must make yourself a schedule. Your schedule should be precise. It should detail what you plan to do, how, when, and for how long. Schedule your time—and keep to your schedule.

It is only when you implement your plans in real time that you will be able to work out any details, limitations, or problems that you have not considered in your planning. Once you have found the schedule that works best for you, stick to it. You will know how well your schedule is working for you by your performance in the markets.

Evaluate Your Progress Regularly

Last, but certainly not least, it is important to continually evaluate the progress of your trading plan. As noted above, the ultimate measure of the plan will be your performance in the markets.

Performance itself, however, will not tell you precisely where you have been strong or weak in your application of the rules and procedures. For this reason, you must constantly monitor your performance and implementation of the trading plan. Keep accurate lists of all your transactions. Refer to your list of trades frequently, and study the reasons for your profits and losses. This list will be the single most valuable source of educational feedback you will have at your disposal. If you keep it up-to-date and if you are totally honest in your record keeping, then you will benefit greatly.

Summary

Recognition of your limitations is your best guide to creating a trading plan, and when combined with realistic goals and thoughtful consideration of system characteristics and performance records, it will help you find success. Maintain and improve upon your success with strict compliance to a schedule, organization, and careful analysis of accurate performance records.

CHAPTER 18

Managing Risk: A Major Key to Success

No matter how experienced a trader is, the possibility of his making losing plays is always present because speculation cannot be made 100 percent safe.

— EDWIN LeFEVRE

Futures trading can be characterized as a highly unstructured environment. There is no prescribed set of rules to guide your behavior. Yet within this open-ended and unstructured setting, various conventions, procedures, systems, and methods exist which, if learned and applied, can facilitate success. On the other hand, failure to learn the "rules of the road" will almost always lead to failure. The fact that considerable money is at stake can cause traders to abandon their discipline and to ignore their rules. But without rules and discipline, profits rarely follow.

If you think of the futures market as a venture with unlimited possibilities, you may begin to see the need for creating rules to guide your behavior above and beyond the existing structure. You need to create your own as an adjunctive structure. This will require you to define the risk you are willing to assume. A good risk management program, if followed properly, will help you to define risk and develop the rules to manage it.

One of the inherent aversions to developing a risk management program is the fear of responsibility. Too many traders want the excitement and the chance to capitalize on the markets without having to apply the rigorous steps necessary to minimize their risk. To become a successful trader, you must be willing to assume responsibility. To be responsible you must make a commitment to manage your risk and be willing to learn from your losses.

Because most trades in the futures markets are closed out as losses, we must use losses as a learning tool. The market, however, is not a patient or reliable teacher. In fact, the market is an inconsistent teacher. Sometimes the market will reward you for doing the wrong thing, and sometimes it will punish you for doing the right thing. As you can easily see, the marketplace is a difficult and unpredictable environment in which to learn.

We must, therefore, pay attention to what we can learn from the market. We must make the most of the market feedback we receive. This feedback, the raw material of our learning, consists primarily of losses, but to some extent, of profits as well. Use the guidelines that follow to develop essential skills for managing risk.

Keep a Trading Record

Keep a detailed record of every trade. The record should include the following information:

1 *Entry and exit dates and entry and exit prices.*

2 *Reason for making the trade.* By forcing yourself to list the reason(s) for each and every trade, you will also be forcing yourself to stick to your trading system rules. You will avoid the temptation of making trades on whims, tips, inside information, or other factors that are not related to your trading system or method. For instance, a valid trading reason according to your system might be "a reversal pattern on this week's soybean chart produced a buy signal." An invalid reason might be "Jim said his cousin's soybean farm is laying off workers." In other words, this practice will force you to think before you act and help reduce impulsive trades that, in the long run, are losing trades.

Adding this simple requirement to your record-keeping system will help you avoid mistakes. It will also give you a permanent record of why you made each trade. If you entered the trade within the parameters of your system and ended up taking a loss, you'll be able to go back over the record in order to evaluate your decision. Perhaps you made a mistake interpreting your indicators. Having clear records is always more reliable than memory.

3 *Reason for closing out the position.* This information is just as important as item 2. It will help you pinpoint the exact reasoning you employed in closing out a trade. Many traders can enter a trade for the right reasons, but they go astray when it comes to closing out. They tend to become emotional once in a trade. Emotion can cause them either to stay too long, riding a loss, or to get out too soon, taking a profit that might have been much larger in the long run. Therefore, make certain you keep a thorough record of why trades were closed out.

4 *Reason for profit or loss.* By studying or analyzing the reasons for your profits or losses (as indicated by items 2 and 3), you will be able to analyze what you are doing right and what you are doing wrong. Generally, you will see that the

reasons for your losses tend to cluster around the same types of errors. These reasons will, most often, be emotional rather than technical.

With most trading systems you'll take as many as six to eight losses out of every ten trades due to the nature of trading systems. However, if you're taking more losses than eight out of ten trades, and if the reasons are not directly due to the system error rate itself, then you will know very quickly by examining your record.

Study the Record Regularly and Frequently

Once you have mastered the record-keeping aspect, you should study the record regularly. If you're an active trader, then study the record at the end of every trading day and review your learning the next morning before the markets open. If you are not an active trader, then once weekly will be sufficient.

I strongly urge you to understand each and every loss and not to trade again until you do. If you study the record and force yourself to learn from it, then your losses will truly help you to grow. Failure to employ losses in the fashion I have outlined means that you are not using your tuition wisely.

Furthermore, by studying your losses, you will be able to determine very quickly what has gone wrong. You can decide if errors were trader errors, system errors, broker errors, or the like. You will know very quickly if your trading system is at fault. If this is clearly the case, then you will be able to change systems. If, on the other hand, you find that you are at fault, you will be able to take the action required to make the changes.

Learn from Your Profits

Don't overlook the importance of learning from profits as well. A profit will let you know when you've done something correctly, but don't be fooled into thinking that profits can only come from correct action. At times, the market will generate a profit whether or not you acted correctly. The market is not entirely consistent. If the market were a bastion of consistency, then there would be no need for this book.

Be very careful about profits that come after you made a trade that was not appropriate or consistent with your trading system. In other words, assume you did something incorrectly, but that you were rewarded with a profit. This outcome is a potentially dangerous because you may be setting yourself up for the beginning of bad trading habits. The profit will reward you for doing something that was not consistent with your system or with effective trading behavior.

If you find that your application of trading rules and principles is resulting in profits most of the time, then you are on the right track and you should stay on it!

Calculate How Much Capital You Should Risk

As I mentioned near the beginning of the book, the more capital you have to start trading, the greater potential you have for surviving the markets. It bears repeating that if, for example, your initial margin on a position is $2,500, then you should have a minimum of $12,500 with which to trade. This 10 percent rule can also be applied to the amount you are willing to risk on each trade. The maximum to risk on any one trade is 10 percent, but you may feel more comfortable risking less. Anything more than 10 percent will affect your ability to survive even a small string of losses.

Use Stop-Loss Orders

It is often said that getting into the market is easy; it's getting out that's tough. One key risk management technique is to place stop-loss orders after you initiate a position. It is easy to think about what you are willing to risk before you get into a trade, but it is another story once you are in the market. Having a stop-loss order in place will automatically limit your downside.

Having a stop-loss order and keeping it in place are two different things, of course. Often, traders will place the stop-loss order in the market, only to cancel when the market gets close to the order. This is a dangerous habit to develop and can lead to big losses. Getting into the practice of using stop-loss orders will protect your equity and keep you disciplined.

Don't Overtrade

One of the pitfalls that even experienced traders fall into is overtrading. The tendency to get caught up in the emotion of the market, especially after a string of winning trades, can make it tempting to trade larger positions, or more positions, than you should. With the relatively low margin requirements, traders can get leverage crazy and a "the bigger the better" mentality starts to set in. This has been the demise of many traders.

Whatever you do, remember that consistency in applying risk management rules is of utmost importance. When you forget this simple fact, your emotions take over and losses will begin to accumulate. Plan your trade, trade your plan, and stick to your rules!

Stand Aside When You're Confused

Many traders feel they must be in the markets at all times. Nothing could be more inaccurate. If you are confused or uncertain, remove yourself from the game and observe for a while. Even if you have been consistent with your application of the trading rules and have done your best to learn from your losses, stand aside if you feel uncertain.

Although a seemingly obvious point, I'll state it anyway: newcomers to the futures markets cannot trade successfully without understanding the ups and downs of trading and recognizing when they have reached the limit of their understanding.

Don't Take Losses Personally

There is no doubt that losses are painful. Every loss hurts, but it can hurt more if your attitude toward losses is a negative one. If you look upon each loss as an opportunity to learn, and if you look upon your initial risk capital as tuition, expecting to lose most of it, your attitude toward losses will be a positive one.

If you do not take each loss as a personal defeat, then you will not allow losses to negatively affect your behavior in the market. Your approach to futures trading should be similar to the approach of any individual entering a new business. You must take about a year to learn the business, and you must not expect your first year to be a winning one.

Futures trading appears to take longer to learn than any other business I know. As a matter of fact, the learning process in futures trading never stops—there are always lessons to learn. If you have the proper attitude toward losses you will learn from them, and the lessons will become ingrained enough that mistakes will become less frequent. The wrong attitude, however, will inhibit the learning process.

Know Your Competition

It has been said that competition is a healthy thing. Although this may be true for the professional athlete, it is not necessarily true for the futures trader. In sports, you know whom you are competing against. In the futures market, however, you do not know your foe. If you envision your rival to be the entire market, then you have set yourself an impossible task, because you will never defeat the entire market.

Who, then, should your competitor be? I maintain that you must always compete with yourself. Do not look at what other traders have done or are doing. Do not attempt to outperform them. Don't set your standards so terribly high that you will never be able to achieve them. The market holds a vast treasure with sufficient wealth for many traders. Naturally, not all traders can be winners. Losers must feed the pot, but the rational futures trader will seek to dip into the pot for only a small portion of its immense wealth.

Be your own chief rival. Compete with your own results. Try to better your own record. There will always be someone who claims to be doing better than you are. This should be of no consequence to you.

The ego of a trader is very important. There are literally hundreds of potentially ego-deflating experiences the market can unleash upon the trader. But the trader will be vulnerable to them only if she opens the door to such experiences. The trader's ego is fragile. Many things can affect it, but the greatest is losses. As you know, many losses are unnecessary. If you know the reasons for certain losses you can eliminate them, thereby protecting your ego and avoiding the many errors a trader can make due to the emotional response of a wounded ego.

Summary

Managing risk involves more than using stop-loss procedures. Risk management is really ego management. A good trader does not let his ego compete with the market or any other trader.

By keeping his ego in check, a trader can stick to a structure that defines what loss is acceptable and signals when to preserve capital. Also, by not taking setbacks personally or trying to stay in a market when confused, a trader will be able to learn from mistakes and losses, as well as from profits.

Afterword

If all economists were laid end to end, they would not reach a conclusion.

— GEORGE BERNARD SHAW

The game of futures trading is not what it appears to be on the surface, but is rather a test of behavior, discipline, emotion, and skill. The facts of futures trading are of secondary importance to the issues of self-control, discipline, self-confidence, and consistency.

We are always tempted to search for better answers, better systems, better methods, and better techniques. This search is the motivating force that drives the consumer to buy literally millions of dollars' worth of computer hardware, software, charts, books, tapes, trading systems, and seminars every year. In their search for the external, most futures traders persistently ignore the value and importance of the internal. As you can tell by now, the emphasis of this book has been on the internal. Much of what I've said in the preceding chapters can be summarized by the following quotation from the ancient Chinese sage Lao-Tze:

> There is no need to run outside for better seeing, nor to peer from a window. Rather abide at the center of your being; For the more you leave it, the less you learn. Search your heart and see if he is wise who takes each turn: The way to do is to be.

My life and time in futures trading have made me understand that no matter what my goals happen to be, each trade is a new challenge and another step on the road to market mastery.

Glossary

Arbing. The execution of a trade conducted from a trading desk to the trading pit by the use of hand signals as opposed to the traditional method of having a runner carry a copy of the order to the pit broker. *See also **Arbitrage.***

Arbitrage. The simultaneous purchase of one commodity contract against the sale of another commodity contract in the same month but on different exchanges in order to profit from distortions in usual or typical price relationships. Spreading one contract against another in different contract months at the same exchange is also a form of arbitrage. *See also **Spread.***

Arbitraging. The process or act of conducting an arbitrage transaction.

Ask price. The price at which a trader or traders are willing to sell. Also known as *offer price.*

Back month. A contract month that is more than 90 days from the current trading month.

Example:	Active Months	Mar	May	Jun	Jul	Dec
	Current Month	Mar				
	Back Months	Jul	Dec			

Alternatively, the term is used to signify a month in which futures trading is taking place with a maturity other than the spot or current month.

Example:	Active Months	Mar	May	Jun	Jul	Dec
	Current Month	Mar				
	Back Months	May	Jun	Jul	Dec	

Bar chart. A graph of horizontal price bars showing the high and low or the open, high, low, and close of given time frames for a given market. Bar charts are used in technical analysis to track price ranges and movements.

Basis. The difference between a cash price at a specific location and the price of the nearby futures contract. The basis price is often used to determine the price a producer will be paid for cash grain crops.

Bid price. The price at which traders are willing to buy in a given market.

Bottom. The lowest price reached during a market move.

Call option. An exchange-traded option contract that gives the purchaser the right, but not the obligation, to buy a commodity futures contract at a stated strike price any time prior to the option's expiration date. The grantor of the call has the obligation, upon exercise, to deliver the long futures.

Example: The buyer (traded)

Option	Strike Price	Expire Date	Trade Price
October 12:	@ 1200	March 9	1.20
Long 1 Mar Sugar #11			

During the dates of October 12 and March 9 of the next year, the March futures market trades at 1400. The buyer exercises the right to be long (the futures) at 1200 (option strike price):

Futures	Long 1	Mar Sugar #11 @ 1200
Market		Mar Sugar #11 @ 1400
(transaction)		Points +200 gain
Buyer paid option		Points - 120
premium:		Net Points 80 gain*

*(less commission and fees upon ultimate sale of the futures contract)

Carrying charges. Those costs incurred in warehousing a physical commodity, generally including interest, insurance, and storage.

Cash settlement. A finalizing mechanism in which a futures contract requirement is satisfied with a cash value calculation. Cash may be given in lieu of the actual commodity or it may be required in addition to physical delivery of a commodity (for example, when commodity quality necessitates a premium or a discount). In finalizing a financial product, such as an index or foreign exchange product, cash settlement is necessary because the contract represents a cash amount rather than a physical product.

Clearinghouse. An agency connected with a commodity exchange, i.e., through which financial settlement is made, through which all futures contracts are reconciled, settled, guaranteed, and later either offset or fulfilled through delivery of the commodity. It may be a fully chartered separate corporation rather than a division of the exchange itself.

Commodity fund. An investment pool, observed as a limited partnership, formed to speculate in commodity futures and options. Participants (investors) will have their original investment increased or reduced by their proportional share of income and trading profits or expenses and trading losses. Also called a *commodity mutual fund.*

Crush spread (crushers). A position entailing long soybean futures contracts and short soybean oil and soybean meal futures contracts in fixed proportions. Its name replicates the positions taken by soybean processors when hedging the later purchase of inputs and sale of products.

Cyclic analysis. Analysis that uses various repetitive patterns such as seasonality and time-based sequences as a basis to determine the future direction of trends and prices.

Day trader. A trader who enters and exits a position during the course of one day.

Delta. A percentage value of the amount that an option premium can be expected to change for a given unit change in the underlying futures contract. The factor takes into consideration the time remaining until an option's expiration, the volatility of the underlying futures contract, and the price relationship. Factors are available from all the clearinghouses offering option trading. They change on a daily basis.

Demand. The quantity of a commodity that potential buyers would want to purchase at a given price based on current conditions (e.g., prices of related goods, expectations, tastes, and so on). The magnitude of demand is inversely related to the price of a given commodity.

Discount broker. A broker who charges lower commissions than most brokers.

Discretionary trading. Customer accounts for which specified employees of a brokerage firm may execute trades without explicit authorization of every individual transaction.

Dollar value (or cash value). The monetary value of the full amount of a commodity or financial instrument represented by a futures contract. This is the price per unit times the number of units.

> *Examples:* Grain futures $5.00/bu x 5,000 bu = $25,000 or
>
> T-bond or T-note future $87^{16}/_{32}$ x $100,000 = $87,500

Elasticity of demand (supply). The percentage change in quantities demanded (supplied) for a given percentage change in price. *Inelastic demand* (supply) would indicate relatively small changes in quantities compared to the price change. *Elastic demand* (supply) would indicate relatively large changes in quantities compared to the price change.

Electronic trading. Trading in which all transactions are processed by computers that match buy and sell orders. Although most futures trading traditionally has been conducted in trading pits at exchanges, many exchanges are now fully electronic.

Elliott wave. The theory proposed by R. N. Elliott holding that prices move in a pattern of five waves. In practice, the theory is quite complex and involves subjective interpretation by the user.

Exercise price. The predetermined price level(s) at which an underlying futures contract or actual commodity may be established upon exercise of an option. For futures options, the exchange sets a price in line with the previous day's settlement price for the underlying futures. From that price, higher and lower exercise prices are established at exchange-determined intervals. Each successive day, new prices for trading options may be established in addition to those currently trading and/or available for trading if warranted by fluctuations in the futures market.

Expiration date. The last day that an option may be exercised into the underlying futures or actual commodity contract. If not exercised or assigned, the option ceases to exist.

Fibonacci ratios. Ratios of market movements based on a mathematical progression that is used to establish price objectives concerning the likely movements in the next cycle. Named after the Italian mathematician who is credited with its discovery, the Fibonacci progression is as follows: 0 ... 1 ... 1 ... 2 ... 3 ... 5 ... 8 ... 13 ... and so on, in which the last number is added to the number directly preceding it to arrive at the next number in the sequence.

Fill or kill order. An order that must be offered or bid immediately at a given price and canceled if not executed. Also known as *immediate order, FOK,* the standard abbreviation is FOK. Generally, a fill or kill order is attempted three times and then cancelled ("killed") if not executed.

> *Example:* Buy 1 Dec COMEX Gold @ 400.00 Fill or Kill
> (may also be written as B 1 Z COMEX GLD @ 400.00 FOK)

Floor manager. A brokerage firm's employee responsible for overseeing and coordinating the activities of all the firm's trading floor personnel, including runners, phone clerks, traders, and assistants.

Floor supervisor. *See* **Floor manager.**

Foreign currency future. A contract requiring the later purchase and sale of a designated amount of money issued by a foreign bank. (A March Swiss Franc contract, for example, would call for the delivery of 125,000 francs during a specified period in March.)

Full carrying charge market. A situation in the futures market when the price difference between delivery months reflects the full costs of interest, insurance, and storage.

Fundamental analysis. The process of determining future price trends in stocks or commodities using fundamental considerations such as supply, weather, government statistics, crop conditions, and demand.

Futures contract. An agreement to later buy or sell a commodity of a standardized amount and standardized minimum quality grade, during a specific month, under terms and conditions established by the federally designated contract market upon which trading is conducted, at a price established in the trading pit.

Futures option. An option contract, exercise of which results in the holder and writer of the option exchanging futures positions.

Good-till-canceled order. An order to buy or sell at a fixed price that remains open until executed or canceled by the customer.

> *Example:* Buy 1 Dec COMEX Gold @ 420.00 Good-Till-Canceled
> (may also be written as B 1 Z COMEX GLD @ 420.00 GTC)

Provision may be made to cancel automatically on a given day.

> *Example:* An order entered on March 10
>> Buy 1 Dec COMEX Gold @ 420.00 Good-Till Mar 15

Hedging. The initiation of a position in a futures market that is intended as a temporary substitute for the sale or purchase of the actual commodity. It entails either the sale of futures contracts in anticipation of future sales of cash commodities as a protection against possible price declines or the purchase of futures contracts in anticipation of future purchases of cash commodities as a protection against the possibility of increasing costs.

Initial margin. Cash or securities required as a good faith deposit to establish a specific, new position in the futures or option market. An initial margin amount is set by the respective exchange. Initial margin is not a partial payment of the purchase.

Intercommodity spread. The purchase and sale of two different, but related, commodities with the same delivery month and trading on the same exchange.

Interest rate future. A contract reflecting the value (and usually the later purchase or sale) of debt instruments (such as T-bond, T-note, federal funds, Eurodollar, or municipal bond futures).

Intermarket spread. The purchase and sale of the same commodity on two different exchanges.

> *Example:* Chicago Board of Trade (CBT)   New York Commodity Exchange (COMEX)
>> Long 5 Mar Silver (1,000 oz. each)   Short 1 Mar Silver (5,000 oz.)

Intramarket spread. The purchase of a commodity and sale of the same commodity of a different contract month or of a different commodity of the same or a different month, both contracts of which are trading on the same exchange.

> *Example:* Chicago Board of Trade
>> Long 5M May Wheat
>> Short 5M July Wheat

Limit order. An order with some restrictions, such as price, time, or both, on execution. Restrictions are set by the client.

> *Example:* Time limit
>> Buy 1 Apr Gold @ 400.00 Opening Only
>> (may also be written as B 1 J GLD @ 400.00 Opening Only)
> *Example:* Price limit
>> Buy 1 Apr Gold @ 390.00 (may also be written as B 1 J GLD @ 390.00)

Liquidity. Refers to the relative ease with which a trader can enter and/or close out a position. Generally, low volume markets are those with poor liquidity.

Local (broker). A floor broker who may trade for customers but primarily does so for his or her own account, continuously buying and selling for quick profits.

MACD. An acronym for moving average convergence-divergence, which is a widely used technical timing indicator developed by Gerald Appel.

Maintenance margin. The monetary value to which an original margin requirement may depreciate and still be considered a satisfactory margin to carry the established position. A minimum is specified by the governing exchange, but it may be the policy of an individual firm to set a minimum higher than that of the governing exchange. Also known as variation allowance. The rule of thumb is maintenance at 75 percent of the original margin requirement.

Example:		
Initial Requirement (one contract)	$4,000.00
Allowable Market Fluctuation (negative)	-1,000.00
Maintenance Margin	$3,000.00

Managed accounts. Customer accounts in which all trades are determined by a trading adviser or fund manager.

Margin. An amount of money deposited by both buyers and sellers of futures contracts to ensure performance of the terms of the contract (the delivery or taking of delivery of the commodity or the cancellation of the position by a subsequent offsetting trade). Margin in commodities is not a payment of equity or down payment on the commodity itself but rather is a performance bond or security deposit.

Margin call. A call from a clearinghouse to a clearing member, or from a brokerage firm to a customer, to bring margin deposits up to a required minimum level.

Market analyst. An individual who follows all important factors potentially affecting the price of the commodity or financial instrument in question. Market analysts typically distribute analyses of past market movement and forecasts of future movement.

Market order. An order to buy or sell a specified number of contracts for a specified commodity month at the best price available at the time the order reaches the trading floor. As long as the execution price represents the best offering at the time of execution and the price received was traded approximately at the time the order entered the trading ring, any price is acceptable.

    Example: Buy 5M May Wheat Market (may also be written as B 5M K WHT MKT)

Market-if-touched order (MIT). A contingency order with a limited price instruction specifying that when the market reaches the required price level it becomes a market order to trade at the next best trading price.

    Example: Buy 1 Dec Gold @ 320.00 Market if Touched (may also be written as B 1 Z GLD @ 320.00 MIT) This buy order is placed below the market and is not to be executed unless and until the market reaches 320.00. At that point, the order becomes a market order and is executed at the best available price; the 320.00 price level cannot be guaranteed.

An MIT can be given as a sell order as well. The significant difference between an MIT order and a stop order is its location for execution relative to current prices.

Market-on-close order. An instruction to buy or sell at the best price available during the closing period of the market on a given day.

> *Example:* Sell 5M May Wheat Market on Close (may also be written as S 5M K WHT MOC)

Market-on-the-open order. An instruction to buy or sell at the best price available during the opening period of the market on a given day.

> *Example:* Sell 5M May Corn Market on the opening (may also be written as S 5M K Crn Mkt opening only)

Execution can take place only during the exchange-specified opening period. If the market trades in the range of 330 to 335, for example, during that time, any price in that range can be the trade price. Trade price need not be the first price traded nor necessarily be guaranteed to be the best price in that range.

Minimum fluctuation. The smallest increment or gradation of price movement possible in trading a given contract. Also known as *minimum price fluctuation, point,* or *tick.*

> *Example:*

Commodity	Basis Point Minimum Fluctuation	Dollar Value
Wheat	1/4 per bushel	$12.50
T-Bonds	1/32 of a dollar	31.25
Gold	10¢ per ounce	10.00
Cattle	2½¢ per pound	10.00
Sugar #11	1/100¢ per pound	11.20

Moving average. A method for averaging near-term prices in relation to long-term prices. Oldest prices are dropped as new ones are added.

> *Example:* Closing prices day
>
> | | | |
> |---|---|---|
> | 1 | | 2.00 |
> | 2 | | 2.01 |
> | 3 | | 2.02 |
> | **Average** (6.03 divided by 3) = 2.01 | | |
>
> Closing prices day
>
> | | | |
> |---|---|---|
> | 2 | | 2.01 |
> | 3 | | 2.02 |
> | 4 | | 2.03 |
> | **Average** (6.06 divided by 3) = 2.02 | | |

As a new day is added, the oldest is dropped. In this example moving averages are not restricted to day measurements, however. Any constant unit measure can be applied, and the average can be of as few as two units to whatever number of units the user chooses.

Naked option. A short option position in which the seller does not possess any position in either options or futures that will satisfy exercise of the short option position.

One-cancels-the-other order. An order designating both sides or the same side of a trading range with different months, markets, commodities, or prices. When the condition of one is reached and executed, the other is canceled.

    Example: Buy 5M July Soybeans   575 or
                   5M August   579 One Cancels Other

This order may be executed by buying either July or August soybeans. Once either month has been purchased, the other is automatically canceled by the broker. The choice of month traded is left to the broker, who is guided by the dictates of market conditions.

Open interest. The total number of futures contracts of a given commodity that have not yet been offset by opposite futures transactions nor fulfilled by delivery of the commodity; the total number of open transactions. Each open transaction has a buyer and a seller, but for calculation of open interest, only one side of the contract is counted.

Option writer. The seller in an option trade that creates an option contract. The terms *short* and *grantor* are synonymous with *writer* and *seller.*

Or-better order. *See* **Limit order.**

Oscillator. A type of technical analysis tool used in forecasting price movements.

Out trade. A trade that does not appear initially when the clearing process is completed.

Out-trade clerk. An employee of a clearinghouse charged with helping to resolve problems with unmatched trade confirmations (out trades). The clearinghouse will not recognize a trade (or thus give a trader the desired position) without a matching confirmation enabling the creation of the contra position.

Overbought, oversold. The belief that the price of a market has gone up too high or has declined to a price level that is too low, respectively. *Overbought* and *oversold* are subjective terms based on indicators and analysis. Stating that a market is overbought or oversold in no way assures that the market will decline.

Pit. An area of the exchange floor designated for executing orders for a given commodity.

Point and figure chart. A chart constructed to detail a continuous flow of price activity without regard to time. Plotting direction is determined by a preset number of price changes in sequential order.

Position trader. A trader who holds trades or positions for an extended period of time (also known as an *investor*).

Premium. The additional payment allowed by exchange regulations for delivery of higher-than-required standards or grades of a commodity against a futures contract. In speaking of price relationships between different delivery months of a given commodity, one is said to be "trading at a premium" over another when a commodity's price is greater than that of the other. In financial instruments, a dollar amount by which a security trades above its principal value.

Price order. *See* **Limit order.**

Put option. An exchange-traded option contract that gives the purchaser the right, but not the obligation, to enter into an underlying futures contract to be short the commodity at a stated strike price any time prior to the expiration of the option. The grantor of the put has the obligation, upon exercise, to deliver the short futures contract.

Quote board. A mechanism for displaying current prices on commodity futures contracts. It is situated so as to be easily seen from most positions on the trading floor. Whereas quote boards were once large mechanical displays, they are now fully electronic.

Regression. A method of statistical analysis that measures quantitative correlations between different variables. It is one method commonly used to weight hedges (hedge ratios).

Relative strength indicator. A technical analysis tool introduced by Welles Wilder that attempts to indicate when the market has moved excessively in one direction and is likely to undergo a technical reversal.

Round trip. *See* **Round turn.**

Round turn. The combination of an initiating purchase or sale of a futures contract and the offsetting sale or purchase of an equal number of futures contracts of the same delivery month. Commission fees for commodities transactions cover the round turn.

Scalper. An active trader who attempts to profit on small price changes by buying and selling on very short term (i.e., within the current trading day); a floor trader who trades only his or her own account and creates liquidity by buying and selling continuously.

Seasonality. The condition of being affected by or occurring during a particular period of the calendar year. This factor determines a repeatable pattern influencing supplies and prices.

Example: Price Behavior:

	Price	
Commodity	High	Low
Wheat	December through May	August through September
Cotton	July	November through December

Short selling. Generally, selling a security, commodity, or other instrument that is not already owned. In futures, a short position not closed out will require the short seller to make delivery of the underlying asset.

Spot month. The nearest month (or current month) in which futures trading is still possible and notices can be issued to the long position holder advising that delivery is about to be made. Depending on the commodity, delivery may be the physical commodity or cash settlement in lieu of the commodity.

Example: On the Chicago Board of Trade for October Silver:

Last Trading Day	The fourth last business day of the month
First Notice Day	The last business day of the month preceding the delivery month
Last Notice Day	The next-to-last business day in the delivery month

Spread. The purchase of one futures contract and sale of another, in the expectation that the price relationships between the two will change so that a subsequent offsetting sale and purchase will yield a net profit. Examples include the purchase of one delivery month and the sale of another in the same commodity on the same exchange, or the purchase and sale of the same delivery month in the same commodity on different exchanges; the purchase of one commodity and the sale of another (e.g., wheat vs. corn or corn vs. hogs); or the purchase of one commodity and the sale of the products of that commodity (soybeans vs. soybean oil and soybean meal).

Standardization. The uniformity of terms and contract specifications of the futures markets to effectively interface with the cash (spot) markets enabling the transfer of economic risk and recording control (clearance).

Stochastics. A technical timing indicator popularized by Dr. George Lane. This indicator is often used to determine trend, in particular "overbought" and "oversold" conditions.

Stock index. A group of stocks selected as representative of the stock market or some industry sector. Changes in the value of the stock index are a way of measuring the changes in the stock market.

Stock index future. A contract reflecting the value of a selected group of common stocks. Currently, all stock index futures are broad-based indexes reflecting movements of the overall market. These contracts can be used to hedge against or speculate on market moves. There is no physical delivery against any stock index futures. All are cash settlement contracts.

Stop order. *See* **Limit order.**

Straddle (futures). Similar to futures spread, a strategy entailing long and short positions in related futures contracts.

Straddle (options). A strategy that entails the purchase (sale) of both calls and puts; is designated a long or short straddle, accordingly.

*Strike price. See **Exercise price.***

Supply. The quantity of a commodity that potential sellers would order for sale at different prices based on current conditions. The quantity of commodity supplied is positively related to price.

Technical analysis. The process of determining future price trends in stocks or commodities using chart patterns, trend lines, trading volume, open interest, mathematical formulae, and other tools not based on fundamental considerations such as supply and demand.

Tick value. The change in the dollar or cash value of a contract when a futures price changes by the minimum possible price fluctuation (one tick). The tick value is the dollar price equivalent of one tick times the number of units in the futures contract.

> *Examples:* In most grain futures, 1/40/bu x 5,000 bu = $12.50,
>
> or in 6,000 futures, 100/oz. x 100 oz. = $10.

Top. The highest price reached during a market cycle.

Trade checking. The process of reconciling trade confirmations reflecting transactions that have been executed in the trading pits.

Trading range. The range of prices over which market action has been taking place during the time frame under study. The trading range is calculated by subtracting the low from the high of a given time frame.

Volatility band. The range of prices around current market levels that are within the likely trading range.

Volume. The number of contracts that have changed hands during a given period of time.

Whipsaw. A term used to describe the conditions experienced by traders who have had stop orders executed as a result of volatile market swings. They are unanticipated in that the traders' intentions were for the stop orders to be executed on market movements indicative of a sustained trend.

Index

About Bloomberg

Bloomberg L.P., founded in 1981, is a global information services, news, and media company. Headquartered in New York, the company has nine sales offices, two data centers, and 85 news bureaus worldwide.

Bloomberg, serving customers in 126 countries around the world, holds a unique position within the financial services industry by providing an unparalleled range of features in a single package known as the BLOOMBERG PROFESSIONAL™ service. By addressing the demand for investment performance and efficiency through an exceptional combination of information, analytic, electronic trading, and Straight Through Processing tools, Bloomberg has built a worldwide customer base of corporations, issuers, financial intermediaries, and institutional investors.

BLOOMBERG NEWS®, founded in 1990, provides stories and columns on business, general news, politics, and sports to leading newspapers and magazines throughout the world. BLOOMBERG TELEVISION®, a 24-hour business and financial news network, is produced and distributed globally in seven different languages. BLOOMBERG RADIO℠ is an international radio network anchored by flagship station BLOOMBERG® WBBR 1130 in New York.

In addition to the BLOOMBERG PRESS® line of books, Bloomberg publishes *BLOOMBERG MARKETS™, BLOOMBERG PERSONAL FINANCE®,* and *BLOOMBERG WEALTH MANAGER®*. To learn more about Bloomberg, call a sales representative at:

Frankfurt:	49-69-92041-200	São Paulo:	5511-3048-4500
Hong Kong:	85-2-2977-6600	Singapore:	65-212-1200
London:	44-20-7330-7500	Sydney:	61-2-9777-8601
New York:	1-212-318-2200	Tokyo:	81-3-3201-8950
San Francisco:	1-415-912-2980		

For in-depth market information and news, visit the Bloomberg website at **www.bloomberg.com,** which draws from the news and power of the BLOOMBERG PROFESSIONAL™ service and Bloomberg's host of media products to provide high-quality news and information in multiple languages on stocks, bonds, currencies, and commodities.

About the Author

Jake Bernstein, president of MBH Commodity Advisors, Inc., is an internationally known commodities analyst, trader, and financial consultant. A longtime educator in the field of stocks and commodities, he has been a featured speaker at investment conferences and trading seminars around the world. His articles have appeared in *Futures Magazine, Money Maker, Barron's, FarmFutures,* and other financial publications. He has appeared on numerous radio and television business shows, including *Financial News Network, JAGfn, WebFN, CNBC,* and *Wall Street Week,* and is a weekly guest commentator on business television in Chicago and Los Angeles. Mr. Bernstein is the author of several dozen books on trading and analyzing the futures and stock markets. His newsletters and advisory services are read and used internationally by traders, investors, brokers, financial institutions, and money managers. He can be contacted via e-mail at jake@trade-futures.com.